GW00685114

797,885 Books

are available to read at

www.ForgottenBooks.com

Forgotten Books' App
Available for mobile, tablet & eReader

ISBN 978-1-330-43937-1
PIBN 10040255

This book is a reproduction of an important historical work. Forgotten Books uses
state-of-the-art technology to digitally reconstruct the work, preserving the original format
whilst repairing imperfections present in the aged copy. In rare cases, an imperfection in
the original, such as a blemish or missing page, may be replicated in our edition. We do,
however, repair the vast majority of imperfections successfully; any imperfections that
remain are intentionally left to preserve the state of such historical works.

Forgotten Books is a registered trademark of FB &c Ltd.
Copyright © 2015 FB &c Ltd.
FB &c Ltd, Dalton House, 60 Windsor Avenue, London, SW19 2RR.
Company number 08720141. Registered in England and Wales.

For support please visit www.forgottenbooks.com

1 MONTH OF
FREE
READING

at
www.ForgottenBooks.com

By purchasing this book you are eligible for one month membership to ForgottenBooks.com, giving you unlimited access to our entire collection of over 700,000 titles via our web site and mobile apps.

To claim your free month visit:

www.forgottenbooks.com/free40255

* Offer is valid for 45 days from date of purchase. Terms and conditions apply.

Similar Books Are Available from
www.forgottenbooks.com

Russia's Agony
by Robert Wilton

Napoleon's Russian Campaign of 1812
by Edward Foord

The Russian Army from Within
by W. Barnes Steveni

The Russian Bolshevik Revolution
by Edward Alsworth Ross

Russian Dissenters
by F. C. Conybeare

Russia Under the Tzars
by S. Stepniak

Slavonic Europe
A Political History of Poland and Russia from 1447 to 1796, by R. Nisbet Bain

The Socialist Soviet Republic of Russia
Its Rise and Organisation, by Jacques Sadoul

The Cossacks
Their History and Country, by W. P. Cresson

The Fall of the Romanoffs
How the Ex-Empress & Rasputine Caused the Russian Revolution, by Unknown Author

Historical Memoirs of the Emperor Alexander I
And the Court of Russia, by Madame La Comtesse De Choiseul-Gouffier

History of the Jews in Russia and Poland, Vol. 1
From the Earliest Times Until the Present Day, by S. M. Dubnow

Russia in 1919
by Arthur Ransome

Life of Alexander II
Emperor of All the Russias, by F. R. Grahame

Barbarous Soviet Russia
by Isaac McBride

Rasputin and the Russian Revolution
by Princess Catherine Radziwill

The Russian Problem
by Paul Vinogradoff

Facts and Fabrications About Soviet Russia
by Evans Clark

Bolshevik Russia
by Étienne Antonelli

Russia and the Great War
by Grigorii Aleksinskii

THE
ROMANCE OF AN EMPRESS

CATHERINE II. OF RUSSIA

FROM THE FRENCH OF

K. WALISZEWSKI

WITH PORTRAIT

LONDON
WILLIAM HEINEMANN
1895

[*All rights reserved*]

First Edition, 2 Vols.,

TRANSLATOR'S PREFACE

'THIS is a romance,' says the writer in his preface, 'in which fiction finds no place. Even legend enters into it no more than it must needs enter into every faithful evocation of the past. The reader's curiosity, however, and his taste for adventure, if he has it, will lose nothing, all the same.' Materials, it seems, for an exact and minute study of Catherine have only of recent years been forthcoming ; now, out of the seventy-two volumes of documents already published by the Russian Imperial Historical Society, scarcely twenty can be found which are not directly concerned with the history of her reign. And there are other materials, scattered in obscure Russian periodicals, other documents, contained in the State Archives in Russia and in France, which have never been consulted, and which are quite out of ordinary reach. Such, M. Waliszewski tells us, are the main foundations of this 'Romance of an Empress,' in which he has endeavoured to present, without fear or favour, the results of a thorough and impartial investigation. One consequence, which is both. interesting and significant, is that the book has been forbidden to be circulated in Russia.

It may be as well to state that the original book is not written in Parisian French; it has the colloquialisms of a foreigner, wishing to be more native than the natives. The translator has not attempted to remove, or even to attenuate, this Russian accent, so to speak. He has endeavoured merely to make his rendering as close as possible to the original

CONTENTS

PART I

THE GRAND DUCHESS

BOOK I

FROM STETTIN TO MOSCOW

CHAPTER I

CHILDHOOD

I

FIFTY years ago there was consternation in a little German town : a railway was to be brought through it, removing, after the manner of railways, old landmarks, cutting through old dwellings, levelling old promenades, where generation after generation had taken the air. Among the objects thus menaced by impious engineers, to the utter despair of the people in the neighbourhood, one tree, a venerable lime-tree, seemed to be held in special reverence. In spite of all, the railway was brought through. The lime-tree was not, however, cut down; it was taken up by the roots and transplanted elsewhere. As a special distinction it was set up opposite the new railway station, where it showed its insensibility to the honour by withering away. Then it was made into two tables : one of them was presented to Queen Elizabeth of Prussia, the other to Alexandra Feodorovna, Empress of Russia. The inhabitants of Stettin gave to this tree the name of *Kaiserlinde*, imperial lime-tree, and, according to their account, it had been planted by a German princess, then known as Sophia of Anhalt-Zerbst (or, more familiarly, Figchen), who had been wont to play with the townspeople's children in the market-place, and who had since become, they knew not how, Empress of Russia, under the name of Catherine the Great.

Catherine had indeed passed a part of her childhood in the old Pomeranian city. Was she born there? It is not often that the old dispute over the birthplace of Homer comes to be renewed over the birthplaces of the great personages of modern history. This uncertainty in the case of Catherine is one of the special peculiarities of her career. No register of any parish in Stettin has kept a trace of her name. In the similar case of the Princess of Würtemberg, wife of Paul I., the explanation is easy : the child was no doubt baptized by a clergyman of the Protestant church, not attached to a parish. But a note has been discovered—apparently authentic—indicating Dornburg as the place where Catherine was born and baptized ; and grave historians have founded on this datum the strangest suppositions. Dornburg was the family seat of the family of Anhalt-Zerbst zu Dornburg—that is to say, of Catherine's family. Had not her mother stayed there about 1729, and had she not frequent occasions of seeing a young prince, barely sixteen years of age, who was enduring, not far from there, a tedious existence with a disagreeable father? This young prince, afterwards known as Frederick the Great, has been designated by a German historian, Sugenheim, as the 'father incognito' of Catherine.

A letter of Prince Christian-August of Anhalt-Zerbst, the official father of the future Empress, seems to take away all appearance of truth from this hazardous conjecture. It is dated from Stettin, May 2, 1729, and states that on that very day, at half-past two in the morning, a daughter had been born to him *in that town.* This daughter can be no other than Catherine. Christian-August ought at least to have known where his children were born, even if he were a little uncertain as to how they came into the world. And further, there is no proof whatever that Dornburg had received within its walls the mother of Catherine, not long before the birth of the latter: indeed, the contrary seems well established. It is far enough from Dornburg and from Stettin, it is at Paris that the Princess of Zerbst appears to have passed a part at least of the year 1728. Frederick, as is well known, never went there, though indeed he nearly lost his head in trying to go. But the imagination of German historians is inexhaustible. In default of Frederick, there was at Paris in 1728, in the Russian embassy, a young man, the bastard of an illustrious family, who certainly must have associated with the Princess of Zerbst. Behold us on the trail of another romance, another anonymous paternity! The young man was called Betzky, and became afterwards a personage of importance. He died in St. Petersburg at an advanced age, and it was reported that Catherine, who showered kindly and gracious attentions upon the old man, was accustomed, when she visited him, to bend over his arm-chair and kiss his hand. This was enough for the German translator of the memoirs

of Masson, whose conviction we should find it
hard to share. At this rate we might indulge
in similar suppositions in regard to every
illustrious birth in the history of the eighteenth
century.

Catherine, then, who was later to be called
Catherine the Great, was born, according to all
appearances, at Stettin, and her parents, by law
as by nature, so far as we know, were called
Prince Christian-August of Zerbst-Dornburg, and
Princess Jeanne-Elizabeth of Holstein, his legitimate wife. A time was to come, as we shall see,
when the least actions of this child, so obscurely
brought into the world, were to be traced day
by day, and almost hour by hour. It was her
revenge upon destiny.

But what, in 1729, would be signified by the
birth of a little Princess of Zerbst? The princely
house so named, one of those with which the
Germany of the period was swarming, formed
one of the eight branches of the house of Anhalt.
Up to the time when an unexpected chance
brought unexampled fame, none of these branches
had attained any particular distinction, and within
a short time the final extinction of the whole line
had cut short this dawn of notoriety. Without
history up to 1729, the house of Anhalt-Zerbst
had ceased to exist in 1793.

II

The parents of Catherine did not live at
Dornburg. Her father had something else to do :
he had, in fact, to make his way in the world.
Born in 1690, he had entered the Prussian army,

and had seen active service in Holland, in Italy, and in Pomerania, fighting against the French and against the Swiss. At thirty-one he had won his epaulettes as Major-General. At thirty-seven he married the Princess Jeanne-Elizabeth of Holstein-Gottorp, younger sister of that Prince Karl-August who had already all but sat on the throne of Russia by the side of Elizabeth. Appointed commandant of the Anhalt-Zerbst regiment of infantry, Christian-August had to betake himself to his regiment, and to the garrison life, at Stettin.

As husband and father, Christian-August was a model. He adored his children, but when Catherine came into the world he had been expecting a son, and his dissatisfaction saddened the early years of Catherine's childhood. When this period of her life came to be inquired into— and a time came when it was zealously inquired into—the memory of those who had witnessed it was already fading. She herself was by no means willing to revive the recollection, and she replied to questionings on the subject with a reserve which was, for her, unusual. 'I see nothing interesting in it,' she wrote to Grimm, the most intrepid of questioners. Nor were her own recollections very exact. 'I was born,' she said, 'in Greifenheim House, on the Marien Kir-chenhof.' There is not, and there never was, a house of that name at Stettin. The commandant of the 8th regiment of infantry lived at 791 Dom Strasse, the house of the president of the Chamber of Commerce of Stettin, von Ascher-leben. The quarter in which this street was situated was called Greifenhagen. The house has

changed owner and number : it belongs to-day
to the Councillor of State Dewitz, and is No. 1.
On a piece of the whitewashed wall there is
to be seen a black patch, the sole trace left by
the sojourn of a great empress : a little smoke
caused by a chafing-dish lighted the 2nd May
1729 before the cradle of Catherine.   The cradle
is gone : it is at Weimar.

Baptized under the names of Sophia Augusta
Frederika, in honour of three of her aunts,
Catherine was generally known as Figchen, or
Fichchen, according to the orthography of her
mother — apparently a diminutive of Sophia
(Sophiechen).   Not long after her birth her
parents moved into the château of Stettin, where
they occupied the left wing, close to the church.
Figchen had for herself three rooms, of which
the one in which she slept was next to the bell-
tower.   Thus was she enabled to prepare her
ears for the task of hearing, in time to come,
the deafening carillon of the orthodox temples,
without too much disturbance—a providential
arrangement, perhaps.   It was there that she was
brought up, very simply.   Often did the streets
of Stettin see her playing with the neighbours'
children, none of whom, most assuredly, ever
thought of calling her Your Highness.   When
the mothers of these children paid a visit to the
château, Figchen went before them and respectfully kissed the hem of their robe.   So it was
ordained by her mother, who had wise notions
on the subject—a rare occurrence with her.

Figchen had, nevertheless, a great many
masters to look after her education, besides a
governess, who, of course, was French.   French

teachers and governesses were at that time to be found in all the German houses of any importance; one of the indirect consequences of the revocation of the Edict of Nantes. They taught the French language, the French manners, and the French gallantry. They taught what they knew, and most of them knew nothing else. Thus Figchen had Mlle. Cardel. She had also a French chaplain, Péraud, and a writing-master, also French, called Laurent. Some native masters completed this well-furnished collection of pedagogues. A certain Wagner taught Figchen her maternal language. For music she had another German, named Roellig. In later days it often pleased Catherine to call up the recollection of these first instructors of her youth, half tenderly, half with a sort of wicked childish wit. She gave a place apart to Mlle. Cardel, 'who knew almost everything without having learnt anything, very much like her scholar'; who told her that she had 'an awkward disposition'; and who was always telling her to keep back her chin. 'She considered it excessively sharp,' Catherine tells us, 'and she said that by sticking it out I knocked against everybody I came across.' The good Mlle. Cardel had probably little thought of the encounters to which her pupil was destined. But she did more than setting up her mind and getting her chin into line. She made her read Racine, Corneille, and Moliére. She contested her with the German Wagner, with his Teutonic pedantry, his Pomeranian dulness, the insipidity of his *Prüfungen*, of which Catherine always kept a painful recollection. Certainly she com-

municated to her something of her own temperament, the Parisian temperament, we should say
nowadays—quick, alert, ready-witted.   And—
must we admit it?—she rendered her a still
greater service, to all appearance, in saving
her from her mother, and not only from the
blows that she was wont to shower down for
a yes or a no—'out of ill-temper, never for any
reason'—but especially from that quite other
temperament that belonged, as we shall see
later, to the wife of Christian-August: a temperament made up of intrigue, of deception, of
low instincts and petty ambitions, in which
was reflected the whole soul of many genera-
tions of Germanic princelings.   After all, Mlle.
Cardel really deserved the furs that her pupil
hastened to send her on arriving at St. Petersburg.

An important part of the education thus organised was made by Figchen's frequent journeys
in the company of her parents.   Residence at
Stettin had no particular attractions for a young
woman bent on pleasure and a young military
commandant who had been through half Europe.
Chances of change were thus welcome, and with a
large family connection such chances were never
wanting.   There were Zerbst, Hamburg, Brunswick, Eutin, everywhere relations, everywhere
hospitality, not very sumptuous as a rule, but
cordial.   It was at Eutin, in 1739, that the Princess Sophia saw for the first time the man whom
she was to deprive of a throne after having
received it from him.   Peter Ulric of Holstein, son
of a cousin-german of her mother, was then eleven
years of age.   She herself was ten.   This first

meeting, which, at the time, passed unnoticed, did not give her a favourable impression—at least so she declared later, when she came to write her memoirs. The child seemed to her a weakling. She was told that he had a bad disposition, and, what appears incredible, that he had already a taste for drink. Another excursion left in her young imagination a much more profound trace. In 1742 or 1743, at Brunswick, at the house of the Dowager-Duchess who had brought up her mother, a canon of the church, expert in chiromancy, bethought himself to see in her hand no less than three crowns, though he could see none in the hand of the pretty Princess of Bevern, for whom they were seeking just then a high marriage. To find a crown along with a husband —that was the common dream of all these German princesses.

At Berlin Figchen saw Frederick, but without his paying her more attention than was natural, or her caring greatly what he thought of her. He was a great king on the threshold of a magnificent career ; she was but a little girl, destined, to all appearance, to be the ornament of some infinitesimal court lost in the depths of the empire.

All this was but the common life and education of all the German princesses of the time. Later on Catherine attempted, by a sort of coquetry, to bridge over the gaps and insufficiencies of this education. 'What would you have ?' she said ; ' I was brought up with the idea of marrying some little neighbouring prince, and I was taught as much as that demanded. Mlle. Cardel and I had no thought of *this*!' The Baroness von

Printzen, maid of honour to the Princess of Zerbst, did not hesitate to declare that, on her part, with the closest opportunities of observing the studies and progress of the future empress, she had never seen in her any exceptional qualities or faculties. She expected her to turn out 'an ordinary woman.' Mlle. Cardel was equally far from thinking, to all appearance, that in looking after the behaviour of her pupil she was (as the enthusiastic Diderot was one day to declare) 'the candlestick bearing the light of the age.'

III

There was something, nevertheless, in this mediocre existence that might already remind the Princess Sophia of her future destiny. She was but a little German Princess, brought up in a little German town, with a desolate sandy waste for horizon. But on this region lay the mighty shadow of a neighbouring power. This very province, not so long before, had seen a strange uniform in its towns, had felt the growing prestige of a power, newly come into Europe, and already terrifying and astonishing the nations, awakening infinite hopes and fears. At Stettin even, the details of the siege held against the armies of the great White Czar were fresh in all memories. In the family of Figchen, Russia, the great and mysterious Russia, her innumerable soldiers, her exhaustless riches, her absolute sovereigns, furnished a favourite theme for discussion, into which, perhaps, there came some vague longings, some obscure presentiments. Why not? With the marriages which had united a daughter of Peter I. to a Duke of Holstein, a grand-daughter of Ivan, the brother of Peter, to a Duke of Brunswick, a whole network of alliances, affinities, and reciprocal attractions had been established between the great monarchy of the North and the vast tribe of meagre German sovereignties bordering on the immense empire. And the family of Figchen was brought into particular association with all this. When, in 1729, Figchen met her cousin Peter Ulric at Eutin, she knew that his mother had been a Russian Czarevna, a daughter of Peter the Great. She knew, too, the story of that other daughter of Peter the Great, Elizabeth, who had so nearly been her mother's sister-in-law.

And now, all unexpectedly, came the news of the accession to the crown of Russia of this very Princess, the sorrowing *fiancée* of Prince Karl-August of Holstein. On December 9, 1741, by one of those *coups de théâtre* which were so frequent in the history of the Northern court, Elizabeth had put an end to the reign of the little Ivan of Brunswick and to the regency of his mother. How the echo of this event must have sounded in the ears of Catherine and her family! Separated by the cruelty of fate from the husband of her choice, the new Empress, it was known, kept a tender feeling, not only for the person of the young Prince, but for all his family. She had but lately asked for the portraits of his surviving brothers: she was not likely to forget his sister. The predictions of the palmist canon must have come back to the mind of Figchen's mother. Certainly she did not fail to write at once to her cousin, and to send her congratulations. The reply was quite encouraging. Amiable, affectionate even, Elizabeth showed herself grateful for all these kind attentions, and demanded yet another portrait—that of her sister, the Princess of Holstein, mother of Prince Peter Ulric. Evidently she was making a collection of them. What was all the mystery about?

The mystery was soon unveiled. In January 1742 Prince Peter Ulric, 'the little devil,' as the Czarina Anna Ivanovna was accustomed to call him, rendered uneasy by his too close relationship with the reigning house of Russia—the little cousin whom Figchen had one day met—disappeared suddenly from Kiel, where he usually lived, and reappeared a few weeks later at St. Petersburg. Elizabeth had sent for him in order to proclaim him solemnly as her heir.

Here, at all events, was an occurrence of no uncertain significance. It was the Holstein blood—Figchen's mother's—that triumphed in Russia to the exclusion of that of Brunswick. Holstein or Brunswick, the posterity of Peter the Great or that of his elder brother Ivan, both deceased without direct male heirs: the whole history of the house of Russia since 1725 had been implicated in this dilemma ; now Holstein had got the upper hand, and the fortune of the new Prince Imperial, as yet scarcely established, began to reflect itself upon his obscure German relations. It extended even to Stettin. In the month of July 1742 the father of Figchen was raised by Frederick to the grade of Field-Marshal —a politeness evidently intended for Elizabeth and her nephew. In September a Secretary of the Russian Embassy at Berlin brought to the Princess of Zerbst the portrait of the Czarina in a frame of magnificent diamonds. At the end of the year Figchen accompanied her mother to Berlin, where the celebrated painter Pesne was intrusted with the painting of her portrait. Figchen knew that the portrait was to be sent to St. Petersburg, where, no doubt, Elizabeth would not be the only one to admire it.

A year passed without bringing anything decisive. At the end of 1743 the whole family was found at Zerbst : the extinction of the eldest branch had recently caused the succession of Christian-August's brother to the principality of that name. Christmas was gaily kept. There was this new good luck, there were doubtless some happy hopes for the future, dreams, perhaps, more audacious still. The new year was beginning gaily, when an express courier, who had ridden post-haste from Berlin, brought startling news to the petulant Jeanne-Elizabeth and her graver spouse. This time the oracles gave open voice, and palmistry won a clear triumph. The courier brought a letter from Brümmer, Master of the Household of the Grand Duke Peter, formerly Peter Ulric of Holstein, and this letter was addressed to the Princess Jeanne-Elizabeth, inviting her to come at once, *with her daughter*, to the Imperial Court of Russia.

CHAPTER II

ARRIVAL IN RUSSIA—MARRIAGE

I

BRÜMMER was an old acquaintance of the Princess Jeanne-Elizabeth. He had been the tutor of the Grand Duke, and had doubtless accompanied his pupil to Eutin. His letter was long, and filled with minute directions. The Princess was to lose as little time as possible in preparing for the journey, and she was to reduce her suite to the bare necessary—a maid of honour, two maids, an officer, a cook, three or four lackeys. At Riga she would find a suitable escort, which would conduct her to the place of residence of the court. It was expressly stipulated that her husband was not to accompany her. She was to keep absolute silence as to the purpose of her journey. If she were questioned, she was to answer that she was going to see the Empress in order to thank her for all the kindness she had shown her She might, however, confide in Frederick II., who was in the secret. A bill of exchange on a Berlin banker, to cover the expenses of the journey, accompanied the letter. The sum was modest—10,000 roubles,—but it was important, Brümmer explained, not to attract attention by sending a large sum. Once in Russia, the Princess should want for nothing.

It was evidently in the name of the Empress that Brümmer sent this invitation, so much like an order, and these peremptory instructions. But he gave no further explanation as to the intentions of the Czarina. Another explained it for him. Two hours after the arrival of the first courier, a second followed, bearing a letter from the King of Prussia. Frederick dotted all the i's, and he did not fail to take to himself all the credit of Elizabeth's choice of the young Princess of Zerbst to be the companion of his nephew and successor. He had in truth had something to do with it, and in this manner.

Naturally, there had been no few matrimonial competitions in regard to 'the little devil,' now heir to so splendid a crown. Soon every notable person at court, the most intriguing court in Europe—from the ex-tutor of the Grand Duke, the German Brümmer, to the physician-in-ordinary of Elizabeth, the Frenchman Lestocq,—had a candidate of his own, and a following for his candidate. Now it was a French Princess, now a Saxon Princess, daughter of the King of Poland, now a sister of the King of Prussia. Backed by Bestoujef, the all-powerful Chancellor of the empire, the Saxon project had at one moment the greatest chances of success. 'The court of Saxony, rampant slave of Russia,' wrote Frederick later, 'desired the success of Marianne, second daughter of the King of Poland, for the increase of its own credit. . . . The Russian ministers, whose venality would, I think, have put the Empress herself up to auction, sold a premature contract of marriage; they received large sums of money, and the King of Poland nothing but words.'

Sixteen years of age, pretty, well brought up,

the Princess of Saxony was not merely a suitable match ; the alliance would serve as basis of a vast combination, destined, so Bestoujef thought, to reunite Russia, Saxony, Austria, Holland, and England, three-quarters of Europe, against Prussia and France. The combination fell through, and Frederick did his best to aid its fall. He refused, however, to checkmate it by putting forward his sister, the Princess Ulrica, who would have suited Elizabeth. 'Nothing would be more barbarous,' he said, 'than to sacrifice the Princess.' For a time he left his envoy Mardefeldt to his own resources, which were small, and to those of his French colleague, La Chétardie, which, for the moment, were no better. Mardefeldt had been in disgrace for some time, and Elizabeth had been on the point of demanding his recall. As for La Chétardie, after having played so important a *rôle* at the accession of the new Czarina, he was foolish enough to let slip a position for which he had fought so hard. He had left his post, and, on his return, had not met with the same favour. His court did nothing on his behalf, and obliged him to be always asking for instructions. He would inquire 'if the king had still the same repugnance that he had shown at the accession of the Czarina to the marriage of the Grand Duke with one of the Princesses (*avec une des Madames*).'

But Frederick was on the watch. It was he who had had the idea of sending to St. Petersburg the portrait painted by Pesne at Berlin. A surviving brother of the mother of Figchen, Prince August of Holstein, had been commissioned to present it to the Czarina. Pesne was getting old, and the portrait, it appears, was not good. It had nevertheless the good fortune to please the Empress and her nephew. At the decisive moment, in November 1743, Mardefeldt received orders to put resolutely forward the Princess of Zerbst, or, if she would not do, one of the Princesses of Hesse-Darmstadt. In default of personal influence, the Prussian agent and his French colleague succeeded in winning over Brümmer and Lestocq, and victory (so La Chétardie testifies) was the price of this alliance. 'They have impressed upon the Czarina that a Princess of an important house would be less docile. . . . They have adroitly made use of some priest to insinuate to her Majesty that, seeing the small difference between the two religions, a Catholic Princess would be more dangerous.' Perhaps in the same order of ideas they dwelt on the agreeable insignificance of the Prince of Zerbst, 'a good fellow in his way, but of a quite unusual stupidity,' says La Chétardie. In short, at the beginning of December, Elizabeth charged Brümmer to write the letter which, a few weeks later, revolutionised the peaceful court in which Catherine had grown up under the benevolent eye of Mlle. Cardel.

II

The preparations of the Princess Jeanne-Elizabeth and her daughter were as brief as Brümmer could have desired. Figchen did not even wait for a new outfit. 'Two or three dresses, a dozen chemises, the same amount of

stockings and handkerchiefs'—that was all that
she took with her. Since they were to want for
nothing, haste and away! 'She only lacks wings
to go quicker,' wrote Brümmer to Elizabeth.
There is no evidence that the Princess took
much trouble to give any sort of *éclat* to her
daughter's first appearance in Russia. In following the correspondence which she carried on at
the time with Frederick, one is surprised to see
how small a place was taken in her plans by
the future Grand Duchess. Was it really on
account of Figchen's chances of marriage that
she was taking the journey to Russia? It might
well be doubted : she scarcely makes the slightest
allusion to it. It is of herself that she thinks
chiefly, the vast projects that swarm in her
brain, and that she is in hopes of developing on
a stage worthy of her; the services that she
professes to render to her royal protector, and
for which she seems to claim a decent recompense in advance. So we shall see her act at
St. Petersburg and at Moscow.

Did Figchen know what was in the air, and
for what reason, good or bad, she had been told
to pack up her things? The point is contested.
She must have been aware that it was something more than a simple excursion like those
she had made to Hamburg and to Eutin. The
extent and the vigour of the debates between
her father and mother before leaving, the unusual solemnity of the leave-taking with her
uncle, the reigning Prince, Jean Louis, and the
not less exceptional magnificence of the present
—a beautiful blue stuff embroidered with silver
wire — with which he accompanied his last

effusions : all that betokened something extraordinary.

The departure took place on the 10th or 12th
of January 1744, and was without incident.
There is still shown at the Rathhaus of Zerbst
the cup in which the Princess Jeanne-Elizabeth
drank the health of the notabilities of the town,
gathered together with great ceremony to bid
her farewell. This is probably only a legend.
One incident, however, occurred at the moment
of departure. After having tenderly embraced
his daughter, Prince Christian-August put in her
hands a large book which he bade her preserve
with care, adding, mysteriously enough, that she
might soon have occasion to consult it. At the
same time he confided to his wife a manuscript in
his handwriting, which she was to pass on to her
daughter, after having absorbed and meditated
upon its contents. The book was the treatise of
Heineccius on the Greek religion. The manuscript fruit of Christian-August's recent watches
and meditations was entitled *Pro Memoria*, and
dealt chiefly with the question whether Figchen
could not, 'by some arrangement or other,'
become Grand Duchess without changing her
religion. This was the great concern of Christian-August, and the conjugal controversy which
had accompanied the preparations for departure,
and which had awakened the attention of
Figchen, had but this one object; Christian
August showing himself intractable on the
subject, and Jeanne-Elizabeth much more disposed to admit the necessities imposed by the
new destiny of her daughter. It was for this
reason that Figchen's father had resolved to

arm his daughter against the temptations that might fall in her way. The treatise of Heineccius was to serve this purpose. It was the heavy artillery of the fortress. In the *Pro Memoria* followed considerations and recommendations of another order, in which the German practical spirit had its share; not without some reflection of the petty ways of a court like that of Zerbst or Stettin. The future Grand Duchess was advised to show the greatest respect and the most entire obedience towards those on whom her future would depend. She would place the good pleasure of the Prince her husband above that of all the world. She would avoid too intimate relations with no matter whom of her associates. She would speak to no one in asides in a public assembly. She would keep her pocket-money to herself, so as not to come under the dependence of a *maîtresse de cour* Finally, she would take care to meddle with none of the affairs of government. All this was expressed in a jargon which gives a curious specimen of the current anguage of the time, the German that Frederick professed to despise—not without reason. 'Nicht in Familiarité oder Badinage zu entriren, sondern allezeit einigen Égard sich möglichst conserviren. In keine Regierungssachen zu entriren um den Senat nicht aigriren;' and so forth.

Two months later Figchen thanked her father with effusion for his 'gracious instructions.' We shall soon see how much she profited by them.

At Berlin, where the two princesses stayed for some days, the future Empress saw Frederick

the Great for the last time in her life. At
Schwedt, on the Oder, she said good-bye for
ever to her father, who had accompanied the
travellers thus far. He returned to Stettin;
Jeanne-Elizabeth set out for Riga, by way of
Stargard and Memel. The journey, especially at
this time of the year, was anything but agreeable.
There was no snow, but the cold was so intense
that the two women were obliged to cover their
faces with a mask. Then there were no comfortable quarters in which to rest. The orders
of Frederick, who had commended the Countess
of Reinbek—the name under which the Princess
was travelling—to the care of the Prussian burgo-
masters and posting-house keepers, served them
in little stead. 'As the rooms in the posting-
houses were not warmed,' wrote the Princess,
'we had to take refuge in the landlord's room,
which was just like a pig-sty; husband, wife,
watch-dog, fowls, and children all slept pell-mell
in cradles, beds, mattresses, and behind the stove.'
It was worse still beyond Memel. There were
not even post-horses to be had. Horses had to
be borrowed from the peasants: not less than
twenty-four were required to drag the four heavy
berlines in which the Princess and her suite were
travelling. Sledges had been fastened on behind
the carriages, in preparation for the snow that
might be found further north. This gave a
more picturesque air to the caravan, but did not
hasten its progress. The advance was slow, and
Figchen had an indigestion through drinking the
beer of the country.

They arrived at Mittau on the 5th of February,
in a state of exhaustion. Here they met with a

better reception, and the pride of Jeanne-Elizabeth, secretly wounded by the familiarity that the
Countess of Reinbek had had to endure from
posting-house keepers, received its first satisfaction. There was a Russian garrison at Mittau,
and the commandant, Colonel Voïeïkof, exerted
himself to do the honours of the place to so
near a relative of his sovereign. Next day
they reached Riga.

And suddenly, as in a pantomime, the scene
changed. The letters of the Princess to her
husband were quite effusive over this unexpected
coup de théâtre; the civil and military authorities
presenting themselves at the entrance to the
town, under the command of the Vice-Governor,
Prince Dolgorouki, another high functionary,
Siemiène Kirillovitch Narychkine, ex-ambassador
at London, with a state chariot, cannon firing
salutes on the way to the castle. And what
splendour in the castle, prepared for the reception
of these foreign guests ! Rooms magnificently
decorated, sentries at all the doors, couriers on all
the staircases, drums beating in the court. The
salons, lit by a thousand tapers, are crowded with
people : court etiquette, kissing of hands, obeis-
ances to the ground, magnificent uniforms, marvellous toilettes, dazzling diamonds, velvet, silk,
gold, a profusion never seen, never heard of
before. To Jeanne-Elizabeth it seems as if her
head is turning, as if she is in a dream. 'When
I sit down to table,' she writes, 'the trumpets in
the house, the drums, flutes, and hautboys of the
guard outside, sound a salute. It always seems
to me that I must be in the suite of Her Imperial
Majesty or of some great princess ; it never

enters into my head that all this is for poor me, accustomed as I am to have only the drum beaten for me, and sometimes not even that.' She takes all the honour, however, and with the greatest delight. As for Figchen, we know nothing of the impression produced on her by all this riches and magnificence, so suddenly unfolded before her. Without doubt, it must have been profound. Russia, the great mysterious Russia, opened before her, giving her a foretaste of future splendours.

On February 9th they set out for St. Petersburg, where, by the will of the Czarina, they were to stay for a few days, before rejoining her at Moscow, and see that their toilettes were conformed to the fashion of the country. This was Elizabeth's delicate way of repairing the deficiencies, known or guessed, of Figchen's wardrobe. Assuredly, with her three dresses and her dozen chemises, the future Grand Duchess would cut a sorry figure at a court where all the splendours met together. The Czarina herself had 15,000 silk dresses, and 5000 pairs of shoes! Catherine did not mind, in later days, recalling her poverty at the time when she arrived in her new country. She seemed to herself to have paid her debt.

Needless to say, the heavy German berlines with their odd equipment had been left behind at Mittau. Another sort of train was now to conduct the two travellers on their way to fortune. The Princess of Zerbst describes it thus : '(1) a detachment with a lieutenant of cuirassiers of the corps of His Imperial Highness, named the Holstein Regiment ; (2) the Chamberlain, Prince Narychkine ; (3) an equerry ; (4) an officer of the

Ismaïlovski Guards, who fills the place of gentle-man-in-waiting ; (5) a major-domo ; (6) a confec-tioner ; (7) cooks and under-cooks, to I know not what extent ; (8) a butler and under-butler ; (9) a man for the coffee ; (10) eight lackeys ; (11) two grenadiers of the Ismaïlovski Guards ; (12) two quarter-masters ; (13) any number of sledges and stable-boys.—Among the sledges is one named *Les Linges*—Her Majesty's linen, that is. It is scarlet, and decked with gold, lined inside with sable. It has silk cushions, coverings of the same stuff, above which is placed one that has just been sent me with the pelisses (a present from the Empress, brought by Narychkine). My daughter and I are to have this sledge, where we shall lie at full length. La Kayn (maid of honour of the Princess) has one to herself, not such a fine one.' Further on, Jeanne-Elizabeth grows yet more eloquent over the perfections of the marvellous imperial sledge : 'It is extremely long. The top is like our German chairs. It is hung with red cloth striped with silver. There is fur all round the bottom. On that are placed a feather bed and damask cushions ; above that again, a satin covering, very neat and nice, on which one lies down. Under one's head are yet more cushions, and one puts over one the furred coverings, so it is exactly like being in a bed. For the rest, the long space between the driver's seat and the covered part serves for two purposes, and is at the same time useful in regard to the comfort of the conveyance, because, whatever rut it passes over in the road, it can pass over without jolting ; and the bottom of this space is made up of boxes, in which one can put what one likes. By day it serves for the gentlemen in attendance, and by night for the servants, who can sleep there at full length. These constructions are drawn by six horses, harnessed two and two, and cannot be upset. It is all the invention of Peter the Great.'

Elizabeth had left St. Petersburg on the 21st January. Nevertheless, a large number of personages belonging to the Court and a part of the diplomatic corps were still there. The journey to Moscow, at this epoch, was quite an affair. It necessitated the moving, not only of people, but of furniture as well. The departure of the sovereign displaced a hundred thousand people, and emptied an entire quarter of the town. The French and Prussian Ambassadors had no intention of letting any one whatever be beforehand with them in regard to the two princesses. La Chétardie, in his despatches to Amelot, boasted that he knew both mother and daughter intimately. He had recently met with them at Hamburg, on his return to Russia. Both exerted themselves to the utmost. The Princess of Zerbst found herself in an atmosphere of homage, of assiduity, of forced flattery, in which already intrigues and rivalries began to show themselves. She was in her element, and she flung herself into it with delight, holding receptions, giving audiences, from morning to night, surrounding herself with prominent personages, essaying the most complicated moves of the game of politics. At the end of a week she was out of breath. Her daughter held out better. 'Figchen southenirt die Fatige besser als ich,' wrote the princess to her husband. And she noted this trait, which seems already to indicate the future Semiramis: 'It is the grandeur of her surroundings that sustains the courage of Figchen.'

The grandeur! that, indeed, is what seemed most to impress the mind of this girl of fifteen, initiating her into the mysteries of her future destiny. At the same time she learnt of what this grandeur was made, and how it was attained. She was shown the barracks from which, so short a time before, Elizabeth had set out to conquer a throne. She saw the wild grenadiers of the Préobrajenski regiment, who accompanied the Czarina on the night of the 5th December 1741. And the one true lesson, the living lesson of things, spoke to her awakening mind.

In the mind of her mother certain anxieties intrude themselves into the intoxication of the present hour. Across the crowd of compliments there pierce certain dim warnings, certain veiled threats. The all-powerful Bestoujef remains always hostile to the projected alliance, and he has not thrown up the game. He counts on the Bishop of Novgorod, Ambrose Jouchkievitch, disapproving of the too close relationship between the Grand Duke and the Princess Sophia, or won over, as people said, by the Saxon court with a thousand roubles. The influence of this prelate is considerable. But Jeanne-Elizabeth has no lack of courage. She has, too, for her further confidence in her own success, two reasons worth all the arguments of her adversaries:— first, her extraordinary levity of temperament, which made her give herself the name of Will-o'-the-Wisp; and secondly, her own opinion of herself, of her resources for intrigue, of her aptitude in surmounting the gravest difficulties. What, after all, has to be done? Merely to overcome the opposition of a minister who is unfavourable to her. For that there is a remedy, which has already been discussed by her and Frederick on her passage through Berlin: it consists in suppressing the opposition by suppressing the minister. Frederick has had it in mind for some time. Well, she will overthrow Bestoujef as soon as she has reached Moscow. Brümmer and Lestocq will aid her.

It is with this fine project in her mind that she once more starts on her way.

III

The journey, this time, is very different from that between Berlin and Riga. The posting-houses on the way are almost palaces. The sledges skim over the firm ice. They push forward night and day, in order that they may reach Moscow by the 9th of February, the Grand Duke's birthday. For the last relay, at seventy versts from Moscow, sixteen horses are harnessed to the famous sledge constructed by Peter the Great, and the distance—some fifty miles— is covered without a stoppage in three hours. This headlong course is all but interrupted by a fatal accident. In passing through a village, the lumbersome vehicle, which once again carries the fortunes of Russia, grazes the corner of a cottage. The blow detaches from the roof of the sledge two great bars of iron, which come near crushing the two sleeping princesses. One, indeed, strikes Jeanne-Elizabeth on the neck, but the pelisse in which she is enveloped softens the blow : her daughter is not even awakened. Two grenadiers of the Préobrajenski regiment, sitting on the front part of the sledge, are dashed to the ground, bleeding and dislocated. Leaving it to the villagers to pick them up, the horses are whipped up, and at eight o'clock in the evening they halt at Moscow, before the wooden palace, the *Golovinski Dvarets*, inhabited by the Czarina.

Elizabeth, all impatience, is waiting for the newcomers behind a double row of courtiers. Her nephew, more impatient still, disregarding etiquette, and not giving the travellers time to take off their furs, dashes into their room and gives them the warmest greeting. Soon after, they are conducted to the presence of the Czarina. The interview is all that could be wished ; nor does it pass without a touch of feeling, which seems of good augury. After having gazed attentively at the mother of the future Grand Duchess, the Empress turns aside and goes quickly out of the room. It is to hide her tears, for she has seen certain traits in the face of the princess which remind her of her unforgotten sorrow. The princess, instructed by Brümmer, has not forgotten to kiss the imperial hand, and Elizabeth is gratified by these testimonies of excessive respect.

Next day, Figchen and her mother are simultaneously raised to the rank of Dames of the Order of Catherine, at the desire of the Grand Duke, as Elizabeth assures them. 'We are living like queens, my daughter and I,' writes the Princess of Zerbst to her husband. As for the all-powerful Bestoujef, there is no need for the Princess to organise a cabal against him. There is one already formed by the French and the Prussian parties, supported by the Holsteiners who have been attracted to Russia by the fortune of Peter-Ulric. Lestocq directs, or seems to direct, the affair; putting forward, in opposition to Bestoujef, Count Michael Vorontsof, who has taken part in the accession of Elizabeth. We need not here paint the portrait of the minister whom Jeanne-Elizabeth would thus put in check, one of the most astonishing diplomatic free-lances of the age, for he has served many before finally offering his services to Russia. Does Figchen's mother really represent to herself the gravity of the struggle into which she is entering, and the power of the adversary whom she has against her? It is not probable. But she remembers that Frederick has promised her the Abbey of Quedlinbourg for her younger sister, if she succeeds in her enterprise, and she means to have her abbey. In Frederick's mind the fall of Bestoujef serves as the signal of a great political upheaval, which may lead to the closer union of Russia, Prussia, and Sweden. How glorious for the Princess of Zerbst, to link her name with the accomplishment of such a task! She feels within herself the power to achieve it. She is a woman, and she comes from Zerbst: let that be her excuse. She imagines herself still in the midst of the little intrigues, the frail plots, that she has known before; and it is this that constitutes her great mistake, till one day her eyes open to the reality of things, and she sees the immensity of the abyss near which she has unknowingly ventured. As

for the marriage of her daughter, she will have
no more to do with it. 'It is a settled thing,'·
she writes to her husband. Figchen has won the
suffrage of all; 'cherished by the sovereign,'
loved by the heir apparent.' And what has the
heart of the future wife to say to all this? Has
the recollection of that first meeting at Eutin with
the sickly 'child of Kiel' given place to more
favourable impressions? That is not a point
that enters into the calculations of her mother.
Peter is Grand Duke; one day he will be
Emperor. The heart of her daughter would be
made of different stuff from the hearts of all
German Princesses, past and present, if she were
not satisfied with her chances of happiness under
such conditions. Let us see nevertheless what
has happened to the sickly child since the unexpected change in his fate.

IV

Peter was born at Kiel, February 21, 1728.
The minister at Holstein, Bassewitz, wrote to St.
Petersburg that the Czarevna Anna Petrovna
had given birth to 'a robust and healthy boy.'
It was a phrase of court flattery. The child was
not robust, and never could be. His mother
died three months later; of consumption, said the
doctors. The feeble health of the future Emperor
caused his education to be neglected. Up to the
age of seven he is in the hands of governesses,
French governesses, at Kiel as at Stettin. He
has also a French master, Millet. At this point
he is suddenly put under the discipline of the
officers of the Holstein Guard. He becomes a

soldier before he is a man, a soldier of the barracks, of the mess, of the guard-room, of the field-parade. So he acquires a taste for the low side of soldiering, its vulgarities, its hardships, its minutiæ. He goes through his drill, he mounts guard. In 1737, at the age of nine, he is sergeant, and he stands, musket in hand, at the door of a room in which his father is giving a sumptuous dinner to the officers. Tears run down the child's cheeks as he sees the succulent dishes file past under his eyes. At the second course his father has him relieved, appoints him lieutenant, and allows him to sit down to the table. After he had come to the throne, Peter was wont to refer to this incident as the happiest recollection of his life.

In 1739, on the death of his father, there is a complete change of regulation. He has a head tutor, under whom are several others. This head tutor is the Holsteiner Brümmer, whom we know already. Rulhière has eulogised this man 'of rare merit,' whose sole error, according to him, was that of 'bringing up the young Prince after the greatest models, considering rather his station than his abilities.' Other testimonies that have come to us in regard to this personage are much less favourable. The Frenchman Millet said of him that 'he was good for training horses, and not princes.' He treated his pupil, it seems, brutally, inflicting on him preposterous punishments utterly unsuited to the delicacy of his health, such as depriving him of food, or inflicting on him the torture of kneeling for a long space of time on dried peas spread on the ground. At the same time, as the little Prince, 'le diablotin,' who persisted in living despite the objection of the Empress Anne—was at once heir to the throne of Russia and to that of Sweden, he was taught alternately Russian and Swedish, according to the chances of the moment. The result was that he knew neither language. When he came to St. Petersburg in 1742, Elizabeth was astonished to find him so backward. She handed him over to Stählin, a Saxon, who had come to Russia in 1735, and who was Professor of Eloquence, of Poetry, and of the Philosophy of Gottschedt, of the Logic of Wolff, and of many other things besides. To his functions as professor he joined the exercise of a great number of talents. He wrote official verse for the Court *fêtes*, translated Italian operas for her Majesty's theatre, designed medals destined to record some victory over the Tartars, directed the choir of the imperial chapel, and composed mottoes for the court fireworks.

What became of Peter's education in the midst of all this may be easily imagined. Brümmer still remained with the child in his position of master of the household—grosser and more brutal than ever, according to Stählin's report. One day the latter was obliged to interfere in order to hinder actual violence; the Holsteiner was making for the young Prince with raised fists, while Peter, half-dead with fright, shouted to the guard to come to his aid.

Under such training the character of Catherine's future husband contracted vicious habits and ineradicable defects; he was at once violent and cunning, cowardly and braggart. He already astonished the candid Figchen by his lies, as he was afterwards to astonish the world by his cowardice. One day, as he amused himself by thrilling her with records of his prowess against the Danes, she inquired naïvely at what time these exploits had happened. 'Three or four years before my father's death.' 'But you would only be seven!' He reddened with anger. Weakly withal, uncomely in body as in mind, he was a crooked soul in an impoverished and prematurely ravaged body. Figchen would certainly do ill to count on his affection, sincere as it appeared in the eyes of Jeanne-Elizabeth, to assure her establishment in Russia. Was he even capable of love, this young man who cut so sorry a figure?

Happily for her, Catherine was well able to depend on her own resources. The account she herself gives of this period of her life would be scarcely credible if we had not wherewith to verify the accuracy of her story. She was hardly fifteen, and already we find in her that just and penetrating perception, that soundness of judgment, that marvellous sense of the situation, and that admirable good sense which, later on, formed so large a part of her genius,—which were, perhaps, her genius. To begin with, she realises that to remain in Russia, to make a figure, to play a *rôle*, it is needful to become a Russian. Without doubt her cousin Peter had never thought of it. But she sees well the discomfort and the dislike that he creates about him with his Holstein jargon and his German manners. She gets up in the night to repeat the lessons that her Russian master, Adadourof, has set her. As she never takes the precaution of dressing, and walks barefoot in the room to keep herself awake, she takes a chill.   Soon her life is in danger.

'The young Princess of Zerbst,' writes La Chétardie (March 26, 1744), 'is ill with peripneumonia.'   The Saxon party takes courage—uselessly, if we may believe the French diplomatist, for Elizabeth is resolved, whatever happens, that they shall never profit from the event.   '"They shall gain nothing," she said the day before yesterday to MM. de Brümmer and Lestocq; "for if I have the misfortune to lose this dear child, may the devil take me if ever I have a Saxon princess."'   Brümmer also confided to La Chétardie that, 'in the distressing extremity that must be faced and considered, he had laid his plans, and that a Princess of Armstadt [sic], a charming person, who had been thought of by the King of Prussia in case the Princess of Zerbst were to fail, would have the preference over every other.'   The prospect of this substitution, reassuring as it is, is far from delighting La Chétardie. 'We shall lose much,' he declares, 'seeing how I am looked upon by the Princesses of Zerbst, mother and daughter, and their persuasion that I have contributed to the future prepared for them.'

While rival ambitions thus fight over her, the Princess Sophia struggles with death.   The doctors prescribe blood-letting.   Her mother opposes it.   It is referred to the Empress; but the Empress is at the convent of La Troitza, absorbed in the devotions to which she abandons herself in her passionate, though intermittent way, putting a certain passion into all that she does.   Five days pass; the patient waits.   At last Elizabeth arrives with Lestocq, and orders the blood-letting. The poor Figchen loses consciousness. When she returns to herself, she finds herself in the arms of the Empress, who, to console her for the prick of the lancet, makes her a present of a diamond necklace and a pair of earrings worth 20,000 roubles. It is the Princess Jeanne-Elizabeth who notes the price. Peter himself becomes generous, and gallantly offers a watch covered with diamonds and rubies. But diamonds and rubies have no power over the fever. In twenty-seven days she is bled *sixteen* times, sometimes four times in twenty-four hours. At length the youth and robust constitution of Figchen get the better alike of the disease and the treatment. It appears, even, that this long and severe crisis has had a decisive and singularly happy influence over her destiny. While her mother has succeeded in rendering herself insupportable to everybody, always in opposition to the doctors, in dispute with the attendants, scolding and tormenting her own daughter, she, on the other hand, has known how to win all hearts, and, despite her condition, to render herself liked and loved by all. There is a story of a certain piece of stuff—the famous blue stuff embroidered with silver, the present of her uncle Louis—that Jeanne-Elizabeth took it into her head, one knows not why, to try to take away from the poor Figchen. It is easy to imagine the excitement caused in the sick-chamber by this pitiful incident: a concert of reprobation against the unnatural mother, a concert of sympathy in favour of the daughter, victim of such unfeeling treatment. Figchen gave up the piece

of stuff, and lost nothing by it. And she had
other triumphs. Her very illness endeared her
to the Russian heart, for it was known how she
had come by it. The image of the young girl,
barefooted, heedless of the winter weather, con-
ning over by night the unfamiliar sounds of the
Sclavonic tongue, already haunted the imagination, was already a legend. And it was said
that, at the most dangerous point of the crisis,
her mother had wished to summon a Protestant
pastor to her bedside. 'No,' was her reply;
'what for? Send for Simon Todorski.' Simon
Todorski was the orthodox priest who had had
charge of the religious education of the Grand
Duke, and who was now to undertake that also
of the Grand Duchess.

What were the sentiments, at this time, of
the Princess Sophia on this delicate subject?
It is difficult to be sure. Certain indications
favour the supposition that the treatise of Heineccius and the objurgations of the *Pro Memoria*
of Christian-August had produced on her a somewhat profound impression. 'I pray God,' she
wrote to her father, still at Königsberg, 'to
strengthen my soul with all the force it will
need in order to resist the temptations to which
I prepare to see myself exposed. He will accord
this grace to the prayer of your Highness and of
dear mamma.' Mardefeldt, for his part, showed
some anxiety. 'There is one point,' he writes,
'that causes me infinite embarrassment: it is
that the mother believes, or pretends to believe,
that this young beauty could never embrace the
Greek religion.' He tells how he had one day
to have recourse to the pastor, in order to calm

the mind of the Princess, frightened by the lessons of the Pope. Here, nevertheless, is what Catherine thought later, no doubt looking back on her own experience, of the difficulties that line the way to the bosom of the orthodox church on the part of a German Princess brought up in the Lutheran religion, of the time required for surmounting them, and of the course and progress of the moral problem. Writing to Grimm on August 18, 1776, in reference to the Princess of Würtemberg, whom she destines for her son Paul, she expresses herself in these terms : 'As soon as we have her, we will set about her conversion. We shall need quite fifteen days. . . . To hasten it all on, Pastoukhof has gone to Memel to teach her the A B C and the Confession in Russian : *conviction will come after.*'

However it may have been, the refusal to see the evangelical minister—a repudiation of the faith of her childhood—coming from the dying lips of the future Grand Duchess, and the appeal for the aid of Todorski—an anticipatory confession of the orthodox faith — received a ready belief. From that time the position of Figchen in Russia was assured. Whatever might come about, she was sure for the future to find it in the hearts of this *naïf* and profoundly religious people, whose beliefs she had espoused, and who testified its gratitude by immediately espousing her interests. The link that was to unite this little German Princess to the great Sclavonic nation, whose language she was but beginning to stammer ; the compact that for near a half-century was to associate their destinies in a single glorious fortune, to be broken only

by death ; this link, this compact, were from this
moment found and formed.

On April 20, 1744, the Princess Sophia
appears for the first time in public after her
illness. She is still so pale that the Empress
sends her a pot of rouge. But, notwithstanding,
she attracts all eyes, and she feels that all eyes
look on her kindly. Already she pleases and
attracts. She brightens and warms about her
the glacial atmosphere of a court which she is
one day to render so brilliant. Peter himself
shows himself more attentive and more con-
fiding. Alas! his gallantry and his confidence
are of but one kind. He tells his future wife
the story of his intrigue with one of the maids
of honour of the Empress, the Princess Lapoukhine, whose mother has recently been exiled
to Siberia The *freiline* has to quit the court
at the same time. Peter would like to have
married her, but resigned himself to the will
of the Empress. Figchen blushes, and thanks
the Grand Duke for the honour he has done
her in making her the third party to his
secrets. Already it is evident what sort of
future lay before these two creatures so little
made for one another.

V

During this time the Princess Jeanne-Elizabeth is quite given over to her enterprises in
the higher diplomacy. She makes friends with
the Troubetzkoï family, and with the bastard
Betzky himself, whose bustling personality
begins to make itself felt. She has a *salon*,

which is the meeting-place of all the adversaries
of the actual political system, all the enemies
of Bestoujef: Lestocq, La Chétardie, Mardefeldt,
Brümmer. She forms cabals, she plots, she
intrigues. She goes forward with all the ardour
of an hysterical woman, and all the heedlessness
of an airy brain. She thinks she has secured
her success, and also her Abbey of Quedlinbourg. She already sees herself complimented
by Frederick, and assuming, in short, the *rôle*
of his ambassador at the court of the North,
his best, his most precious ally. She sees
nothing of the abyss at her feet.

On the 1st of June 1744 Elizabeth has
betaken herself once more to the convent of
La Troitza, this time with full ceremony and
the pomp of a solemn pilgrimage, taking half
her court with her, and journeying on foot.
She has formed the vow, on coming to the
throne, that she will repeat this ceremony
every time that she visits Moscow, in memory
of the refuge that Peter I. had found in the
ancient monastery, at a time when his life was
in danger through the revolt of the *Strelitz*.
The Princess Sophia, still too weak, is not able
to accompany the Empress, and her mother
remains with her. But after three days a
courier arrives, bearing a letter from Elizabeth:
the two Princesses are to rejoin the Imperial
cortège, and assist at its solemn entrance within
the walls of La Troitza. Scarcely are they
installed in a cell, where the Grand Duke
comes to pay them a visit, when the Empress
herself enters, followed by Lestocq. She seems
greatly agitated. She orders the Princess

Jeanne-Elizabeth to follow her into a neighbouring room. Lestocq accompanies them. The interview is long. Figchen pays no heed to it, occupied in listening to her cousin's usual extravagant chatter. Little by little her youth and vivacity get the better of the constraint which the Grand Duke's presence generally inspires, she enters into his childish mood, and both fall to laughing and playing with great gaiety. Suddenly Lestocq returns: 'This is soon to be put a stop to,' says he brusquely; then, addressing the Princess Sophia: 'You had better see about packing up.' Figchen remains dumfounded, and, as the Grand Duke demands what it all means, Lestocq contents himself with adding: 'You will soon see.'

'I saw clearly,' writes Catherine in her memoirs, 'that he (the Grand Duke) would have abandoned me without regret. For my part, his disposition being what it was, I should have viewed his loss with indifference, but not that of the crown of Russia.' Was it possible that this girl of fifteen was already thinking about the crown? Why not? Writing her memoirs forty years afterwards, supposing that she really wrote them as they have come to us, Catherine may, and indeed must, have forced the note of her childish impressions. 'My heart,' she tells us, referring to this period, 'foresaw nothing good in the future; ambition alone sustained me. I had, deep down in my heart, an indefinable something which never let me doubt for an instant that I should become the Empress of Russia.' Here the exaggeration is evident, and the *à posteriori* attitude stares one in the face. But the throne in company with Peter might well allure the imagination of the precocious child; 'expectations' far more distant have at all times figured in the matrimonial bill, and *fiancées* of fifteen, now as ever, know very well how to cash them.

After Lestocq comes the Empress, very red, and the Princess Jeanne-Elizabeth, very agitated, her eyes full of tears. At the sight of the sovereign the two youngsters, who had been sitting on the ledge of the window, their legs dangling, and, taken aback by what Lestocq had just said, had not moved from their place, jump down precipitately. One sees the picture. It seems to disarm the Empress's wrath. She smiles, goes up to them, embraces them, and goes out without a word. Then the mystery begins to clear up. For more than a month the Princess of Zerbst had been unconsciously walking over a mine that had been dug for her by the enemies whom she fancied it so easy to dispose of. And the mine had just exploded.

The Marquis La Chétardie had returned to Russia at the age of thirty-six, with the reputation of being the most brilliant diplomatist of the day. Tall, well made, an imposing and accomplished cavalier, he seemed destined to take a great place at a court where everything was decided by favour, where success depended on the power of pleasing, and where he, it was said, had already had the good fortune to please. He had his plan, a very ingenious, perhaps a too ingenious, plan, whose adoption he had already secured, not without difficulty, at the court of Versailles. It placed the fall of Bestoujef, that is to say the abandonment of the Austrian policy defended by this minister, as the price of an arrangement long debated between the two courts, eagerly desired by Elizabeth, obstinately refused by France. It related to the title of Imperial Majesty, tacitly allowed to the Czars of Russia since Peter the Great, but not yet inscribed on the protocol, and consequently absent from the official documents emanating from the chancellor of the Most Christian King. La Chétardie had obtained credentials containing the longed-for title. He kept them by him, to give to the successor of Bestoujef, after his dismissal. Elizabeth was well aware of it, and soon it was known to every one at the court. Until matters were arranged, the French diplomatist, relying on his personal ascendency, affected to deal directly with the Empress, over the head of her chancellor. This was relying too much on his powers; it showed, too, a singular error in regard to the character of Elizabeth. The portrait of the daughter of Peter I. has been often sketched, and we have been able to arrive at a probably exact idea of this singular sovereign's ways of living and ruling. She was at once restless and indolent, avid of pleasure and nevertheless fond of affairs, spending hours over her toilette, keeping a signature or an order waiting for weeks or months, and yet authoritative withal; voluptuous, pious, incredulous, and superstitious; passing, from moment to moment, from excesses which ruined her health to religious exaltation which impaired her intellect: *une névrosée*, as we should say to-day. The Baron de Breteuil relates, in one of his despatches, that, in 1760, she was in the act

of signing the renewal of the treaty concluded in
1746 with the court of Vienna, and had already
written 'Eli .   ' when a wasp settled on the
end of her pen. She stopped, and it was six
months before she made up her mind to finish the
signature. Of her appearance, the Princess of
Zerbst has left us this pleasant sketch :—

'The Empress Elizabeth is very tall; she had
formerly an extremely good figure. She was
getting fat when I knew her, and it always
seemed to me that what Saint Evremond says in
his portrait of the famous Duchess de Mazarin,
Hortense Mancini, might have been said of the
Empress : " De ce qu'elle a la taille déliée une
autre l'aurait belle." It was then true to the
letter. Never was a head more perfect; it is
true that the nose is less so than the other
features, but it is well enough in its way. The
mouth is unique : there never was such another ·
it is all graces, and smiles, and sweetness. It
could never look sour, could never take any but
a gracious shape ; reproaches from it would be
adorable, if it could ever proffer reproaches.
Two rows of pearls show through the coral of two
lips that must be seen to be imagined. The eyes
are full of sensibility ; yes, that is the effect they
make upon me. One might take them for black,
but they are really blue. They inspire all the
sweetness with which they are animated. . . .
Never was a forehead more pleasing. Her hair
grows in such a manner that with a touch of the
comb it seems to have been cunningly arranged.
She has black eyebrows, and hair naturally
cendrée. Her whole form is noble, her bearing
fine, her presence full of grace ; she speaks well,

with an agreeable voice ; her gestures are correct.
In short there never was one like her. Her
complexion, her neck, her hands—never were
any such seen. Believe me, I know what I am
talking about, and I am speaking without prepossession.'

As for her mind, the pen of the Chevalier
d'Éon opposes to this gracious *ensemble* a terrible
counterpart :—

'Under an air of apparent *bonhomie*, she
(Elizabeth) has a sharp and incisive intelligence.
If one is not buttoned and cuirassed beforehand
against inspection, her eye glides under your
clothing, lays you bare, pierces open your breast,
and when you discover it, it is too late : you are
naked, the woman has read you to the root of
your heart, has rummaged your very soul.
Her frankness and good nature are only a mask.
In your France, for example, and in all Europe,
she has the reputation and the name of *clément*.
On her accession to the throne, indeed, she swore
on the venerated image of St. Nicholas that no
one should be put to death during her reign.
She has kept her word *to the letter*, and not a
head has as yet been cut off, it is true ; but two
thousand tongues, two thousand pairs of ears
have been. . . . You know, no doubt, the story
of that poor, interesting Eudoxie Lapoukhine ?
She did some wrong perhaps to her Majesty, but
the gravest wrong, be sure, was to have been her
rival, and fairer than she. Elizabeth had her
tongue pierced with a red-hot iron and twenty
strokes of the knout administered by the hand of
the hangman, and the unhappy creature was
pregnant, and near the birth. . . . You will find in

her private life the same contradictions. Now impious, now fervent, sceptical to the point of atheism, bigoted to the point of superstition, she passes whole hours on her knees before the image of the Virgin, talking with her, interrogating her with ardour, and demanding of her in what company of the Guards she should take the lover of the moment. . . . I was forgetting one thing. Her Majesty has a pronounced taste for strong liquor. It happens to her sometimes to be indisposed to the extent of falling in a swoon. . . . Then her dress and her corsets have to be cut. She beats her servants and her women.'

It is easy to see what difficulties must have been found by La Chétardie in his relations with a princess of so strange a humour, and on what slippery ground the Princess of Zerbst was venturing in his company. For she had become his associate, and had ended by pinning all her faith to him. Mardefeldt was quite out of the battle, Brümmer had little by little drawn away from the party, and Lestocq tacked about, with the native suspiciousness of his shrewd instinct. Despatches from Versailles exhorted the Marquis to prudence, ending by peremptorily ordering him not to make too uncertain a bargain on the strength of the expected gratitude for the Imperial title. After all, the matter was not of such grave importance, 'the King is Emperor in France.' It was much better to pay the Czarina 'a kind of flattery,' by showing her the king's letter. This would, perhaps, induce her to force the minister's hand in favour of the conclusion of the wished-for alliance. La Chétardie declared himself ready to obey, but there was some difficulty in doing so : it was needful to 'catch and keep' the Czarina, for at least a quarter of an hour, and this he could not do.

Meanwhile, Bestoujef put himself on the defensive. With the assistance of an employé of the chancellor's, Goldbach, a German, perhaps a Jew, an expert in the art of deciphering, so much cultivated at that period, he intercepted and brought to light all the correspondence of the French ambassador, which he suddenly planted before the eyes of the Empress, bringing specially to her notice the passages which personally concerned her, the passages in which La Chétardie deplored the idleness and frivolity of the sovereign, her unrestrained love of pleasure, and her very coquetry, which caused her to change her toilette four or five times a day. One can imagine Elizabeth's anger, and the consequences. Having deliberately refrained from making use of his credentials, La Chétardie was without official standing. A simple note from the chancellor's office gave him orders to quit Moscow and Russia within twenty-four hours. The Empress even demanded the return of a portrait that she had given him on the cover of a snuff-box set with diamonds. The snuff-box he could keep.

But it was not La Chétardie only who was compromised. His despatches had revealed to the Empress the part taken by the Princess of Zerbst in the abortive intrigue. They showed her at the court and in her own intimacy playing the part of spy in the service of Prussia and France, giving secret information to La Chétardie and Mardefeldt, corresponding secretly with

Frederick. That is what was meant by the enigmatical scene at the convent of La Troitza.

The Princess of Zerbst escaped with a good fright, with a taste of the truth that she had to hear from the lips of Elizabeth, and with the irrevocable loss, not only of the credit she had fondly hoped to acquire at court, whose secret springs she only now began to realise, but also of that to which she might legitimately have laid claim. 'The name of the Princess of Zerbst,' wrote La Chétardie's successor, d'Albion, a year after these events, 'was frequently met with in the intercepted letters of M. de La Chétardie. From that time the Empress took a decided dislike to her. . . . Her best course would be to return to Germany.' This, indeed, is what she did, but not without having assisted at the single victory of which a chance remained to her under a sky now so overcast,—the single one of which she seemed to have lost sight, almost to the point of letting it escape her.

VI

The person of Figchen had passed through this crisis unhurt. From this moment, indeed, and as if her proved innocence had pleaded her cause with even her adversaries and the enemies of her fortune, her triumph became certain, and her marriage with the Grand Duke finally assured. One delicate point still remained to be settled, the solemn admission of the Princess Sophia into the Greek Church. The Princess of Zerbst had done her best to carry out the injunctions of her husband. She had tried to fortify her own faith and the faith of her daughter. She had also made inquiry if the precedent of the wife of the Czarevitch Alexis, who had retained her position in the Protestant Church, might not be utilised for the benefit of Figchen. On this last point the result of her investigation was unsatisfactory. But the news that she gave of it to the pious and scrupulous Christian-August was accompanied by reassuring statements. She had gone over the creed of the Greek Church with Simon Todorski, she had compared it carefully with Luther's catechism, and she had arrived at the conviction that there was no fundamental difference between the two religions. As for Figchen, she had not taken so long to find out that she could save her soul in the orthodox religion. Heineccius evidently did not know what he was talking about, and Methodius harmonised admirably with Luther. The arguments of Simon Todorski on this subject were irresistible. He was a clever man, this archimandrite. He had seen the world, and had been a student at the University of Halle. Christian-August was not at first easy to move. 'My good Prince of Zerbst,' wrote Frederick, later on, 'was most restive on this point. . . . He replied to all my arguments, "My daughter shall not join the Greek Church."' Happily there was another Simon Todorski at Berlin. 'Some priest,' continues Frederick, 'whom I knew how to win over . . . was complaisant enough to persuade him that the Greek rites were similar to those of the Lutherans. After that he was always saying "Lutheran-Greek, Greek-Lutheran, it is the same thing."' In the course of June, a courier, sent by Elizabeth, returned with the Prince's official authorisation of the marriage and conversion of the Princess Sophia. The good Christian-August declared that he had perceived the finger of God in the circumstances which had led to this determination.

June 28th was fixed for the public profession of the young catechumen, and the day following, the feast of St. Peter and St. Paul, for the betrothal. The approach of this ceremony did not fail to cause some emotion to Figchen. The letters that she received in great numbers from her relations in Germany were not all of a reassuring kind. One can see to what comment of all kinds this unexpected destiny of the little princess would give rise in the minds of those among whom she had lived till now. The tendency was not generally too favourable. A little jealousy mingled perhaps with the apprehensions that seemed inspired only by a tender solicitude. The lamentable history was recalled of that unhappy Charlotte of Brunswick, the wife of Alexis, deserted by her husband, forgotten by the Czar. And had not the far-off Russia been fatal to all that German family, which had thought to find there a future of glory and greatness? All that came to the future Grand Duchess in long contorted phrases of Teutonic jargon, stuffed with French, in which she saw more of envy than of true consideration, but which made her sometimes tremble as she gazed anxiously into the future.

No one certainly would have thought so among the crowd of courtiers who, at ten o'clock in the morning of the 28th June 1744, thronged the entrance to the imperial chapel of the *Golovinski Dvarets.* Dressed in an 'Adrienne' robe of red cloth of Tours laced with silver, a simple white ribbon about her unpowdered hair, Figchen was radiant with youth, beauty, and modest assurance. Her voice did not tremble, her memory did not hesitate an instant, as she pronounced in, Russian the creed of her new faith before the moved assembly. The Archbishop of Novgorod, he who had formerly declared himself against the marriage, shed pious' tears on receiving her profession of faith, and all the assistants felt bound to imitate him. They had wept the same, it is true, at the conversion of Peter - Ulric, who had made grimaces during the ceremony, and had amused himself at the expense of the officiant. This sensibility was a part of the ceremony. The sovereign testified her contentment by presenting the catechumen with a clasp and collar of diamonds, which the expert Jeanne-Elizabeth estimated at 100,000 roubles.

But what would the good Christian-August have said if he had heard his daughter declare before God and man : 'I believe and I confess that faith alone doth not suffice for my justification?' Did not Figchen herself need some effort to pronounce these words, which separated her finally from her past? Those who would find here the influence of the Parisian philosophers on her youthful mind have somewhat confused their dates. It is extremely probable that at this moment the future friend of Voltaire did not know of that writer's existence. On leaving the chapel she found herself at the end of her strength, and she could not appear at dinner. But it was no more either Figchen or the Princess Sophia-Frederika who had crossed with unsteady feet the threshold of this temple of golden icones. That day, in the official liturgy, a prayer was introduced for the 'Orthodox (*Olagovierna*) Catherine Aleksieïevna.' The Princess of Zerbst explained to her husband, it is true, that Catherine had simply been added to Sophia, 'as occurs at confirmation.' As for Aleksieïevna, that sur-name, according to the usage of the country, stood for 'daughter of Augustus,' Augustus having no nearer translation in Russian. The good Christian asked no questions. He had had for some time to lay in a provision of credulity, and there were special graces, no doubt, for the benefit of German princes with marriageable daughters abroad.

The betrothal took place next day in the *Ou-spienski Sobor.* The Princess of Zerbst herself placed the rings upon the fingers of Catherine Aleksieïevna and her future husband—two little marvels, these rings, worth quite 50,000 écus, said she. Some writers, Rulhière among others, affirm that Catherine received on this occasion the title of heir to the throne, with right of succession in case of the Grand Duke's death. The fact is contested by the most recent Russian authorities. It would have required an official manifesto, and there is no trace of this. The future Grand Duchess continued to win all hearts by the per-fect grace and seemliness of her attitude. Her mother herself observed with satisfaction that she blushed every time that the exigencies of her newly acquired rank obliged her to take pre-

cedence over her who had given her birth. **She**
had soon to find out that her daughter, notwithstanding, seized the opportunity afforded **by her**
new position to escape from a tutelage that had
long weighed upon her.   Nor was she alone in
finding herself now out of place and unwelcome
in the position in which she was obliged to live.
The Princess of Zerbst was treated in general
as a 'stranger,' and she aroused no sympathy.
Catherine, for the first time in her life, had now
money of her own—30,000 roubles—which had
been sent to her by Elizabeth, '*pour son jeu,*' as
the phrase was at the Court of Russia—an
amount which seemed to her an inexhaustible
treasure.   She soon drew upon it largely, and,
at first, very commendably.   Her brother had
just been sent to Hamburg to finish his studies.
She declared that she would pay the cost of his
maintenance.   She had her own court, of whom
the principal functionaries, chamberlains and
gentlemen of the bedchamber, were carefully
chosen outside of the coterie that the Princess
of Zerbst professed to keep in her interests and
in those of Frederick.   The son of the chancellor
himself, Peter Bestoujef, was one of the number.
This was one disappointment the more for the
Princess of Zerbst, and she did not fail to give one
more instance of her want of tact by showing it.
Her bad temper, bursting forth on any occasion
and at the expense of every one, put the finishing
touch to her unpopularity.   There were violent
scenes between her and the Grand Duke, which
afforded the latter an opportunity for showing off
his guard-room manners and language at the
expense of his mother-in-law.

Catherine, nevertheless, rapidly took root in her new situation   She even seized the occasion to become more intimately acquainted with the vast domain that she would one day be called to govern.   She made, in the company of the Grand Duke and of her mother, the journey to Kief which, forty years after, she was to make over again with ·such pomp and splendour, and the impression of this journey was destined never to be effaced from her memory, but to have a visible influence on her mind and even on the character of her future government.   Journeying five hundred miles without ever leaving the domains of Elizabeth, without ever seeing anything but crowds prostrate before the omnipotence of the Czarina, the little German Princess, accustomed to the narrow horizons of the puny sovereignties of her country, felt the rise and development in her of an idea of grandeur and force absolutely without limits.   It was this idea that, become Empress, she felt to be incarnated in her, and destined to subdue the world.   At the same time, with her young, clear-eyed sagacity, her already just perception of things, she perceived the seamy side of all this pomp and splendour, this magnificent empire one day to be hers.   At St. Petersburg, at Moscow, she had till now had before her eyes only the throne glittering with gold, the diamond-starred court, the outer drapings of the imperial majesty, lined with a somewhat barbarous showiness and a half-Asiatic luxuriousness, but so much the more imposing. She now found herself face to face with the roots and sources of this unparalleled splendour: she saw the Russian people as they were, she saw

them with astonishment, with affright. They
were sordid and savage, half-clothed, shivering
with cold and hunger in their smoky hovels, and
bearing like a cross the double yoke of misery
and servitude. The lamentable vices of the
social and political organisation, frightful abuses
of power, forced themselves upon her. And all
those attempts at reform, all those generous
instincts, all the liberal ideas that were to mark
the first part of her reign, had their origin in this
first rapid vision of things.

On her return to Moscow she had also to make
experience of another side of the picture: the
little annoyances inseparable from so elevated a
rank. One evening at the theatre, in the Grand
Duke's box, opposite to that of the Empress, she
observed the angry looks of the Empress turned
in her direction. Presently the obsequious Lestocq, with whom the sovereign had just been
conferring, presented himself before her, and
drily, almost brutally, with the visible intention of
making the rigidity of his attitude felt, explained
to her the reason of the Czarina's anger. Catherine had got into debt—17,000 roubles, besides
the 75,000 francs that she had spent in a few
months. Her treasure had slipped between
her fingers, one day to shed a shower of gold
through the empire, through all Europe. But
what was she to do? Was she to content herself
with the three dresses that she had brought to
Russia? She had had, at first, to borrow the
very bedclothes of her mother. She could not
decently continue in such a fashion. Then, too,
she had soon found out that in this court, as
much and more than in that of Zerbst, presents

make friends, and that a person in her position had no other means of paying for so indispensable an outlay. The Grand Duke himself had a marked predilection for this means of forwarding the good terms on which he hoped to keep with his *fiancée*. Finally, the Countess Roumiantsof had her own way of reading the responsibilities of her position as lady in waiting—a responsibility which seemed to her to lie in the direction of perquisites.

In her memoirs, from which we take these details, Catherine is very severe upon those who were at this time in attendance on her, nor does she spare the Grand Duke himself, with whom, in spite of his generosity, her relations, up to the present, had not been specially cordial. Perhaps she gave way to the temptation of blackening this corner of the picture. A letter in her writing, which dates from this period, seems to justify the supposition. The Grand Duke had been attacked by a pleurisy, in the month of October, and was obliged, despite his impatience, to keep his room. This is what Catherine writes to him (we respect the style and orthography of the document) :—

'Monsiegneur, ayant consulté ma Mére, sachant qu'elle peut beaucoup sur le grand-maréchal (Brümmer), elle m'a permis de lui en parler et de faire qu'on vous permettent de jouer sur les instrumens. Elle m'a aussy chargée de vous demander, Monseigneur, sy vous voulez quelques Italiens aujourd'hui aprés Midy. Je vous assure que je deviendray folle en Votre place sy on m'otois tous. Je vous prie au Nom de Dieu, ne lui montrez pas ses billets.

CATHERINE.'

This may do something to rehabilitate the Princess of Zerbst herself from the accusations of crabbed and cross-grained temper that her daughter was fond of bringing against her memory. Two months later, in December, we find Catherine imploring, with tears and prayers, that she may be allowed to see her betrothed, who, having recovered from the pleurisy, has just been attacked by another and more dangerous disease. On his way from Moscow to St. Petersburg, at Hotilof, Peter was brought to a stop: smallpox had manifested itself. It was of this disease that the betrothed of Elizabeth had died. The Czarina promptly sent Catherine and her mother out of the way to St. Petersburg, and took up her place by the bedside of her son. Catherine wrote the tenderest letters to her betrothed, letters in which, for the first time, she used the Russian language. The letters, it is true, were really written by her Russian master, Adadourof, whose writing she copied.

This second stay at St. Petersburg was marked for Catherine by the arrival of Count Gyllemborg, an envoy from Sweden, who brought news of the marriage of the heir to the throne, Adolph-Frederick, Catherine's uncle, with the Princess Ulrica of Prussia. Catherine had already met the Swede at Hamburg, in 1740. He had then recognised in her 'a philosophical mind.' He now wanted to know how the philosophy was getting on, and urged her to read Plutarch, the life of Cicero, and the *Causes de la Grandeur et de la Décadence des Romains*. In return, Catherine offered to the grave philosopher her portrait, 'the portrait of a philosopher of fifteen,' composed by her in his honour, according to the custom of the age. The original of this composition, which she laid claim to later on, was unluckily burnt by her, and no copy is to be found in the papers of Count Gyllemborg, which are preserved in the university of Upsal. In her memoirs Catherine states that, on seeing this juvenile work in 1758, she was astonished at the truth and depth of the characteristics she had there noted. It is to be regretted that she has not given us the chance of verifying this appreciation.

Peter was not able to set out for St. Petersburg till the end of January. Castéra relates that Catherine, having embraced her betrothed with every sign of the greatest delight, fainted away as soon as she had reached her room, and did not recover consciousness for three hours. The smallpox had not improved the appearance of the Grand Duke. The marks on his face, and an enormous wig in which he was muffled to hide other ravages, rendered him almost unrecognisable. The Princess of Zerbst was alone in finding him better looking than ever—as she reported to her husband. Castéra no doubt exaggerated in his story, as he was accustomed to do, and the Princess remembered that letters sent through the post at St. Petersburg were copied without extra charge. However that may have been, the preparations for the marriage commenced soon after this auspicious, or inauspicious, return.

VII

Such a ceremony had never yet been seen in Russia. The marriage of the Czarevitch Alexis,

son of Peter I., had taken place at Targau, in
Saxony, and, before his time, the heirs to the
throne of Moscow were not future Emperors.
Inquiries were made in France, where the marriage of the Dauphin had just been celebrated,
and also at the court of Saxony. From Versailles
and from Dresden arrived abundant memoranda,
minute descriptions, drawings even, giving the
minutest details of the pomps to be imitated, to
be surpassed. As soon as the ice was broken up
on the Neva, English and German vessels followed one another with equipages, furniture,
draperies, liveries, ordered from every corner of
Europe. Christian-August sent a present of
Zerbst goods, heavy pieces of silk broidered with
gold and silver, much thought of at that time.
Flowered silks were in fashion then, gold or
silver on a clear ground. England was specially
noted for them, and Zerbst came next in order,
in the opinion of connoisseurs.

After many alterations, the date of the ceremony was at last fixed for the 21st August. The
festivities were to last till the 30th. The Grand
Duke's physicians would have wished for a longer
postponement. In March Peter had again had
to take to his bed. A year seemed scarcely long
enough to set him on his feet again entirely.
But Elizabeth would not wait. It has been
suggested that she was in a hurry to get rid of
Catherine's mother. Probably she had more
serious reasons for showing impatience. Peter
was in such uncertain health, that the succession
to the throne was anything but assured, and the
remembrance of the young Ivan, shut up in his
prison, still haunted her. In June 1745 an un-

known man had been found, poniard in hand, in Elizabeth's bedroom. He had been put to the torture, but had preserved silence. It appears, nevertheless, on the best authority, that Jeanne-Elizabeth continued to make herself very disagreeable. There was no dirty business in which she is not implicated during the last weeks of her residence in Russia. She plots and plans and intrigues without cease She even goes so far as to accuse her daughter, declaring that she is having nocturnal *rendezvous* with her betrothed. The Empress intercepts her correspondence and carefully examines it. She does not invite her husband to the ceremony which is about to take place. The Princess of Zerbst has long held out the hope of this invitation to her husband, telling him to hold himself ready, putting him off from day to day and from month to month. Frederick himself, misled by Mardefeldt, has raised similar expectations in the mind of his field - marshal. At length Jeanne-Elizabeth has to confess that there is more chance of her being herself sent away before the ceremony.

The Princess's brother was the only one of the family to be present; thanks to the treachery, it is said, of Bestoujef. Homely, uncouth, poor-spirited August of Holstein was not a nice relative to produce in public. The English ambassador Hindford declares in his despatches that he never saw so fine a procession as that which conducted Catherine to the church of Our Lady of Kasan. The religious ceremony began at ten o'clock in the morning, and was not over till four o'clock in the afternoon. The orthodox church does things conscientiously. During the following days there was a constant succession of *fêtes*. Balls, masquerades, state dinners and suppers, the Italian opera, the French plays, illuminations, fireworks, nothing was wanting to the programme. The Princess of Zerbst has left us a detailed description of the most interesting day, the day of the wedding :—

'The ball did not last beyond half-past one in the morning ; after which Her Imperial Majesty, preceded by the masters of the ceremonies, the grand master of household, the grand marshal, and the grand chamberlain of the Grand Duke's court, and followed only by the bride and bridegroom, holding one another's hands, by me, by my brother, the Princess of Hesse, the mistress of the robes, the *staats dames*, the *cammer frelen*, and some *frelen*, directed her steps to the nuptial chamber, which the men all quitted as soon as the ladies had entered, and the doors were closed, while the bridegroom entered the dressing-room. First the bride was undressed. Her Imperial Majesty took off the crown from her head ; I waived, in favour of the Princess of Hesse, the honour of putting on the chemise. The mistress of the robes put on the dressing-gown, and the rest of the ladies helped to adjust the most magnificent déshabille imaginable.

'Except this ceremony,' observes the Princess of Zerbst, 'there is much less undressing of bride and bridegroom than there is with us. Not a man dares enter after the bridegroom has gone to undress for the night. The " garland " is not danced, and the garter is not handed round.

'As soon as the Grand Duchess was dressed, her Imperial Majesty went into the Grand Duke's room, where the Master of the Hunt, Count Razonmovski; and my brother had aided him to undress. We followed the Princess in. He was dressed much like the bride, but he did not look near so well. Her Imperial Majesty then gave them her benediction, which they received kneeling. She embraced them tenderly, and left the Princess of Hesse, the Countess of Roumiantsof, and myself, to put them to bed. I tried to speak to her of the thanks and gratitude I owed her, but she only laughed at me.'

We owe to the pen of Jeanne-Elizabeth a description of the suite of rooms reserved for the bride and bridegroom :—

'It consists of four large rooms, one more beautiful than another. The principal room is the richest; the hangings are of cloth of silver embroidered with silk, of the finest possible shading; the furniture all matches: chairs, curtains, *portières*. The bedroom is in red velvet, almost scarlet. It is embroidered with columns and garlands in raised silver; the bed is in the middle. The furniture all matches. It is all so fine, so majestic, that you cannot see it without being transfixed with admiration.'

The series of *fêtes* ended with a ceremony of a unique kind, never afterwards to be repeated. For the last time the *Diedouchka* (grandsire) of the Russian Fleet, a ship constructed by Peter the Great himself, according to the legend, was set afloat. By a ukase dated September 2, 1724, that monarch had ordered that the ship should be thus launched on the 30th August of every year, and kept the rest of the time in the monastery of Alexander Nevski. After his death, ukase and ship were alike forgotten. It was only in 1724 that Elizabeth thought of it. She attempted the ceremony again the following year, on the occasion of her nephew's marriage, and then it was done with for ever. A raft had to be made to support the ship, which could no longer hold water. Elizabeth went on board in great pomp, and kissed the portrait of her father, which was suspended to a mast.

A month later, the Princess of Zerbst parted for ever from her daughter and from the court of Russia. In taking leave of the Empress, she threw herself at her feet, and asked pardon for all the trouble that she had caused her. Elizabeth drily replied that 'it was too late to speak about it, but that if the Princess had always been so humble, it would have been better for everybody.' In her own account of the parting scene, Jeanne-Elizabeth only speaks of the graciousness of the Empress, of the reciprocal tenderness, of the tears of regret shed by both. As we have already seen, the court tears were at that time current coin, and Jeanne-Elizabeth, despite the failure of her political enterprises, did not lack diplomacy in what she wrote.

A terrible blow overtook her at Riga. A letter of Elizabeth, which reached her there, charged her to demand at the court of Berlin the immediate recall of Mardefeldt. This meant absolute ruin to the hopes that Frederick himself, generally more wide awake, had founded on the Princess's intervention with the Empress; hopes that she had done her best to encourage. It so happened that on the very day of the departure of Jeanne-Elizabeth from St. Petersburg, October 10, 1745, the Empress had discovered the measures which were being taken by Frederick to induce the new husband of the Princess Louise-Ulrica, and the brother of the Princess of Zerbst, to confirm his claim to the Duchy of Holstein. Frederick conceived that the possession of this Duchy was incompatible with that of the throne of Russia. At the same time came the news of the first successes of the Prussian army in Saxony (at Sorr, September 30), and the Council of the Empire, instantly convoked, decided that it was advisable to send a body of soldiers to the support of the King of Poland, attacked in his hereditary domains. From that time Mardefeldt, the friend and political ally of the Princess of Zerbst, and consequently of her brother, became impossible at St. Petersburg.

Thus had Jeanne-Elizabeth succeeded in making her daughter Grand Duchess of Russia, and with very little trouble on her part. On every other point, notwithstanding that she had put forth all the resources of her intelligence and of her indefatigable activity, her failure had been complete. Among other things, we may note in passing, she had endeavoured to make her husband a Duke of Courland, and with the same want of success.

Nevertheless, Catherine gave way to tears, not mere court tears, over the departure of this restless mother of hers. And well she might. It was a mother, after all, and the single person, amidst all her new splendours, whose affection she could not call in question, however little she might agree

E

with her advice. Her absence left a great void about her. It is from this moment, in such a solitude, the great element of strong natures, that the real education of the future Empress was to begin, an education of which Mlle. Cardel had not dreamed.

CHAPTER III

TIIE SECOND EDUCATION OF CATHERINE

I

DESPITE her precocity, Catherine was still only a child. Despite her orthodox name and her official title, she was only a stranger, brought by chance into Russia that she might hold high rank there, and one to whom it was no easy thing to hold herself on the level of so high a station. If she were ever to forget it for a moment, as she would seem to a certain extent to have done, there was always some one to remind her of it sharply enough. It seems that once having attained her end, once married, Mlle. Cardel's pupil somewhat relaxed the propriety of demeanour which had hitherto gained for her unanimous approbation. The 'gracious instructions' of Christian-August appeared to have escaped her memory. She was soon to receive others, somewhat less paternal.

On the 10th or 11th of May 1746, less than nine months after the marriage, two documents concerning the Grand Duke and Duchess were presented for signature to the Empress. Their object appeared to be to fix the choice and regulate the conduct of the two 'persons of distinction' who were to be assigned to their Imperial Highnesses as master of the household and mistress of the robes. Their real end was quite other. Under pretext of filling a place in the official list of offices, it was really two tutors and spies who were set over Catherine and her husband. They were put to school again, so to speak. And, under colour of indicating the programme of this complementary education, it was an act of accusation that was drawn up against the young people, whose conduct had rendered necessary the application of such a measure. The mover in this matter, the concocter of the two documents, was Bestoujef in person.

This work of the chancellor has been preserved. It abounds in truly extraordinary revelations, so extraordinary, indeed, that we should treat them with incredulity if we were not able to check them by another testimony. This testimony is to be found in Catherine's memoirs. The author of the memoirs repeats in almost identical terms everything that is said by Bestoujef of the doings and sayings of Catherine and her husband at this period of their life. In certain respects the pen of Catherine is even more frank than that of the chancellor, and it is from her that we learn the most dubious details, even in respect to herself.

The 'person of distinction' assigned to the Grand Duke as companion will make it his business, we read in the chancellor's report, to correct certain unseemly habits of his Imperial Highness, as, for example, that of throwing the contents of his glass at the servants who wait table, that of greeting every one who has the

honour of approaching him, including even the
strangers who visit his court, with gross jests and
indecent pleasantries ; that of disfiguring himself
in public with grimaces and with incessant con-
tortions of all his members.

'The Grand Duke,' we read in the memoirs,
'passed his time in childish pursuits unworthy of
his age. . . . He had a theatre of marionettes in
his room, the stupidest thing in the world. . . .
The Grand Duke passed his time literally in the
company of valets.   The Grand Duke put all
his suite under arms : the servants, the huntsmen,
the gardeners, all had muskets on shoulder .
the corridor of the house served as guard-
room. .   The Grand Duke grumbled at me on
account of what he termed my excessive devotion ; but having no one but me to speak to
during mass, he ceased complaining. When the
Grand Duke learnt that I fasted on Fridays, he
grumbled at me more than ever.'

The same figure of the ill-bred, unmannerly
child with vicious instincts stands out in both
reports, even more prominently, in some respects,
in the second.

Let us now look at Catherine's share in the
matter.   There are three principal complaints
brought against her by the chancellor : negligence in the observances of the orthodox religion ;
prohibited interference with the affairs of state,
those of the empire and those of the Duchy of
Holstein ; excessive familiarity with the young
lords of the court, the gentlemen in waiting, and
even the pages and valets. This last point is
evidently the most serious ; and it is on this that
Catherine enlarges in her memoirs, in the

clearest fashion, leaving no doubt whatever as to the familiarity, to say no more, of her relations at this time with three at least of the young people at court, the three brothers Tchernichef, all tall, well-made persons, extremely in favour with the Grand Duke The eldest, André, the most brilliant of the three, was the favourite of Peter, and soon of Catherine. She called him affectionately her 'petit fils'; he gave her the name of 'petite mére.' Peter not only tolerated this intimacy, he encouraged it, and pushed it to excess, even to the forgetfulness of the most elementary proprieties. He carried everything to excess, and cared little for impropriety of demeanour in himself or in those about him. While Catherine was still only betrothed, André had reminded him that the daughter of the Princess of Zerbst was destined to be -called Grand Duchess of Russia, and not Mme. Tchernichef. Peter burst out laughing at this explanation, which seemed to him extremely droll, and it only served to make him give his friend the name of 'fiancé de Catherine.' 'Votre fiancé,' he said to her in speaking of the young man. Catherine, for her part, tells us that she was remonstrated with by one of her *valets de chambre*, Timofeï Jevreïmof, who felt it to be his duty to warn her of the perils to which she was exposing herself. She pretends, it is true, to have acted in all innocence and ignorance, either of evil or of danger. Timofeï also warned Tchernichef, who, on his advice, feigned illness for a time. This was during the carnival of 1746. In April, when the court was moved from the Winter to the Summer Palace, -Tcherni-

chef reappears, and tries to get into Catherine's
room.   She bars the way, but without thinking
of fastening her door, which would certainly
have been more prudent.   She holds it half-
open, and continues a conversation which no
doubt she finds interesting.   Suddenly there
comes on the scene Count Devierre, one of the
heroes of the Seven Years' War, at present
chamberlain at the court, and spy also, it would
seem.   He informs the Grand Duchess that the
Grand Duke wishes to see her.   Next day the
Tchernichefs are sent away from the court, and
the same day the 'distinguished·lady' charged to
look after the conduct of Catherine makes her
appearance.   The coincidence is significant.   Nor
does Elizabeth stop there.   She imposes both on
Catherine and on Peter a sort of 'retreat,' in the
course of which Simon Todorski, the zealous
archimandrite and Bishop of Pskof, is instructed
to interrogate them on their relations with the
Tchernichefs.   The Tchernichefs themselves are
put under arrest, and undergo a similar interro-
gation, more pressing still, and no doubt less
mild.   No one confesses to anything.   Nevertheless Catherine speaks of a correspondence
that she has found means to carry on with André
Tchernichef, even while he is in prison.   She
wrote to him, he replied; she gave him commissions, which he executed.   Let us assume
that at this time she acted innocently.   Later on
we shall have to be less indulgent.

It was certainly a singular and unfortunate
idea, as the event proved, to attempt to treat a
married woman and a Grand Duchess of Russia
as if she were a little girl.   Catherine was ex-

pressly forbidden to write directly and personally to any one, even to her father and mother. She was only to sign the letters written for her at the Ministry of Foreign Affairs, that is to say, under the secretaryship of Bestoujef. This was actually to invite Catherine to engage in a secret correspondence, so much in vogue then. She was not long in doing so. Just then there arrived at the court of St. Petersburg an Italian gentleman of the name of Sacromoso, a Knight of Malta. A Knight of Malta had not been seen in Russia for a long time. He was received with great honour. He was present at all the *fêtes*, and at both the official and private receptions. One day, in kissing the Grand Duchess's hand, he slipt into it a note : 'From your mother,' he murmured, so as to be heard by no one. At the same time he pointed out a musician in the Grand Duke's orchestra, a compatriot of the name of Ololio, as the man who would take charge of the reply. Catherine deftly hid the note in her glove. It was not the first time, no doubt. Sacromoso had not deceived her : it was really her mother who had written to her. Having written her answer, she followed attentively, for the first time—for she had no taste for music—the concerts of the Grand Duke. The man who had been pointed out to her, seeing her approach, carelessly drew his handkerchief out of his vest-pocket, so as to leave the pocket wide open. Catherine threw her letter into this improvised letter-box, and the correspondence was started. It lasted during the whole time that Sacromoso was at St. Petersburg. Thus was put to nought the wisdom of statesmen and the power of an Empress, for having failed to reckon with that other power of youth, and that other wisdom, which bids that its power be not abused.

II

We may here pause for a moment to throw a rapid glance over the surroundings in which Catherine found herself placed, through so many long years of initiation. The Russia of the eighteenth century is a building all front, a piece of scene-painting. Peter I. endeavoured to put his court on a European footing, and his successors did their best to maintain and develop his work. At St. Petersburg as at Moscow, Elizabeth is surrounded with all the pomp and splendour of other civilised countries. She has palaces in which there are suite after suite of rooms, the walls covered with tall mirrors, the floors inlaid, the ceilings painted by great artists. She gives *fêtes* which are crowded with courtiers dressed in velvet and silk, laced with gold, starred with diamonds; where the court ladies appear in the newest fashions, with powdered hair, rouged cheeks, and a killing patch at the corner of the lips. She has her retinue, her *état de maison*, her train of chamberlains, of maids of honour, of officers of the court, and of servants, which, for number and splendour of uniforms, has not its equal in Europe. According to certain contemporary accounts, which modern Russian writers have perhaps too implicitly believed, the imperial residence of Peterhof exceeds in magnificence that of Versailles. To judge of the matter, we must look a little closely into all these splendours.

And, to begin with, they have for the most part something precarious and ephemeral which takes off much of their value. Her Majesty's palaces, like those of her most opulent subjects, are almost entirely made of wood. When they catch fire, and that often happens, all the treasures with which they are heaped up, furniture and works of art, disappear in the disaster. They are rebuilt always in a hurry, without an attempt to make a durable piece of work. The palace at Moscow, three kilométres and a half in circumference, burns in three hours under the eyes of Catherine. Elizabeth gives orders that it is to be rebuilt in six weeks, and she is obeyed. It is easy to imagine what the construction is like. The doors will not shut, the windows let in the draught, the chimneys smoke. The house of the high priest of Moscow, in which Catherine takes refuge after the burning of the palace, catches fire three times while she is there.

Then there is no idea of comfort or convenience in these outwardly imposing structures. Everywhere sumptuous reception-rooms, magnificent galleries for balls and gala dinners, and scarcely a corner to live in—only a few little rooms without light or air. The wing of the summer palace at St. Petersburg, in which Catherine lives, looks out on one side on the *Fontanka*, which at that time is a pool of fetid mire; on the other, upon a court a few feet square. At Moscow it is worse still. 'They stowed us away,' writes Catherine, 'in a wooden wing built during the autumn, so that the water dropt from the ceiling, and all the rooms were dreadfully damp. This wing contained two ranges of five or six rooms each, of which the one looking on the street was mine and the other the Grand Duke's. In my dressing-room were stowed away all my waiting-maids and other servants, so that there were seventeen women and girls in one room, a room which had, it is true, three large windows, but no outlet except through my bedroom, which they had to pass through every time they went in and out. . . . Besides that, their dining-room was one of my anterooms.' At length another communication with the outer world was made for this feminine establishment, by means of a single plank going from the window to the ground and serving as a ladder. Surely that is different enough from Versailles!

Catherine sometimes regretted her modest dwelling-place by the clock-tower of Stettin, or sighed after the castle of her uncle John at Zerbst, or that of her grandmother at Hamburg, heavy, but solid and spacious constructions in cut stone, dating from the sixteenth century. And she took her revenge on the discomforts that met her at every turn by rhyming these verses that have been found among her papers :—

> 'Jean bâtit une maison
> Qui n'a ni rime ni raison :
> L'hiver on y gèle tout roide,
> L'été ne la rend pas froide.
> Il y oublia l'escalier,
> Puis le bâtit en espalier.'

And not merely were Elizabeth's palaces built in this way, they were furnished to match. The affectation of settled furniture was then an unknown thing. The things belonged to the person, and were taken about from place to place. It was a sort of survival of the nomad life of the Eastern people. Hangings, carpets, mirrors, beds, tables and chairs, the luxuries and the necessities, followed the court from the Winter to the Summer Palace, from thence to Peterhof, and sometimes to Moscow. It goes without saying that some of these things got damaged or lost on the way. This resulted in an odd mixture of magnificence and destitution. One ate off gold plate on lopsided tables which had lost a leg somewhere. In the midst of masterpieces of French or English cabinet-work, there was nothing to sit down on. In the home of the Tchoglokofs, which Catherine inhabited for some time at Moscow, she found no furniture at all. Elizabeth herself was often no better looked after. But she used every day a cup that Roumiantsof had brought from Constantinople by her order, and which had cost 8000 ducats.

Corresponding with this outward disorder and dilapidation was the private license to which, despite the appearance of extreme pomp and refined etiquette, the very dignity of the throne abandoned itself. Some idea of this may be gathered from the following anecdote, which is told by Catherine in her memoirs. A little while before the intervention of Bestoujef, which had brought about such changes in the environment of Catherine and her husband, Peter was guilty of an action which may well have contributed, if not to provoke, at all events to justify, the severities of the chancellor, and to have determined the Empress to approve them. The room in which the Grand Duke had set up his marionettes communicated by a door, which had been closed up since the installation of the young court, with one of the *salons* of the Empress. In this *salon* Elizabeth sometimes had little private dinners of a few persons only. There was a table so arranged that the presence of servants could be dispensed with. One day Peter heard a noise in the room, the sound of many voices, and the clink of glasses. He bored several holes in the door with a gimlet, and, looking through, saw the Empress sitting at table with the master of the hunt, Prazoumofski, her favourite of the moment, wearing a mere dressing-gown. With this friendly couple were a dozen of the courtiers. Peter was immensely amused by the sight, and, not content with enjoying it himself, he hastened to ask Catherine to take part in the amusement. The Grand Duchess, more prudent, declined the invitation. She even warned her husband of the impropriety and danger of the proceeding. He paid no heed to her, and, in her place, brought in the ladies of her suite, made them get up on chairs and footstools in order to see better, and arranged a whole amphitheatre before the door, behind which was exposed the dishonour of his benefactress. The incident was soon found out, and Elizabeth was extremely angry. She even went so far as to remind her nephew that Peter I. had also had an ungrateful son. It was a way of saying that his head was no more firmly planted on his shoulders than was that of the unfortunate Alexis. Every one at the court soon heard of the incident, and was amused in turn.

As for Catherine, no doubt she learnt, if not a

moral lesson, which may be doubted, at least a lesson in practical wisdom.   If she, in after days, had her favourites in their dressing-gowns, she took care not to be overlooked through a keyhole. She either concealed them, or flaunted them before the world in all the magic of an incomparable *mise en scène*.   But she learnt from Elizabeth, at this period, other precious lessons.   If she refused to violate the secret of the private banquets in which the Empress forgot herself and her state, she was assuredly present, just after the departure of the Princess of Zerbst, at the state festival in yearly celebration of the day on which the daughter of Peter the Great had ascended the throne.   In the great hall of the Winter Palace the tables were laid for 330 under-officers and soldiers of the regiment which had then accompanied Elizabeth in the conquest of her crown.   The Empress, in captain's uniform, wearing top-boots, a sword by her side, and a white feather in her cap, took her place in the midst of her 'comrades.'   The dignitaries of the court, the head officers, and the foreign ministers were seated at table in a neighbouring room.   No doubt it is from having seen and thought over such sights in early life that Catherine was able, at the right moment, to put on the warlike livery with such easy grace, and to win in her turn the enthusiasm and support of these same grenadiers, ready themselves, thanks to the lessons of the past, to strike, and to strike hard.

The Grand Duke, though more generally called elsewhere by his pleasures and his amours, was sometimes, for a change, very attentive to his wife.   These were not her most agreeable

moments.   During a whole winter he spoke to
Catherine of nothing but his project of building
near his country house a place of rest and recreation in the form of a Capuchin monastery.   To
please him she was forced to design, over and
over again, the plan of this establishment, which
he was for ever altering.   Nor was this the worst
she had to put up with.   The presence of the
Grand Duke brought with it other trials, such, for
example, as the constant neighbourhood of a pack
of hounds, who infected the place with an intolerable stench.   The Empress having forbidden
this kind of amusement, it occurred to Peter to
hide his kennel in the bedroom, where Catherine's
nights soon became a martyrdom   By day the
barking and the piercing cries of the beaten
animals left her not a moment's repose.   When
the pack was quiet, Peter seized his violin and
walked from room to room, merely endeavouring
to make the greatest possible noise with the instrument.   He had a taste for uproar.   He had
also, from an early age, and increasingly, a taste
for drink.   From 1753 he got drunk 'almost
daily.'   And on this point Elizabeth was unhappily, and for an obvious reason, unable to
exercise the needful repression.   From time to
time the Grand Duke returned again to his
marionettes.   Once Catherine found him in full
uniform, booted and spurred, and with drawn
sword, standing before a rat suspended in the
middle of the room.   She found that there had
been a military execution : the unhappy rat
having devoured a paste sentinel placed before
a cardboard fortress, a council of war, solemnly
assembled, had condemned it to be put to death.

With her vigorous youth, and the ardour of her temperament, Catherine could nevér have endured such an existence, had she not contracted certain habits capable of diverting her by taking her away from this wretched interior. In summer, during her stay at Oranienbaum, she rose at dawn, slipped on a man's suit, and started for the chase, in the company of an old servant. 'There was a fishing-boat,' she tells us, 'by the shore; we crossed the garden on foot, our guns over our shoulders, we got into the boat, he and I and a pointer, and the fisher who was taking us, and I shot at the wild ducks in the reeds on both sides of the Oranienbaum canal.' Besides the chase, horsemanship gave occasion for staying out of doors. Elizabeth herself was a passionate horsewoman. She felt obliged, however, at one time, to cool the growing ardour of Catherine in this kind of exercise. With that taste for masculinity which always haunted her, the Grand Duchess liked to sit astride her horse, like a man. The Czarina fancied she had discovered one of the reasons which hindered her from having children. Catherine thereupon procured a saddle so arranged that she was able to mount as if it were a side-saddle, and to regain her favourite position as soon as she was out of Elizabeth's sight. A 'divided skirt' aided her in this performance She took lessons of a German groom, the teacher of the corps of cadets, and by her rapid progress won a prize of silver spurs. She was also very fond of dancing. One evening, in one of the frequent balls with which Elizabeth enlivened the court, the Grand Duchess made a wager with Mme. Arnheim, the wife of the

Saxon minister, that she would not be the first
to be out of breath.   She won the wager.

III

It was in such distractions, and in the reading of Bayle's *Dictionary* and other less serious
books, that Catherine was passing her time, when,
in 1754, a long-looked-for event came to bring a
great change into the monotony of her life.   She
became a mother.

How did this come about?   The question
may seem strange : yet there is no point in the
whole biography of Catherine which has given
rise to more controversy.   It must be remembered that ten years had elapsed since the
Grand Duchess's marriage, ten years during
which her union with Peter had remained without
issue, while the relations between husband and
wife had become more and more frigid.   A letter
of the Grand Duke to his wife, published at
the end of the Russian translation of the memoirs
of Catherine, and belonging to the year 1746,
seems to indicate that the rupture was already
complete.   Here is the letter, textually :—

'MADAME,
          Je vous prie de ne point vous incommodes
cette nuis de dormir avec moi car il n'est plus le tems
de me tromper, le lit a été trop étroit, après deux
semaines de séparation de vous aujourd'hui après
mide.

Votre
très infortuné
mari qui vous ne
daignez jamais de
ce nom.   PETER.'

At the same time, and in spite of her retired life, and the careful watch kept over her,
Catherine was exposed to many temptations,
was engaged in pursuits where her virtue was
constantly in peril, and was plunged, so to speak
(to use the phrase of a Russian historian), in
an atmosphere of love. As she says in her
memoirs, without being absolutely pretty, she
was attractive : that was 'her *fort.*' She called
forth love in every direction. In the summer of
1749, a part of which was spent at Raïova, a
property belonging to the Tchoglokofs, she was
in a state of mortal dulness. She there saw
nearly every day the young Count Razoumofski,
who lived near, and who used to ride over to
dinner or supper and back to his château at
Pokrovskoïe, a distance of nearly forty miles
each way. Twenty years later Catherine asked
him what had induced him to come over every
day to share the *ennui* of the Grand Ducal Court,
when at his own house he had, whenever he
pleased, the best company in Moscow. 'Love,'
replied he, without a moment's hesitation.
'Love? But who could you have been in love
with at Raïova?' 'You.' She laughed aloud.
It had never occurred to her.

It was not always so, however. Tchoglokof
was ugly, Razoumofski too discreet. Others
came forward who had neither the defect of the
one nor the defect or merit of the other. In
the first place, one of the three exiles of 1745,
Zahar Tchernichef, reappears at the court in
1751. He finds that Catherine is handsomer
than ever, and does not hesitate to tell her so.
She hears him with pleasure. He takes ad-

F

vantage of a ball at which, according to the custom then (and until quite recently), people exchanged 'mottoes,' little pieces of paper containing verses more or less ingeniously turned, to present her with a *billet-doux* full of passionate declarations. She enjoys the joke, and keeps it up with the best grace in the world. He wishes to force his way into her room in the guise of a lackey; she merely points out the danger of the undertaking, and the correspondence by 'mottoes' goes on again. A part of this correspondence is to be seen. It was published anonymously, as a specimen of the style employed by a lady of rank, in the eighteenth century, in writing to her lover. The contents seem to leave no doubt that it was not Zahar Tchernichef who could lay claim to this title.

After the Tchernichefs came the Saltykofs. There were two brothers of this name among the chamberlains of the Grand Ducal Court. The family was one of the oldest and most important in Russia. The father was general aide-de-camp; the mother, *née* Princess Galitzine, had rendered services to Elizabeth in 1740, about which the Princess of Zerbst was particularly well informed. 'Mme. de Soltickof succeeded in captivating whole families. She was Galitzine. Further, she was beautiful, and she manœuvred in a way that ought to be forgotten as soon as possible. She went with one of her waiting-women into the barracks of the Guards, she abandoned herself, she drank, she gambled, lost, let them win. . . . She had for lovers the 300 grenadiers who accompanied her Majesty.' The elder of the two brothers was not handsome; or, as Catherine put it, he could rival the unfortunate Tchoglokof in both wit and beauty. The younger, Sergius, was 'beau comme le jour.' In 1752 he was twenty-six years of age, and he had been married for two years to a *freiline* of the Empress, Matrena Pavlovna Balk, a love-match. It was at this epoch that Catherine fancied he was paying court to her. She went almost every day to see Mme. Tchoglokof, who, being in an interesting condition, kept her room. Always finding the handsome Sergius there, she began to doubt whether he came entirely to see the mistress of the house. It will be seen that she had acquired some experience. It was not long before the handsome Sergius explained himself more definitely. The surveillance of Mme. Tchoglokof was just now more easy-going than usual. He arranged to divert that of the husband, who, himself in love with the Grand Duchess, might be more troublesome. He pretended to discover that the good Tchoglokof had a remarkable talent for poetry. Highly flattered, he would retire into a corner to fill up *bouts-rimés*, or to turn into verse the themes that were liberally supplied to him. Meanwhile, there was a chance of uninterrupted talk. The handsome Sergius was not only the handsomest man at the court, he was a man of resources; 'a demon for intrigue,' says Catherine. She heard his first declarations in silence. She certainly could not have thus intended to discourage him from going on. At last she asked him what he wanted of her. He had no difficulty in painting, in the most vivid colours, the happiness that he had pictured for himself. 'And your wife?' said she. It was almost a confession, and it reduced to a very fragile obstacle the distance which still separated them. He was by no means taken aback, and resolutely threw the poor Matrena Pavlovna overboard, speaking of a youthful error, declaring that he had been mistaken in his choice, and that 'the gold had soon changed into lead.' Catherine assures us that she did all she could to turn him aside from his pursuit, even to the point of insinuating that he had come too late. 'How do you know? My heart may be already lost.' It was not a happy means. The truth is, as she admits, that the difficulty she had in getting rid of her handsome admirer came mainly from herself; she liked him extremely. A hunt was organised by the poet Tchoglokof, in the course of which the occasion so long sought by Sergius presented itself. They were alone. The *tête-à-tête* went on for an hour and a half, and to bring it to an end Catherine had to have recourse to heroic means. The scene is charming, as Catherine describes it in her memoirs. Before going, Saltykof would have her admit that he was not indifferent to her. 'Yes, yes,' she murmured at last, 'but go.' 'Good, I have your word,' cried the young man, putting spurs to his horse. She would take back the fatal word. She cried after him, 'No, no!' 'Yes, yes!' he cried from the distance. And so they parted; doubtless, to meet again.

Shortly after, it is true, Sergius Saltykof was obliged to leave the court; indeed, on account of the scandal which his relations with the Grand Duchess had caused. Elizabeth severely re-

primanded the Tchoglokofs, and the handsome
Sergius received a month's *congé*, with instructions to go and see his family in the country.
He fell ill, and was only able to return to court
in 1753, when he once more joined the inner
circle, mainly of young people, that had formed
around Catherine, in which there was now another
cavalier of high rank and fine bearing, Leon
Narychkine, who was already playing the part
of court fool, which he was to keep up through
so great a part of the future reign, but for the
moment, no doubt, aiming at something more
than that. Catherine was now on the best terms
with the two Tchoglokofs. She had succeeded
in making a friend of the wife, on the ground
that she repelled the advances of her husband ;
and in making the husband himself her slave, by
cunningly tantalising him with expectations. She
thus had the confidence of both, and was able to
count on their discretion. Whether from prudence or from natural inconstancy, the handsome
Sergius seemed now more reserved, so that by a
change of parts it was now Catherine who complained of the lack of his attentions. But soon a
fresh intervention of the supreme power, and this
time quite unexpected, gave a new turn to the
second chapter of the old romance. The point is
a little difficult to explain ; it would be yet more
difficult to believe, were it not for the testimony
of Catherine herself. This is the story she gives
in her memoirs. At a few days interval, Sergius
and herself were summoned, one before the
chancellor Bestoujef, the other to a confidential
interview with Madame Tchoglokof, and both
received, on the subject which occupied them so

closely, hints which must have surprised them not
a little. Speaking in the Empress's name, the
governor and guardian of the Grand Duchess's
virtue, and of the honour of her husband, explained
to the young woman that there were state reasons
which must override all other considerations,
even the legitimate desire of a wife to remain
faithful to her husband, if that husband proved
incapable of confirming the peace of the empire
by ensuring the succession to the throne. In
conclusion, Catherine was peremptorily ordered
to choose between Sergius Saltykof and Lev
Narychkine, and Madame Tchoglokof was persuaded that she preferred the latter. Catherine
protested. 'Well, then, the other,' said the *gouvernante*. Catherine kept silence. Bestoujef,
with somewhat more reserve, spoke after the
same manner to the handsome Sergius.

In due course Catherine became *enceinte*, and
after two miscarriages gave birth to a son on the
20th September 1754. Who was the father of
the child? The question is a natural one, and
all that we know on the subject leaves it still an
open question. Physically and morally, especially
morally, Peter resembled his legitimate father.
Few, however, of his contemporaries were willing to admit the hypothesis of this paternity.
Various suppositions were current at the time.
'The child,' wrote the Marquis de l'Hôpital, 'is,
they say, the Empress's own, which she has
changed with the Grand Duchess's.' In a later
despatch, it is true, the marquis took back his
story, saying that he had been better informed ;
but Elizabeth did much to give it credit, and her
conduct at the time of the Grand Duchess's con-

finement was calculated to lend colour to the rumours which were in the air. The child had no sooner been born, and thereupon summarily baptized, than the Czarina ordered him to be taken away, and disappeared after him. Catherine did not see her child again for six weeks. She was left alone with her chambermaid, without even the necessary attentions which her situation demanded. The bed on which she had been delivered was placed between a door and two enormous windows, through which a cutting draught entered. As she was in a constant perspiration, she wished to return to her ordinary bed. *La Vladislavova* dared not take upon herself to grant this request. Catherine wanted something to drink. The answer was the same. At last, after three hours, the Countess Chouvalof came on the scene, and gave her some assistance. That was all. She saw no one else either that day or the following. The Grand Duke was feasting with his friends in a neighbouring room. After the solemn baptism of the child, the mother received, on a plate of gold, as a sort of recompense for her trouble, a ukase of the Empress, presenting her with 100,000 roubles and some trinkets. The trinkets were so valueless that Catherine tells us she would have been ashamed to give them to one of her women. She was glad of the money, for she had now a good many debts. Her joy was of short duration. A few days afterwards Baron Tcherkassof, the Empress's treasurer, 'the Cabinet Secretary, according to the official designation, came to beg back the amount. The Empress had given a second order of payment for the same amount, and there

.was not a kopeck in the treasury. Catherine knew very well that it was a trick of her husband. Peter had been very angry on hearing that she had received 100,000 roubles, while he had had nothing, he who had at least equal rights, it seemed to him, to the imperial munificence. To calm him, Elizabeth, to whom signatures cost nothing, had made another demand on her treasury, without a thought of the difficulty of her treasurer. At the end of six weeks the 'purification' of the Grand Duchess was celebrated with great pomp, and on this occasion she was allowed to see her child. She admired it. She was allowed to hold it during the ceremony; then it was again taken away. At the same time she learnt that Sergius Saltykof had been sent to Sweden with the news of the little Grand Duke's birth. At that time, for a nobleman occupying his position at the court of Russia, a change of place of this kind was rarely a favour. For the most part it was the application of a sort of judicial measure, even when it was not an actual punishment. From this point of view, the departure of the young chamberlain was not without its significance.

We shall not insist further. This historical question, turning as it does on a disputed paternity, has, to our thinking, we must admit, a very secondary importance. So far as Catherine is concerned, the only really important point in the history of the intellectual and moral development of her personality—which is what we are studying—is the uncontested and incontestable presence of the handsome Sergius beside the cradle of her first child, with Lev Narychkine, Zahar

Tchernichef, and perhaps others in the background. And there is also this kind of incomplete maternity of hers, outrageously suspected by public rumour, cruelly curtailed by an abuse of power which is almost a violence, and in which something equivocal seems to hide under the cloak of etiquette, so counter to the most natural rights and functions. There is, too, the isolation and abandonment, now more profound and sorrowful than ever, into which the young wife and mother sinks, between the empty cradle and the long deserted nuptial couch.

IV

If Catherine had been a vulgar, or even an ordinary, woman, the existence in which she was thus placed would doubtless have served to add one or many chapters to the *chronique galante* of the eighteenth century. Sergius Saltykof would have had a successor, the Grand Duke new motives to doubt the virtue of his wife; but that would have been all. Catherine was not an ordinary woman; she has superabundantly proved it. Nor was she one of those who make the martyrs of the domestic hearth. She replaced the handsome Sergius; she entered definitely, blindly, on a path which was to lead to the most colossal and the most cynical display of imperial licence known to modern history; but she did not allow herself to become absorbed in it. In abandoning herself, her honour, and her virtue to ever-new distractions, to pleasures followed with an ever-increasing ardour, she never meanly forgot her rank, her ambition, and the

supremacy that a near future was to signalise.
On the contrary, she drew herself together, she
fell back upon her own resources, and carried yet
further forward her self-culture, that adaptation
of her mind and character to a vaguely-realised
destiny, of which we have indicated the commencement.

It is at this moment that we see her more
actively absorbed than ever in the study of the
Russian language and literature. She reads all
the Russian books that she can lay her hands on.
They do not give her the idea of a very high
intellectual level. She is unable afterwards to
remember the name of any of these books, except
a Russian translation in two volumes of the
Annals of Baronius. But she obtains from her
reading a conviction destined never to leave her,
a conviction which is to imprint a definite stamp
upon her future reign, and to make it a sort of
continuation of that of Peter the Great: her
adopted country's absolute necessity of taking
pattern from the West, in order to raise itself to the
height of its newly-acquired position in Europe.

At the same time she gives herself seriously to
the study of serious books. Despite the recom-
mendation of Count Gyllemborg, and the attention she had paid to it, she had not read the
*Considérations sur la Grandeur et la Décadence des
Romains*. She now makes the acquaintance of
Montesquieu, reading *L'Esprit des Lois*, which is
only laid aside for the *Annals* of Tacitus and the
Histoire Universelle, as she calls it, which, no
doubt, means the *Essai sur les Mœurs et l'Esprit
des Nations* of Voltaire.

Tacitus impresses her by the vivid reality of

his pictures, and by the striking analogy which she finds in them with the men and things around her. Across all the space of time and circumstance she perceives the unchangeable identity of certain types which compose human nature, and certain laws which it obeys. She sees the reproduction of the same traits of character, the same instincts, the same passions, the same combinations of interests, and the same formulas of government, reproducing the same consequences. She learns to disentangle the play of elements so differently associated, and yet unvarying; to penetrate their inner mechanism and appreciate their true value. Her hard and dry mind—the philosophical mind with which the Swedish diplomatist credited her — finds itself singularly at home with the abstract, detached, impersonal manner of judging of events and their causes peculiar to the Latin historian; his way of soaring above humanity, which he seems to observe as a disinterested spectator, having himself other claims on existence.

It is, however, Montesquieu who attracts and satisfies her the most. He does not confine himself to presenting the facts, he theorises upon them. He provides her with formulas ready made, which she appropriates with ardour. She makes them her Breviary, to use her own picturesque expression. She declares later that this book, *L'Esprit des Lois*, ought to be 'the Breviary of every sovereign of common sense.' This is not to say that she understands it. Montesquieu was probably, during a good half of the eighteenth century, the most widely read, and the least understood, man in Europe. No

doubt Catherine and others found in him a good
store of ideas and theories, which they were
ready to apply in an isolated manner. As for
appropriating the doctrine as a whole, in its true
spirit, few indeed were capable of that. And as
for applying it *en bloc*, to use a modern phrase,
that occurred to no one. As a matter of fact it
would have led, and the author of *L'Esprit des
Lois* was probably himself far from realising it,
to an utter upset of the political and social *régime*
of the time, and to a revolution more radical than
that which the end of the century saw accomplished. What this doctrine attacked was the
principle itself of the vices which he analysed,
the abuses which he pointed out, the catastrophes
which he foresaw, in the constitution of human
societies. Now, to suppress this principle was
not merely to overturn such and such an institution or manner of government, nor even, nor
mainly, such and such a government itself, it was
to set aside the great idea which governed the
world, and which is perhaps to govern it for
ever; it was to substitute an ideal, and perhaps
unrealisable, equilibrium of natural forces for the
sharp, constant battle of interests and passions
which has for all time constituted human life,
which is perhaps life itself.

Of all that Catherine is still unaware. But
she has pleased to attribute to herself a 'republican soul,' after the fashion of Montesquieu,
without too closely considering what that meant
in the thought of the illustrious author, without
caring too much what it meant in hers. The
idea pleased her as it pleased so many; she
adopted it as she might have done a feather or

a flower in fashion. A certain prepossession against the abuse of despotism, the admitted necessity of substituting, in the conduct of men and things, the counsels of universal reason for the inspirations of individual caprice; there was a vague liberalism in that, no doubt. Catherine was one day to astonish the world by the revolutionary boldness of certain maxims flung in the face of Europe in an official document. She had copied them out of Montesquieu and Beccaria, but without understanding them. When their meaning was revealed to her in their passage from theory to practice, no doubt she was taken by surprise. But she continued to govern in a reasonable, and even, to a certain point, liberal, way. Montesquieu had done his work.

What she is prompt in understanding, with the reflective mind and the infallible good sense with which nature has endowed her, is that there is a flagrant contradiction, apparently inevitable, between the hatred of despotism and the state of a despot. This established fact must certainly clash with the overbearing instincts that are already at work in her. It will one day set her at variance with her philosophy, or at all events with certain philosophers. Meanwhile, some one is found to prove to her that what she fears is vain, and this, too, is a philosopher, Voltaire. Doubtless the introduction of caprice in the sway of human destinies is a fault, and may become a crime; doubtless it is reason that should govern the world, but still there must be some one to act as its representative here below. This once granted, the formula is seen at once: the despotic government may be the best sort of government possible; it is indeed the best, if it be reasonable. To this end it must be *enlightened.* All the political doctrine of the author of the *Dictionnaire Philosophique* lies in that, and also the explanation of his admiration, undoubtedly sincere, for the Semiramis of the North. Catherine has realised this formula: she is enlightened by philosophy, by that of Voltaire in especial; she governs reasonably, *she is reason itself,* set over the direction of forty millions of men; she is a divinity, the prototype of those that an odd deviation of intelligence and a grotesque freak of imagination were to instal over the altars profaned by the orgy of revolution.

It is thus that Voltaire becomes the favourite author of Catherine. This time she has found her man, the master *par excellence,* the supreme director of her conscience and her thought. He instructs without alarming her, accommodating the ideas that he gives her with the passions that she has. With that, he possesses, for all the ills of humanity, which he points out with Montesquieu, which he deplores with him, a number of simple remedies, within easy reach, and of easy application. Montesquieu is a great scientist working on broad lines. According to him, it would be needful to begin at the beginning and change everything. Voltaire is an empiric of genius. He takes one by one the sores that he discovers on the human body, and professes to heal them. An ointment here, a cautery there, and all will be gone, the sick man will be well. And what clearness of language, what limpidity of thought, with what

wit! Catherine, like most of her contemporaries, is charmed, dazzled, fascinated, by this
great magician of the art of writing, and, like
them, by his defects as much as by his qualities,
more perhaps; by what there is of superficiality
in his vision of things, of childishness sometimes in his conceptions, of injustice often in
his judgments, and especially by the licentious,
irreligious, and irreverent side of his attacks
on established beliefs, for which the philosophical tendencies of the time, and the need of
liberty, then agitating the minds of men, were
not alone accountable. If Voltaire did not aid
Catherine to exchange the Lutheran religion
for the orthodox faith, he did much at all
events to allay the memory of this doubtful
step, and to save her, if not a remorse, at least
some uneasiness of mind, at the same time that
he set her at ease in regard to certain other
transactions, which could not harmonise with
the rigid morals of any catechism, Greek or
Lutheran. Essentially intellectual as was the
immorality of the author of *La Pucelle*, it lent
itself also to other interpretations, which might
justify every sort of liberty, including that of contemporary morals. For that too Voltaire was
popular, and for that he was liked by Catherine.

No doubt also he took hold on her by other
nobler parts of his genius, by the humanitarian
ideas which made him the apostle of religious
tolerance, by the generous outbursts which forced
all Europe to applaud in him the defender of
Calas and Sirven. Catherine certainly owed
him some of her best inspirations.

But to him, as to Montesquieu and Tacitus,

she owed especially, at this period, a certain intellectual gymnastic, a certain flexibility in the handling of great political and social problems, a sort of general preparation, in short, for her future work.

And at the same time, with the rapid ripening of her intelligence in its contact with these great minds, and the corresponding development of her practical qualities, she acquires new tastes and habits which bring with them other benefits. She begins to find pleasure in the society of some of those serious personages who had frightened her in her childhood. She seeks the company of certain old women, far from being in favour at a court such as Elizabeth's, and she holds long conversations with them. She thus makes progress in the Russian language ; she follows up the information she has derived from *la Vladislavova* as to the ins and outs of a society that she desires to know so intimately. She gains, too, many a friend and ally, destined one day to be of the greatest service.

Thus was the second education of Catherine brought about.

BOOK II

IN PURSUIT OF POWER

CHAPTER I

THE YOUNG COURT

1

AFTER having given birth to the heir to the throne, Catherine had not merely to endure the singular treatment that we have recorded, she found herself, by the very fact of this birth, relegated to the second place. She was still a person of high rank, but of great show rather than of great importance. She had ceased to be the *sine quâ non* of the dynastic programme, the necessary being on whom were fixed the eyes of all the world, from the Empress to the humblest subject of the empire, all waiting for the great event. She had accomplished her task.

It was, nevertheless, not long after this decisive event that she came, little by little, to assume a *rôle* such as no Grand Duchess had ever played before, or was ever to play again, in Russia. What this so-called 'young court' was, that of Peter and Catherine, during a period of six years, from 1755 to January 5, 1762, the day of Elizabeth's death, nothing in the history

G

of any other country, or of Russia itself at any other time, can give an idea. At certain moments the diplomatists sent to St. Petersburg were embarrassed to know to whom they should address themselves ; some, among others Hanbury Williams, the English ambassador, did not hesitate to knock at the lesser door.

A detailed account of this epoch would take us beyond our limits We will indicate only its most salient features, namely, the entrance of Catherine into the political arena, her *liaison* with Poniatowski, and the violent crisis brought about by the fall of the all-powerful Bestoujef, in the course of which the future Empress played her first game on the ground of her future triumphs, and gained her first victory.

It was love that brought Catherine into the domain of politics. She was destined to perpetually mingle these two elements, so divergent in appearance ; and it was her art, or her good fortune, to almost always obtain a good result from a mixture which was so often unlucky to others. Her first escape from the narrow limits within which Elizabeth had tried to keep her for ever was an intervention in the affairs of Poland. Now it certainly did not occur to her to interest herself in these affairs until she had become interested in those of a certain handsome Pole. And she had to be helped even to this discovery.

In 1755 a new ambassador came to St. Petersburg from England, then desirous of renewing the treaty of subsidies which, since 1742, had included Russia in its system of alliances, anxious also to make sure of the support of the Russian forces in the event of a rupture with France. Guy Dickens, the then ambassador, found himself at a loss in so bustling a court as Elizabeth's, where a state question was settled between a ball, a play, and a masquerade. At his own wish, a new man was found, more fitted to cope with the difficulties of the post. This was Sir Charles Hanbury Williams, a happy choice, for the friend and boon-companion of Robert Walpole had been trained in a good school, and he never missed a ball or a masquerade. He was not long, however, in finding that he was after all no further forward. His attentions to Elizabeth seemed to be quite agreeable to her, but, politically speaking, were of no avail. Whenever he tried to get on the positive ground of no matter what negotiation, the Czarina evaded the question. Where he would find an Empress, he found no more than an amiable dancer of the minuet, and sometimes a Bacchante. At the end of a few months he came to the conclusion that Elizabeth was not a woman with whom one could have any serious talk, and he decided to look elsewhere. Foiled by the present he looked to the future. The future was the young court.

But there again he was repelled by the aspect of the future Emperor. It seemed to him at first that he would lose his time as he had done before. But he was clear-sighted, like his countrymen, and his eyes fell upon Catherine. Perhaps he felt the current of other hopes and other deceptions setting in the same direction. Was not the great Bestoujef himself beginning to recant his early beliefs? Williams could not but see the significant advances, the disguised approaches, that were being made to the Grand Duchess. He was prompt in decision. He had heard the rumours of certain adventures in which the handsome Saltykof and the handsome Tchernichef had figured, and, adventurous himself in his way, might he not himself, for a moment, have tried to follow on this romantic trail? At all events he did not waste time over it. Catherine made him welcome, talked with him on any subject, even serious subjects, which Elizabeth would not hear of; but she looked elsewhere. He followed the look, and, being a practical man, he at once chose his part. He left the way open to a young man in his suite. It was Poniatowski.

The obscure origin of this romantic hero, whom an unhappy chance, a chance fatal to Poland, had thus brought into the history of his country, was well known. Williams, who before coming to Russia had for some years been minister at the Court of Saxony, had there met with Poniatowski, the son of a *parvenu*, and the nephew of two of the most powerful Polish noblemen, the Czartoryskis. He interested himself in him, and offered to begin his political education by taking him to St. Petersburg. The Czartoryskis, on their side, were glad to seize the occasion of thus defending, at the Russian court, both their own interests, and, as they understood them, the interests of their country. They were just setting on foot in Poland a new political movement, one of compromise and of cordial understanding with the hereditary enemy, Russia, and of desertion of the traditional allies of the republic, France in particular. They turned their back on the West, and made head for the North, hoping to find a port of refuge for the unhappy vessel, shattered by the tempest, and leaking in every timber, of which they professed to be the pilots. This scheme was precisely in accord with that which Williams himself wished to further.

The future King of Poland was then twenty-two. Pleasant to look at, he could not rival Sergius Saltykof in beauty, but he was an accomplished gentleman of the period; with his varied acquirements, refined manners, cosmopolitan education, and superficial tincture of philosophy, he was an accomplished specimen of the kind, and the first that had come before the notice of Catherine. He personified to her that mental culture and worldly polish of which the writings of Voltaire and of Mme. de Sévigné had given her a notion and a taste. He had travelled, and at Paris he had belonged to that brilliant society whose charm and glitter had taken the admiration of all Europe, a very royalty, and less contested than every other. He was in some sort an emanation of it, and had both its merits and its defects. He could talk playfully on the most abstract questions, and touch lightly on the most risky subjects. He knew how to turn a love-letter gracefully, and to manipulate a commonplace into a madrigal. He had *sensibility*, and he knew the melting mood. He had a stock of romantic ideas, which could give him on occasion an adventurous and heroic air, hiding away, as under flowers, a cold dry nature, an imperturbable egoism, a very depth of cynicism. He united all the qualities likely to take her heart, even to a certain frivolity, always so attractive to her, perhaps by a mysterious affinity with her own firm and stable nature.

On his own account, Poniatowski had a further merit, strange enough, almost incredible, in a young man just come from Paris. 'A severe education,' he tells us in an autobiographical fragment which has reached us, 'had kept me out of all vulgar debauchery; an ambition of winning and holding a place in what is called, especially at Paris, high life, had stood by me in my travels, and a concourse of singular little circumstances in the *liaisons* that I had barely entered upon in foreign countries, in my own, and in Russia, had seemed expressly to reserve me all in all for her who has disposed of all my destiny.'

Bestoujef, too, encouraged the young Pole, who, however, showed a certain distrust in the matter. He had heard gloomy tales of what had happened to young men who had pleased Empresses and Grand Duchesses of Russia, after they had ceased to please. Bestoujef had recourse to Lev Narychkine, who generously consented to show the new favourite the road that he no doubt knew well. Narychkine was always the most accommodating of men. But it was probably Catherine herself who bore down the last resistances. Her beauty alone, had there been no other attraction, would have sufficed. This is how the favoured lover afterwards described it :—

'She was five-and-twenty; she had not long recovered from her first childbed; she was at that perfect moment, which is generally, for women who have beauty, the most beautiful. With her black hair, she had a dazzling whiteness of skin, the colour [*sic*] of the eyelids black and very long, a Grecian nose, a mouth that seemed made for kisses, hands and arms perfect, a slim figure, rather tall than short, an extremely active bearing, and nevertheless full of nobility, the sound of her voice agreeable and her laugh as gay as her humour, which caused her to pass with facility from the most sportive, the most childish amusements, to the driest mathematical calculation.'

Gazing at her, 'he forgot,' said he, 'that there was a Siberia.' And soon those about the Grand Duchess were the spectators of a scene which went far to settle the floating conjectures. Count Horn, a Swede who was on a visit to St. Petersburg, and a friend of Poniatowski, was in the 'set' of the Grand Duchess. One day, as he entered the room, a little Bolognese dog belonging to her began to bark furiously. It did the same to all the other visitors, until at last Poniatowski appeared, and the little traitor rushed up to him with an air of the greatest delight, and with all the tender demonstrations in the world.

'My friend,' said the Swede, taking the new-comer aside, 'there is nothing so terrible as a little Bolognese dog; the first thing I have always done with the women I was in love with is to give them one, and I have always found out by their means if there was any one more favoured than I.'

Sergius Saltykof, on his return from Sweden, was not long in finding out that he had a suc-cessor. But he had no inclination to be jealous. If, later on, Catherine was not particularly con-stant to her lovers, it was certainly the lovers themselves who first set her the example. Even before Poniatowski was in favour, Saltykof carried his insolence to the point of giving rendezvous which he did not keep. One night Catherine waited for him in vain till three o'clock in the morning.

Williams had thus at his disposition, with regard to the Grand Duchess, a powerful influence. He did not, however, neglect other means. He had soon discovered the money difficulties in which Catherine was desperately entangled. In this matter the remonstrances of Elizabeth had been of no avail. Despite her love of order, and even certain *bourgeois* habits of economy, Catherine was all her life a spendthrift. Her taste for display carried all before it, and also her way of considering the utility of certain outlays that the mercenary spirit of her native country had implanted in her mind, and that the experience acquired in her new surroundings had only developed. Faith in the sovereign efficacy of the 'tip' was one of the beliefs to which she remained most faithful. Williams offered his services, which were gladly accepted. The total amount borrowed by Catherine from this source is unknown. It must have been considerable. Williams had *carte blanche* from his government. Two receipts, signed by the Grand Duchess, for a sum-total of 50,000 roubles, bear date July 21 and November 11, 1756, and the loan of July 21 was not the first, for, in asking for it, Catherine writes to Williams's banker : ' I have some hesitation in coming to you *again.*'

It only remained for the English ambassador to put to profit the influence thus acquired ; and the reconciliation that had come about between the Grand Duchess and Bestoujef seemed of good augury.

II.

Bestoujef had triumphed successively over all his enemies, but these victories, in which he had put forth all his strength, had exhausted him. He was growing old, and he felt less and less able to cope with the incessant attacks of rival ambitions, of old grudges, of old thirsts for revenge. Elizabeth herself did not forgive him for having, in some sort, imposed himself upon her. She began to treat him with coldness. She began also to suffer from attacks of apoplexy, and that gave the chancellor food for reflection. The Grand Duke, the Emperor of to-morrow, showed him the same discouraging aspect which had daunted Williams. Not that he imagined it would be very difficult to get into his favour; it would be easy enough, but it would lead to nothing, or rather, it would lead only where Bestoujef absolutely would not go. If Peter had a political idea in his narrow brain, it was his admiration for Frederick. He was Prussian from head to foot. Bestoujef was, had been, and meant to die, a good Austrian. There was still the Grand Duchess. From the year 1754 the idea of a direct understanding with her seems to have been in the chancellor's mind.

The progress of this evolution was rapid. Catherine soon saw a considerable change, and one entirely to her advantage, in the organisation of the staff charged with the service and the surveillance of her person. Her head chamber-maid, *la Vladislavova*, a sort of feminine Cerberus, became all at once as meek as a lamb, after a confidential interview with the chancellor. Not long after, Bestoujef made his peace with the Princess of Zerbst, and offered himself, most unexpectedly, as intermediary in the correspondence which she continued to keep up with her daughter, and which he had himself done his best to put down. Finally, he ventured upon a heroic effort: by means of Poniatowski a document of capital importance was submitted to Catherine on the part of the chancellor. This time Bestoujef had burned his boats, and indeed risked his head; but he opened out before the sad companion of Peter a new horizon, enough to dazzle her and to tempt her growing ambition; he opened to her, in some sort, the way by which she was to arrive at the conquest of the empire: it was a project to settle the succession to the throne. It suggested that, immediately after the death of Elizabeth, Peter should be proclaimed Emperor, but conjointly with Catherine, who should become co-partner in all his rights and all his authority. It need not be said that Bestoujef did not forget himself. He reserved to himself nearly all the power, leaving to Catherine and her husband only what his position as a subject did not allow him to take. Catherine showed on this occasion the tact of which she had already given proof. She was far from discouraging the project, but she made her reserves. She did not believe, she said, in the possibility of its execution. Perhaps the old fox did not believe it any more himself. He went over the scheme again, turned it about, made additions and alterations, submitted it again to the interested party, then made fresh corrections, and appeared absorbed in the task   There was sharp practice on both sides ; but the ice was broken, and there were other points on which it was easy to agree.

Thus was Catherine urged, from two sides at once, to come out of the reserve—a forced reserve, certainly—in which she had hitherto been kept. She was by no means disinclined.   All her tastes and instincts urged her forward.   Held back for a time by a sentiment of prudence which was only too well justified, she ventured timidly at first, then more and more boldly, till finally she brought herself within a hair's-breadth of ruin. It is but just to add that neither Bestoujef nor Williams, the allies of to-day, the adversaries of to-morrow, showed any sort of discretion, first by joining to spread abroad the growing fame of the Grand Duchess, their common work, then in quarrelling over her when events had set them at variance   Bestoujef staked his whole hand, and endeavoured to increase his stake as best he could.   As for Williams, he showed himself per- fectly reckless.   The Englishman joined to a certain practical ability, and a very clear sense of things, an extraordinary dose of imagination and a strange capacity for making blunders.   He had the most chimerical ideas in his head ; he arranged things his own way, and whenever chance or providence disposed them otherwise, he refused to accept his defeat.   He was a very Gascon of England.   When, in August 1755, he had secured the renewal of the treaty of subsidies between England and Russia, he chanted vic- tory.   He had gained-over Bestoujef, conquered

Elizabeth, and beguiled Catherine through the medium of Poniatowski. He already saw a hundred thousand Russians in the field, putting to flight the enemies of his Britannic Majesty. These enemies were of course France and Prussia. Suddenly he learnt that the Treaty of Westminster had been concluded (January 5, 1756) and Prussia was now an English ally. Williams was nothing daunted. The hundred thousand Russians would now have only one enemy to fight instead of two. They would triumph on the banks of the Rhine instead of conquering on the banks of the Spree. They would merely have to march a little further. Meanwhile the adventurous diplomatist put himself at the disposal of Frederick. Frederick had had no envoy at St. Petersburg since 1750; Williams took upon himself to supply the place. By means of his colleague at Berlin he set on foot an active exchange of correspondence, intended to keep his Prussian Majesty *au courant* with what happened in Russia. Elizabeth, on hearing the news of the Anglo-Prussian Treaty, at first refused to ratify her own treaty of subsidies with England; then, on signing the ratification, February 26, 1756, she added a clause which limited it to the single event of England being attacked by Prussia. This was simply to annihilate the treaty, and to make game of both Prussia and England. Williams did not give way even yet. Amidst all this *chassé-croisé* of alliances, this general break-up of European politics which seemed likely to be its result, he remained faithful to his programme, which was to secure the co-operation of the Russian forces against the enemies of England. His hatred of France led him forward blindfold. The Treaty of Versailles, even (May 1, 1756), did not succeed in opening, his eyes. He did not or would not see, that, allied as it now was with Austria, France had become, with regard to Russia, not so much an enemy to oppose, as a natural associate in the new group of rival powers and interests, and a brother in arms in the coming conflict. It was just then that he wished to push forward the union that he had made with the young court and the power that he professed to wield over the dispositions and procedures of the Grand Duchess. In his infatuation he succeeded in making Frederick believe that Catherine had the power and the will to hold back the Russian army, at the very moment when the commands of Elizabeth had sent it into the field; that at least she could keep it inactive. When Frederick was undeceived it was too late: Apraksyne had taken Memel, and inflicted on the Prussian army a sanguinary defeat at Gross-Jaegerdorf, August 1759. But the illusion lasted two years, during which Williams, speaking of Catherine as his 'dear friend,' varied at will her sentiments for or against the King of Prussia, boasted of the information, equivalent to a betrayal of the secrets of state, that he received from her, and ended by imputing to this Russian Princess the position of a common spy in the service of a power with which Russia was at war.

What part was really played by Catherine during this period, one of the most troublous periods of her life, it is difficult to know for certain. Williams, most assuredly, deceived both

Frederick and himself.   German historians are
agreed in accusing the English cabinet of having
retouched the despatches of the presumptuous
ambassador, with whom the cabinet at Berlin was
in communication.   In one particular instance,
Williams appears to have carried his infatuation to the point of inventing a measure and a
letter of Catherine, both entirely imaginary.   It
is no less certain that the attentions of Williams
and the homage of Poniatowski did not permit
the Grand Duchess to remain entirely disinterested in this grave crisis, or even indifferent
to the English interests.   The receipts that the
banker Wolff continued to give on the orders of
the English ambassador had their eloquence.
But, on the other side, the advances of Bestoujef
were not to be lightly regarded by Catherine;
now, the chancellor, whom Frederick had not
succeeded in corrupting, insisted that the pact of
alliance concluded with Austria should be faithfully carried out.   All that must have brought
the political pupil of Montesquieu and of
Brantôme into many a hazardous and perhaps
contradictory undertaking.

Moreover, what she did not do, Poniatowski
did, or seemed to do, for her; and the Pole began
to be very stirring.   He was soon so very much
so, that, in the allied courts of Vienna and
Versailles, he passed for the worst enemy that
they had at St. Petersburg, a man who must be
got rid of at any price.   The unofficial character
of the personage seemed to render the undertaking easy.   Vigorous attempts were made, but
they met with an unexpected obstacle . love had
been left out of the question.   Williams himself

was more easily dislodged from a post in which he seemed to be doing as much or more for Prussia than for England itself. He left in October 1757. Poniatowski remained. But Catherine was thus brought definitely into the field of politics, which had been so expressly forbidden to her.

We must add that her *début* was far from promising. At her first trial she made use of her newly-acquired influence in certain personal interests to which she could not confess, and which were, in certain respects, against the interests of her adopted country as they were then understood by those who had their direction. She had entered politics on account of love; love followed and kept her there. This episode of her life is so decisive that we must dwell upon it yet further.

III

Poniatowski had pleased Catherine because he spoke the language of Voltaire and also that of the heroes of Mlle. de Scudéri. He gained the favour of the Grand Duke by mocking at the King of Poland and his minister, which was an indirect way of doing homage to Frederick. He made no further conquests at St. Petersburg. Elizabeth looked upon him askance, and seemed inclined to give way to the demand of the Court of Saxony that he should be recalled. By what title did he claim a place in the English Embassy, being neither an Englishman nor a diplomatist? The argument was of small avail. Personages more enigmatical still, diplomatic agents even less authorised, swarmed in every court in Europe-

That of St. Petersburg was no exception. D'Éon had just arrived there. Poniatowski, nevertheless, was obliged for the moment to obscure himself. Catherine let him go, being certain that he would come back again. He came back three months later, with the official title of Polish Minister. This was the doing of Bestoujef, who persisted in making himself agreeable.

Finding the ground more solid under his feet, the Pole did not wait long before he began to concern himself in the affairs of his uncles the Czartoryskis, to the detriment of those of his master, the King of Poland; and in those of his friend Williams, to the benefit of the King of Prussia. Frequently Catherine seconded his doings, adding postscripts to the letters he wrote to Bestoujef. Even if her intervention did not appear openly, it was easily to be guessed, and that came to the same thing. There was soon a new chorus of complaints on the part of the French and Austrian ambassadors. At one moment, Douglas, the aide-de-camp of the Marquis de l'Hôpital, fancied the way was open to a good understanding with the young court and with Poniatowski himself. After some indecision and a certain amount of resistance, the Marquis de l'Hôpital came over to his way of thinking, and abandoned his opposition to the presence of the Polish diplomatist in the capital of the North. But at this very moment a violent quarrel broke out between the representative of French interests at St. Petersburg and its representative at Warsaw, the Comte de Broglie. The latter clamoured with might and main for the recall of Poniatowski. Alas! it was the French interests themselves, the influence of France in the East, that were to founder in the conflict of irreconcilable ideas and principles.

In September 1757 Douglas paid a visit to Warsaw, and in a series of conferences with the Comte de Broglie did his best to convince him of the necessity of a radical change of front in regard to the defence of the French interests in the east of Europe. In his eyes the Treaty of Versailles, which had brought France into the system of alliances which included Russia and Austria, would have as its consequence the rupture of the old alliances of the King, both with the Porte and with Poland. The gain of a powerful ally at St. Petersburg would make up for the loss of influence at Warsaw and at Constantinople. There was the problem, and it was this view of things that had convinced both Douglas and the Marquis de l'Hôpital of the possibility of disarming the hostility of the young court, and even of obtaining the support of Poniatowski. From the moment they declared frankly and entirely for Russia, the nephew of the Czartoryskis, occupied in the advancement at St. Petersburg of the Russophilist programme of his uncles, would become their natural ally.

But the Comte de Broglie was by no means disposed to adopt these views. As for those who had to fix his line of conduct in this respect, they were simply precluded from having, on this as on many other points, any clear and definite view at all. Those who presided in France at the direction of foreign affairs, and by this we mean not only the anonymous directors of the private politics of Louis XV., the holders of the 'royal

H

secret,' but also the official ministers, Rouillé, the Abbé de Bernis, or Choiseul, pretended on the contrary, though in an uncertain measure, to reconcile the most irreconcilable things, the change of system with the immutability of principles, the co-operation of the Russian army against a common enemy, with the retention of the old *clientèle*, whether Turkish, Polish, or Swedish, an advance towards an obscurely-realised future with fidelity to the past. If there was a divergence of opinion in this respect between the two powers of direction, between the ministerial cabinet and the mysterious laboratory wherein were elaborated these often contradictory despatches, it was merely a question of limit and degree. Doubtless, while on one side they insisted on seeing in Russia only the barbarous element, with which no understanding was possible, which was merely to be driven back into Asia, on the other they were inclined to look for an ally in the formidable empire created by Peter the Great, an ally, if not too desirable, at all events possible, and perhaps necessary in the more or less distant future; a power, in any case, which had to be reckoned with, and to which it was well to make some concessions, even on the banks of the Vistula. But both parties were agreed in limiting these concessions. More than a century was destined to elapse before a series of cruel deceptions, of sterile efforts, of disasters shared, alas! by those unhappy dependants who were not to be sacrificed, and who were, after all, sacrificed to a common illusion, had at last proved the essential mistake of such a conception of things and of such a scheme. Meanwhile they persisted in the extraordinary resolution of defending Poles, Turks, and Swiss against the Russians, while at the same time in alliance with Russia. As for the Comte de Broglie, he had come, after his long residence in Poland, to identify himself with the Polish party, we might almost say to confound the interests of France, not even only with those of Poland, but with those of one of the parties among which the republic was divided; and this party was precisely the one opposed to the Russian interests and to the powerful Czartoryski family, which would advance those interests and their own with them.

The result of all this was, that the ambassador of the King at Warsaw received in October orders at once official and secret to press for the recall of Count Poniatowski, which he did with all ardour. In November the thing was done. Brühl had given way. 'The blow has been struck,' wrote the Marquis de l'Hôpital to the Abbé de Bernis; 'it must now be followed up.' But he added that the matter had been done much too brusquely. 'The consequence will be,' he said, 'a lively resentment against me on the part of the chancellor Bestoujef, and a bitter grudge on the part of the Grand Duke and Duchess. . . . I cannot help letting you know that, in my opinion, M. le Comte de Broglie has put into all this much too great a heat and passion. He has made it a point of honour towards his party to inflict this mortification on the Poniatowskis and the Czartoryskis. In short, it is his *impegno*.' In general, l'Hôpital found that the Comte de Broglie, 'accustomed to take the lead,' took somewhat too lofty a tone with his colleague, and acted in regard to him more as if he were Minister of Foreign Affairs than Ambassador. This authoritative diplomatist also permitted himself to indulge in certain pleasantries that seemed to his colleague out of place. He had written to d'Éon: 'You will perhaps be surprised at the recall of M. Poniatowski; send him back to me quickly; I have an inexpressible desire to see him again, and pay him my compliments on the success of his negotiations.'

But Poniatowski did not leave. First of all he pretended to be ill, thus putting off his leave of absence from week to week and from month to month. And meanwhile an event happened which changed the whole situation of affairs and the very position of the foes on the European battle-field. France, which before had taken the tone, if not of a master, at least of one who must be respectfully listened to, at St. Petersburg as at Warsaw, had soon to lower its demands. This event was Rosbach (Nov. 5, 1757).

There was no more question for the cabinet of Versailles of imposing its will. The Grand Duchess made her own more emphatically felt by the chancellor Bestoujef. The latter reminded her of the orders of the Prime Minister of Poland, recalling Poniatowski, now put on half-pay. 'The Prime Minister of Poland would go without his bread to please you,' replied Catherine drily. Bestoujef pointed out the necessity of looking after his own position. 'No one will molest you if you do what I wish you to do.' One sees that with the lofty idea of the power of Russia, gained at the cost of the present eclipse of France, a not less lofty idea of her own importance had taken hold of the future Empress. This was another consequence of Rosbach.

And the event justified both suppositions. Brühl, the Saxon Minister, did indeed go without his bread to please the chancellor of all the Russias; Poniatowski received the order to remain at his post, and things returned to their former courses. As for the Marquis de l'Hôpital, he gave up, once for all, his attempts to accommodate himself to a state of things in which he had ceased to have the least weight. He ceased to try to put back the current, and 'let things drift.' He did not even seek to enter into relations with the young court, where he saw 'a little stormy sea,' full of reefs.

It was Poniatowski himself who, six months later, gave the Comte de Broglie the satisfaction that he had no doubt lost all hope of obtaining. To render himself impossible at St. Petersburg, after all he had done there, did not seem an easy thing for him. He succeeded however in doing so. The story has been differently told; we shall follow the narrative of the principal actor in it, which is confirmed, almost throughout, by the testimony of the Marquis de l'Hôpital.

The Grand Duke had not yet said his say in regard to the presence of the Polish diplomatist in Russia, and the relations he had established there. It is true that he was absorbed by a new passion: Elizabeth Vorontsof, the last of his mistresses, had just entered upon the scene. An interference on his part, however, remained a quite possible, if not probable, eventuality. It came in July 1758. Issuing from the château of

Oranienbaum in the early morning, Poniatowski was arrested by one of the pickets of cavalry that Peter planted round his house as in time of war. He was in disguise.   He was roughly seized and hauled before the Grand Duke.   Peter insisted on knowing the truth, which in itself did not seem in the least to trouble him.   'It could all be arranged,' he said, as long as he was taken into confidence.   The silence which the prisoner felt bound to keep exasperated him.   He concluded that this nocturnal visit had been meant for him, and he pretended to believe that his life was in danger.   Had it not been for the presence of mind of a compatriot, recently arrived in St. Petersburg in the suite of Prince Charles of Saxony, Poniatowski might have paid dearly for his imprudence.   But the Grand Duke, none the less, talked for some days of what he would do to this stranger who had tried to elude the vigilance of his outposts.   Catherine was so alarmed that she resigned herself to a great sacrifice : Elizabeth Vorontsof received from her the most unhoped-for advances and civilities.   Poniatowski, on his part, made his supplications to the favourite.   'It would be so easy for you to render everybody happy,' he whispered in her ear, at one of the court receptions.

Elizabeth Vorontsof desired nothing better. The same day, after a talk with the Grand Duke, she suddenly introduced Poniatowski into his Highness's apartment.   'What a fool you have been,' cried Peter, 'not to have taken me into your confidence before !'

And he explained laughingly that he had not the least wish to be jealous ; the precautions taken round Oranienbaum were merely for his personal safety. On this Poniatowski, not forgetting to be diplomatic, broke out into compliments on his Highness's military arrangements, whose perfection he had found out to his expense. The good humour of the Grand Duke increased. 'Since we are all good friends,' said he, 'there is one wanting.'

'And with that,' relates Poniatowski in his memoirs, 'he goes into his wife's room, pulls her out of bed, without leaving her time to put on her stockings or shoes, and without so much as a petticoat, brings her in to us, and says, pointing to me, "Well, here he is, and I hope you will be satisfied."'

They supped gaily together, and the party did not break up till four o'clock in the morning. Elizabeth Vorontsof was obliging enough to make a personal explanation to Bestoujef, in order to convince him that the presence of Poniatowski at St. Petersburg had ceased to be displeasing to the Grand Duke. Festivities were recommenced next day, and for some weeks this astonishing *ménage à quatre* had the best of times together.

'I often went to Oranienbaum,' writes Poniatowski; 'I got there in the evening, mounted by a secret staircase to the Grand Duchess's apartments, where I found the Grand Duke and his mistress; we supped together; after which the Grand Duke departed with his mistress, saying to us, "Now, my children, you don't require me any longer." And I stayed as long as I liked.'

Rumours of the adventure, however, began to circulate at court, and, lenient as every one 'was in matters of this kind, it made a scandal. The

Marquis de l'Hôpital thought it his duty to profit by it in order to renew his demands for the dismissal of Poniatowski. This time he succeeded. Poniatowski was obliged to go. Elizabeth saw that the reputation of her nephew and heir was at stake. Two years later the Baron de Breteuil was charged to do all he could to wipe out the impression caused on Catherine by this painful event. He only half succeeded. It is true that, uniting as he did the position of official representative of French politics with that of secret agent, he had a double part to play, and, while assuring the Grand Duchess 'that his Most Christian Majesty not only would make no opposition to the return of Count Poniatowski to St. Petersburg, but that he was even disposed to lend himself to the measures that were being taken to induce the King of Poland to take up his cause,' he was obliged also, 'without open offence to the Grand Duchess, to avoid granting her wishes.'

The extravagant dualism which had resulted in France from the fantasy of the sovereign in conflict with the serious duties of sovereignty, came out very eloquently in this comedy. Catherine was not duped by it. Having with some difficulty obtained a private interview with the Grand Duchess, Breteuil had to listen to some flattering speeches. 'I have been brought up to love the French,' said she, 'I have long had a preference for them; it is a sentiment that your services bring back to me.' 'I wish,' wrote the Baron after this interview, 'that I could render the fire, the dexterity, and the effrontery that Madame la Grande Duchesse put into this conversation.' But he added sadly : 'All that means, perhaps, and will continue to mean, nothing but the excess of her thwarted passion.'

He judged truly. Poniatowski was to return to St. Petersburg no more—until, indeed, thirty-five years later, a dethroned king. Soon, absorbed by other preoccupations, distracted too by other amours, Catherine herself lost interest in the success of her own and others' tentatives in this direction. But the leaven of spite against France remained in her heart. The more, as she did not, in giving up hope of seeing her Pole again, give up thinking of him. Fidelity, at least a certain fidelity, odd enough at times, it must be admitted, was a part of her character. As she had associated politics with love, she had to keep her love-affairs in line with her other affairs. Now she could sometimes—not always —be consistent in the latter. It is thus that, in all her changes of lovers, she continued to love some of them, even beyond the passing infatuation of the heart and senses. She loved them in another way, more calm, but as definite, if not more so, tranquilly, 'imperturbably,' as the Prince de Ligne was to say. There was a certain *effrontery* also, and even a little cynicism, in the edict that she addressed in 1763 to her ambassador at Warsaw, recommending the candidature of the future King of Poland, and stating that he 'had rendered, during his residence at St. Petersburg, more services to his country than any other minister of the republic.' But there was tenderness as well as a wise forethought in the measures that she took at the same epoch, in order to pay all the debts of this

singular candidate.   In 1764 the supposition
of a marriage which would commingle the two
empires having taken general hold of people's
minds, Catherine had recourse to an ingenious
expedient to reassure her excitable neighbours.
She wrote to Obrescof, her ambassador at Constantinople, that he was to communicate to the
Porte the news of imaginary parleyings undertaken by Poniatowski in view of an alliance with
one of the first families of Poland.   And, her
heart being now disinterested in regard to a
romance thus followed up across time and space,
without her mind and her ambition having lost
interest in it, she gave simultaneous orders to
Count Kaiserling and Prince Repnine, her representatives in Poland ; so that, after his election,
Poniatowski really did marry a Pole, or at least
intended to.   It was a measure designed to calm
the disquietude of the Porte, perhaps also to
raise an insuperable barrier between past and
present.   Alas ! a near future was to remove
from her this care, leaving, in place of the
obstacle she had wished for, a bottomless gulf.
This is how Poniatowski, after he had become
King of Poland, wrote, two years later, to his
representative at the court of St. Petersburg,
Count Rzewuski :—

'The last orders given to Repnine to introduce dissension even in the legislation have
come like a very thunderbolt upon the country
and myself. If it is still possible, make the
Empress see that the Crown she has given me
will become a very Nessus' shirt for me, to burn
and bring me to a fearful end.'

The lover of former days was now, for Catherine, merely the executant of her supreme will in a half-conquered country. She replied by a letter in which she ordered this improvised king, the fragile work of her hands, to let Repnine have his way; if not, 'there will only remain to the Empress the continual regret of having been so much deceived in the friendship, the way of thinking, and the sentiments, of the King.' Poniatowski insisting still, she sent him this last and sinister warning, which already foretells the brutal measures of the Salderns, Drevitchs, and Souvarofs, the future stranglers of the last national resistances : 'All that now remains for me is to leave this matter to its fate. . . . I close my eyes on the consequences, flattered nevertheless that your Majesty should believe me so far disinterested, in all I have done for yourself and for the nation, as not to reproach me with having set up in Poland a target for my arms. They shall never be directed against those . . .' Here the pen of the Empress paused; she had written, 'Those I love'; she erased the words and substituted 'those to whom I wish well'; then she ended with this phrase, which betrays all her thoughts, and which must have sounded in the unhappy Poniatowski's ears like the roll of drums before the fire of the squadron : 'As I shall not withhold them when it seems to me that their use may be useful.'

We shall not have to refer again, other than cursorily, to this *liaison*, destined to such singular and tragic reversion. It held, indeed, a less important place in the life of Catherine than in that of the unfortunate people called to play the part of expiatory victim. After having risked her reputation, which she was no longer afraid of compromising, and her credit, which she knew so well how to keep intact, Catherine finally gained an enormous profit therefrom. We might say that Poland died of it, if nations had not more profound reasons for living and dying. We must now return to the period in which the heyday of this love affair was about to end, and to this strange interior, outwardly so like a prison, a guard-house, and a villa, which screened, indiscreetly enough, so many mysteries.

IV

In her connections, political with Williams and Bestoujef, amatory and political with Ponia-towski, Catherine is no longer the recluse of the past, watched by officers of the court in the guise of spies, ill-treated by her husband, terrorised over by Elizabeth. The chancellor's agents have been mastered one by one, and finally he himself has undergone the same fate. Peter remains the same gross, extravagant, and in-supportable being that he has always been, 'a strange brute, streaked with insanity,' according to St. Beuve's expression. He still knows how to render himself odious. Frequently he comes to bed dead drunk, and between two hiccups he speaks to his wife on his favourite subject, his amours with the Duchess of Courland, who is a hunchback, or with *Freiline* Vorontsof, who is marked with small-pox. If Catherine pretends to go to sleep, he pummels her with hands and feet to keep her awake until sleep takes hold of himself. He is almost always drunk, and he

becomes more and more mad. In 1758 Catherine gives birth to a daughter, the Czarevna
Anna, of whom Poniatowski is supposed to be
the father. At the moment when the pains
of childbed take hold of her, at half-past two
in the morning, Peter, informed of it, arrives,
'booted and spurred, in his Holstein uniform,
a belt round his waist, and an enormous sword
by his side.' On Catherine's inquiry as to why
he has put on these accoutrements, he replies
that 'a friend in need is a friend indeed, that in
this garb he is ready to act as duty bids him,
that the duty of a Holstein officer is to defend
the ducal house, according to his oath, against
its enemies, and that, believing his wife was
alone, he had come to her aid.' He can scarcely
stand on his feet. He has at times, however, as
we have seen, his agreeable moments, an occasional access of good humour or an accidental
complaisance, which he exaggerates, in his usual
extravagant way, but of which his wife has the
benefit. It is partly that, like others, he has
come under the charm of the Grand Duchess,
or at least under the power of her mind and
temperament. He is often obliged to recognise
the wisdom of her counsels, and the accuracy of
her views. He has become accustomed to go to
her in all his difficulties, and little by little there
has come into his dull brain some notion of the
superiority that he is one day to realise so
terribly. At the fatal moment it is this idea,
haunting and discouraging him, which will
paralyse his defence.

'The Grand Duke,' writes Catherine in her
memoirs, 'for a long time called me *Madame la*

Ressource, and, however vexed he might be with me, if ever he found himself in distress on any point, he came running to me at full speed, to have my advice, and, as soon as he had it, he would dash away again at full speed.'

As for Elizabeth, worn out by an irregular life, haunted by terrors which will not allow her to sleep two nights following in the same room, and which have caused her to search through all her empire for a man sufficiently slumber-proof to watch all night by her bedside without dozing, she is now only the shadow of herself.

'This princess,' writes the Marquis de l'Hôpital, under date January 6th, 1759, 'has sunk into a singular state of superstition. She remains whole hours before an image for which she has great devotion; she talks to it, consults it; she comes to the opera at eleven, sups at one, and goes to bed at five. Count Chouvalof is the man in favour. His family have taken possession of the Empress; and affairs go as God wills.'

This new favourite, Ivan Chouvalof, does not fear to awaken the jealousy and the anger of the Empress by paying, under her very eyes, assiduous court to the Grand Duchess, who is now the observed of all. He covets 'the double post,' declares the Baron de Breteuil, 'dangerous as it is.' From the year 1757 the Marquis de l'Hôpital is alarmed and scandalised to see the young court (and the young court, politically speaking, is Catherine) 'break a lance openly with the Empress, establish a sort of counter-cabal.' 'They say,' he observes, 'that the Empress has given up objecting to anything, and leaves them free course.' About the same time, in a conversation in which all the foreign ministers take part, the Grand Duchess, speaking to the ambassador of the King in reference to her love of riding, cries : 'There is not a bolder woman than I ; I am perfectly reckless.' D'Éon, who saw her then, thus depicts her :—

'The Grand Duchess is romantic, ardent, passionate ; her eyes are brilliant, their look fascinating, glassy, like those of a wild beast. Her brow is high, and, if I mistake not, there is a long and awful future written on that brow. She is kind and affable, but, when she comes near me, I draw back with a movement which I cannot control. She frightens me.'

She frightens, indeed, and fascinates a wider and wider circle, making of these persons the slaves of her will, of her ambition, of her passions, now from day to day more ardent. Nor is it only in the domain of politics that she begins to find elbow-room, and if, in one respect, the young court resembles a stormy sea, as the Marquis de l'Hôpital would have it, the Baron de Breteuil sees in it, no doubt, a certain resemblance with the *Parc aux Cerfs*. Licence is everywhere the order of the day, during these last years of the reign of Elizabeth. In March 1755 the Saxon Minister, Funcke, gives an account of the representation at the Imperial Theatre of a Russian opera, *Cephale and Procris*. Elizabeth is present, the Grand Duke, and all the court ; and it is simply the court, with all its depravities, which is put on the stage, in a series of tableaux so revolting that the good Funcke is obliged to draw a veil over them. To this same year belongs the following episode (told in Catherine's memoirs),

which opens a new chapter in the history of
her private life, that of nocturnal rambles, which
render entirely illusory the pretence of surveillance still exercised over her.   In the course of
the winter, Lev Narychkine, who, faithful to his
buffooning instincts, is accustomed to mew like a
cat at the Grand Duchess's door, to announce his
presence, makes the familiar signal one evening,
just as Catherine is on the point of going to bed.
He is admitted, and proposes to go and see the
wife of his elder brother, Anna Nikitichna, who
is ill. 'When?' 'To-night.' 'You are mad!'
'I am quite collected; nothing is easier.'   And
he explains his project, and the precaution to be
taken.   They will pass through the Grand
Duke's apartments; he will never notice them,
as he will certainly be at table with some jolly
boon-companions, if he is not already under the
table.   There is not the least risk.   He puts
it so convincingly that Catherine hesitates no
longer.   She has herself undressed and put to
bed by *la Viudislavova*, while at the same time
she gives orders to a Calmuck whom she has
always at hand, and whom she has trained to a
blind obedience, to procure for her a suit of men's
clothes.   As soon as *la Vladislavova* has gone,
she gets up, and goes off with Lev Narychkine.
They arrive without difficulty at Anna Nikitichna's, whom they find in good health and in
gay company.   They have a delightful time, and
all promise to meet again.   They soon do, and
Poniatowski, naturally, is of the company.   Sometimes they return on foot through the most ill-
famed streets of St. Petersburg.   Then, when
the winter has become too severe, they find

means to renew their pleasures without exposing the Grand Duchess to the inclement nights, and the jolly party ends by transporting itself to the Empress's bedroom, always through the apartments of the Grand Duke, who suspects nothing.

After her second confinement, the nights not being enough for her, Catherine arranges to receive during the day whenever, whoever, and in what manner soever she pleases. Of late she has suffered somewhat from the cold; she thereupon seizes the pretext for arranging by her bedside, by means of an assemblage of screens, a sort of little retreat, where she will be properly screened from the draught. Here she gives frequent hospitality to select visitors, such as Lev Narychkine or Count Poniatowski. The latter comes and goes in a great blond wig, which renders him unrecognisable, and if on the way he is stopped with 'Who goes there?' he answers, 'The Grand Duke's musician.' The 'cabinet,' due to the inventive spirit of Catherine, is so ingeniously constructed that she is able, without quitting her bed, to put herself into communication with those who are there, or, by drawing one of the curtains of the bed, to hide them entirely from view. One day, while the two Narychkines, Poniatowski, and some others are hidden behind this protecting curtain, she receives Count Chouvalof, who comes to see her on behalf of the Empress, and who leaves her without the least suspicion that she was not alone. When Chouvalof has gone, Catherine declares that she is terribly hungry, orders six dishes, and, sending away the servants, she has supper with her friends. Then she draws the curtain again, and, summoning the servants to take away the plates, she amuses herself with their astonishment at the sight of this extraordinary voracity.

Doubtless her maids of honour are well aware of what is going on. But they have other things to do than to be concerned about it. They have their own daily and nightly visitors. To reach their rooms, it is true, they have to pass through that of their *gouvernante*, Mme. Schmidt, or that of the Princess of Courland, honorary directress of the establishment. But Mme. Schmidt, ill nearly every night with the indigestion that she has given herself during the day, generally leaves the coast clear. As for the Princess of Courland, she has a weakness herself for a good-looking man. The Grand Duke's relations with her we have already seen. Nevertheless, on the news that his wife is again *enceinte*, Peter has a momentary fit of ill humour. He does not remember being responsible for it. 'God knows where she gets them,' he grumbles one day before the whole table; 'I don't at all know that the child is mine, and yet I shall have to take the responsibility.' Lev Narychkine, who is present, hastens to report the remark to Catherine. She is not at all concerned. 'You are children,' she says, shrugging her shoulders. 'Go and find him, speak sharply to him, and make him swear that he has not slept with his wife for four months. After that, declare that you will report the fact to Count Alexander Chouvalof, the Grand Inquisitor of the Empire.' She thus calls the head of the terrible 'secret

chancellorship,' which in our days has beén replaced by the famous third section. Lev Narychkine faithfully executes her commission. 'Go to
the devil!' replies the Grand Duke, whose mind
is not quite easy on the subject.

But, despite the assurance that she has shown
on this occasion, the incident gives some uneasiness to Catherine. She sees in it a warning, and
a commencement of hostilities in the decisive
struggle for which she has for some time been
preparing. She accepts the challenge. It is
from this moment, if we may believe her, that she
forms the resolution to 'follow an independent
line,' and we know where these simple words will
lead her. The last agony of Peter III. in the
sinister house of Ropcha comes at the end of
the way she has chosen. But it is at this same
moment that she stands face to face with the
crisis which in some hours and for some months
threatens her with the ruin of all her hopes and
all her ambitions.

V

On February 26th (14th, Russian style), 1758,
the chancellor Bestoujef was arrested. At
the same time field-marshal Apraksyne, commandant of the army sent into Prussia against
Frederick, was removed from command and
brought to trial. These two events, though
they had not really a cause in common, seemed,
in the eyes of the public, to hang together. We
know what had taken place in the course of the
last campaign. The capture of Memel and the
victory of Gross-Jaegersdorf, achieved by Aprak-

syne in August 1757, had transported with joy the allies of Russia, and awakened in their minds the liveliest hopes. Already they saw Frederick lost and at bay, begging for mercy. Suddenly, instead of pushing forward and profiting by its advantages, the victorious army abandoned its position and beat a retreat so precipitately that one would have thought the *rôles.* to be reversed, and the Prussian troops, instead of having received a bloody defeat, to have won another triumph. A great cry of indignation arose in the camp of Frederick's enemies. Evidently Apraksyne had betrayed them. But why? It was known that he was an intimate friend of Bestoujef. It was known, too, that the Grand Duchess had written to him several times by the means and at the suggestion of the chancellor. That was quite enough. Evidently the field-marshal had carried out a plan concocted by the friends, new or old, of Prussia and England. Bestoujef, bought by Frederick, had won over Catherine, whose relations with Williams and Poniatowski rendered her only too likely to be so influenced, and between them both they had induced the victorious general to sacrifice his own glory, the interests of the common cause, and the honour of his flag. France especially was convinced of this. The Comte de Stainville, ambassador of the King at Vienna, was instructed to propose a common application to Elizabeth for the dismissal of Bestoujef. Kaunitz reflected, and finally declined the proposition. He had, meanwhile, received information from St. Petersburg which cleared Bestoujef and Catherine. The representative of the court of Vienna at

St. Petersburg, Esterhazy, did not believe them culpable. The Marquis de l'Hôpital was alone in supporting the accusation. He supported it to the very end. During the inquiry against the ex-chancellor, he wrote :—

'This first minister had found means to win over theGrand Duke and Duchess to use their influence with Apraksyne to hinder him from acting as vigorously and promptly as the Empress ordered him to do. These plots were made under her Majesty's very eyes; but as her health was then very uncertain, she was entirely taken up with it, whilst the whole court was at the disposition of the Grand Duke, and especially the Grand Duchess, who was gained over by the chevalier Williams and by English money, with which this ambassador supplied her by means of her jeweller Bernardi, who has confessed all. The Grand Duchess had the indiscretion, not to say temerity, to write a letter to General Apraksyne, in which she dispensed him from the oath that he had made to her not to bring the army into the field, and giving him permission to put it in action. M. de Bestoujef, having one day shown this letter to M. de Bucow, lieutenant-general of the Empress, who had come to St. Petersburg to push forward the operations of the Russian army, this officer immediately informed M. de Vorontsof, the chamberlain Schwalof, and M. le Comte Esterhazy. This was the first step in M. de Bestoujef's ruin.'

It is almost certain that if the conduct of the chancellor, as well as that of Catherine, appeared somewhat dubious in regard to this circumstance, they had neither of them any hand in the retreat of Apraksyne's army. Catherine took some trouble to clear her conduct and that of her supposed accomplice from all suspicion, and she did so at a time when she need not have minded confessing the truth. The movements of the Russian army after the victory of Gross-Jaegersdorf were made in consequence of three councils of war, held on the 27th August and the 13th and 28th September. General Fermor, who succeeded Apraksyne in command, had been present at these councils, and had voted for the retreat. The army was dying of hunger, and Apraksyne had foreseen that it would be so. The partisans of the Austrian alliance had urged it forward without thinking of providing it with food. Those about Elizabeth, too, had cried, heedlessly enough, 'A Berlin! à Berlin!' But it was thought well to give satisfaction to the clamours of the Austro-French party by sacrificing the marshal. As for Bestoujef, his ruin had long been decided on, and the disgrace of Apraksyne was but a pretext to hasten his. The chancellor's enemies had got scent of his project for eventually associating Catherine with the government of the empire. They insinuated to Elizabeth that among the minister's papers would be found some endangering the safety of her crown. That decided her.

Imagine the terror of Catherine on learning of this formidable event! Would she not seem to be the accomplice of the minister who had come to his downfall on an accusation of a definite state crime? Her letters to Apraksyne were nothing. But the great project which had been formed on her behalf,—what a menace seemed to be suspended above her head! The prison, torture perhaps; and afterwards, what sort of disgrace? the convent? dismissal to Germany? who knows, perhaps Siberia? A cold shiver ran through her veins. This is what all her dreams were to end in!

But she soon took heart again. At this tragic moment we see her rise to the occasion, strong and resolute, calm and full of resources; just as a near future was to show her, when, having done violence to fortune and snatched the supreme power, she was to weave out of the bloody vestments of Peter III. the most magnificent imperial mantle that woman has ever borne. Her education is done; she is now in full possession of all her gifts, natural and acquired, of one of the most marvellous intellectual and physical organisations that have ever been made for combat, for the conduct of affairs, and for the government of men and things. She has not a moment's hesitation. She faces the danger resolutely. The day after the chancellor's arrest there is a state ball, in honour of the marriage of Lev Narychkine. Catherine appears at the ball. She is smiling and unaffectedly gay. The charge of the trial which is on foot has been confided to three high dignitaries of the empire, Count Chouvalof, Count Boutourline, and Prince Troubetzkoï. Catherine goes up to the last-named. 'What are these fine affairs that I have heard of?' says she playfully. 'Have you found more crimes than criminals, or more criminals than crimes?' Surprised by such *aplomb*, Troubetzkoï stammers out some excuse or other. He and his colleagues have done what they have been told to do. They have interrogated the supposed criminals. As for the crimes, they have yet to be found. Somewhat reassured, Catherine goes on to gather further information. 'Bestoujef is arrested,' says Boutourline simply; 'we have now to find out why.'

So nothing has yet been discovered, and it is Catherine who, interrogating the two inquisitors of Elizabeth, and listening to their replies, has made a discovery. In their embarrassed air, in their eyes that dare not meet her own, she has divined the fear that she inspires already. Some hours later she breathes yet more freely: the Holstein minister Stampke has brought her a note from Bestoujef himself bearing these words: 'Have no fear in regard to that you know of; I have had time to burn all.' The old fox was not to be caught in the snare. Catherine can thus go forward without fear. The time is past when, counselled by Madame Kruse, one of her maids of honour, she had replied to the least reproach of the Empress, '*Vinovata matouchka* (I am in the wrong, little mother),' which produced, it seems, a marvellous effect. The Marquis de l'Hôpital, whose advice she seeks, no doubt in order that she may put him on the wrong scent, recommends her to make full confession to the Empress. She is far enough from doing that! To begin with, she makes use of Stampke, of Poniatowski, her *valet de chambre* Chkourine, to keep up an active correspondence with Bestoujef and the other prisoners implicated in the accusation against him, the jeweller Bernardi, the Russian master, Adadourof, and Ielaguine, a friend of Poniatowski. A little servant, who is allowed to look after the ex-chancellor, leaves and takes the letters from a heap of bricks used as a letter-box, which serves also a double purpose, for the love-correspondence with Poniatowski is carried on by the same means. The Pole gives her a rendezvous for the evening at the opera, and Catherine promises to be there without fail, *coûte que coûte.* She finds it no easy matter to keep her word, for at the last moment the Grand Duke, who has made his own plans for the evening, and who does not wish to have them upset by his wife going out with her maids of honour, especially one of them, the *Freiline* Vorontsof, puts in an objection. He goes so far as to countermand the orders that the Grand Duchess has given, and forbids the horses to be put in the carriage. Catherine declares that she will go to the theatre if she has to go on foot; but first she will write to the Empress to complain of the ill-treatment of the Grand Duke, and to ask permission to go back to her parents in Germany. Just this—a forced, humiliating return to her native country, to a narrow horizon, to mediocrity, to the misery of the domestic hearth—is of all things what she now fears the most. Where, even, could she return? Her father is no more; she had mourned his death in 1747. She had even been hindered from mourning it too long; she had been told at the end of a week that that was enough, and that the deceased not having worn a crown, etiquette did not allow her a longer mourning. As for her mother, she herself had had to leave Germany, in consequence of a well-known incident, which had brought about the occupation of the Duchy of Zerbst by Frederick. In August 1757 the Abbé de Bernis had sent a special emissary to Zerbst, the Marquis de Fraignes, 'with the view of inspiring, in the mind of Madame la Grande-Duchesse of Russia, through Madame la Princesse de Zerbst, her mother, the desired feelings.' Frederick, hearing of the presence in his neighbourhood of a French officer, ordered a detachment of his huzzars to capture him. Surprised in his sleep, de Fraignes made a spirited defence. He barricaded himself in his room, shot the first Prussian who crossed the threshold, roused the entire town, and was saved, and taken to the castle. Frederick, who would not be thus balked, sent a whole corps of soldiers with cannon to besiege the refractory Frenchman. De Fraignes at last gave in. The Duchy and town of Zerbst had to pay the expenses of the war. The reigning Duke, who was now the brother of Catherine, sought refuge at Hamburg. The mother took shelter in Paris, where, though she seemed to have suffered for France, and to some extent through it, she was not welcomed. Her liking for intrigue and her restless spirit were feared, though it seemed useful, all the same, to have in her a sort of surety, and a powerful hold upon the Grand Duchess. But it is precisely this which alarmed people at St. Petersburg. On the demand of the vice-chancellor Vorontsof, l'Hôpital had to beg that the princess should be sent back. The reply was, naturally, that she had not been asked to come, that, had it been thought of, she would have been detained at Brussels, but that she could not be turned away, now that she was there, without gravely offending the Grand Duchess, and even without doing wrong to France : 'for France,' wrote de Bernis nobly, 'has always been the refuge of unhappy princes. The Princess of Zerbst, who has suffered partly by reason of her devotion to the king, has more right to it than most.'

Where then would Catherine go if she were to leave Russia ? To Paris ? Assuredly Elizabeth would never consent to lengthen the list of unhappy princes domiciled in France by adding to it a Grand Duchess of Russia. But the more impossible it appeared to Catherine, the more she felt emboldened to beg for it. Elizabeth, on her side, is in no haste to respond to this embarrassing request. She sends word to the Grand Duchess that she will have a personal explanation with her. Days and weeks pass. The examination of Bestoujef and his supposed accomplices goes on apace, and, if one may believe the Marquis de l'Hôpital, who follows feverishly the course of affairs, every day new proofs are discovered of his culpability, without, however, the opportunity of bringing in a sufficiently definite act of accusation to allow of a trial.

Finally Catherine carries the day by main force. One night the Empress's chaplain is awakened with the news that the Grand Duchess is very ill, and desires to confess herself. He goes, and allows himself to be convinced of the necessity of giving the alarm to the Czarina. Elizabeth is frightened, and agrees to what had been asked : for the sake of Catherine's health an interview must be granted, and she grants it.

Of this meeting we know only what Catherine has told us herself. Forty years afterwards her memory may well have deceived her in a few details, and this remark applies to the whole of her autobiography, from which we have, up to now, made numerous excerpts, and from which we must now, unhappily, cease to borrow; for the memoirs stop at this exact point. There is no trace, however, of arrangement or straining after effect in these pages; the narrative rises without preparation and without apparent effort to the most intensely dramatic point. One sees the scene of the interview: the Empress's dressing-room, a vast apartment bathed in semi-obscurity, for it is the evening. At one end, like an altar, the table of white marble before which the Empress passes long hours, seeking the fled dream of her former beauty, shines in the shadow, its heavy ewers and basins of fine gold shedding dull gleams. In one of these basins the sharp eyes of Catherine, attracted by a streak of light, observe a roll of paper, which the hand of the Empress has evidently just thrown there. It is, she feels sure, the incriminating papers—her correspondence with Bestoujef and Apraksyne. From behind a screen comes a stifled murmur of voices: she recognises them. Her husband is there, and also Alexander Chouvalof; doubtless as witnesses. At last Elizabeth appears, frigid in manner, brief in speech, her eyes hard and cold. Catherine throws herself at her feet. Without giving the Empress time to commence her examination, she renews the request she has already made in writing: that she may be allowed to return to her mother. She has tears in her voice:

it is the sorrowful complaint of a child whom strangers have ill-used, and who cries to go back to its own people. Elizabeth is surprised, and somewhat embarrassed.

'How shall I explain your departure?' she says.

'By saying that I have had the misfortune to offend your majesty.'

'But how will you live?'

'As I did before your Majesty deigned to summon me hither.'

'But your mother has had to leave her home. She is at Paris, as you know.'

'In truth she has called on herself the hate of the King of Prussia through her love for Russia.'

The answer is triumphant. Every word tells. The embarrassment of the Czarina increases visibly. She endeavours, however, to reassume the offensive; she reproaches the young woman with her excessive pride. Once, in the Summer Palace, she had been obliged to ask her *if she had a stiff neck*, so difficult did she seem to find it to incline her head before the Empress. The conversation thus turns to a vulgar quarrel of wounded self-esteem. Catherine makes herself humbler and smaller than a blade of grass. She has no recollection of the incident that her Majesty would recall to her mind. Doubtless she is too stupid to have understood the words that her Majesty deigned to address to her. But her eyes—those wild beast's eyes of which d'Éon speaks—are fixed glitteringly upon the Empress. To avoid the look before which Troubetzkoï and Boutourline have trembled, Elizabeth goes to the other end of the room and speaks to the Grand

Duke. Catherine listens. Peter profits by the occasion to make accusations against his wife, whom he fancies already condemned. In violent terms he denounces her wickedness and obstinacy. Catherine flares up: 'I am wicked, I know,' she cries, in a ringing voice; 'I am and I ever will be against those who deal unjustly with me. Yes, I am obstinate with you, since I have learnt that one gains nothing by giving way to your caprices!'

'You see now!' says the Grand Duke triumphantly, addressing the Empress. But the Empress is silent. She has again met the look of Catherine, she has heard the ring of her voice, and she too is afraid. Once more she endeavours to intimidate the young woman. She orders her to avow the culpable relations that she has had with Bestoujef and Apraksyne; to admit that she has written other letters to the latter besides those which have been found. On her refusal, she threatens to put the ex-chancellor to the torture. 'As it pleases your Majesty,' replies Catherine coldly. Elizabeth is overcome. She changes her tone; puts on a confidential air; intimates to Catherine by a gesture that she cannot speak to her openly before the Grand Duke and Chouvalof. Catherine is prompt to seize the indication. Lowering her voice, she says, in a humble murmur, that she longs to open all her heart and mind to the Empress. Elizabeth is touched, and sheds a few tears. Catherine does the same. Peter and Chouvalof are astounded. To put an end to the scene, the Empress points out that it is very late. As a matter of fact it is three o'clock in the morning. Catherine retires, but before she has had time to go to bed, Alexander Chouvalof comes to her from the Empress, to bid her be of good courage, and to announce to her that she shall have another interview shortly with her Majesty. A few days after, the vice-chancellor in person is sent to her by Elizabeth to beg her to think no more of returning to Germany. At last, on the 23rd of May 1758, the two women meet again, and part apparently enchanted with one another. Catherine weeps once more, but it is tears of joy that flow from her eyes, 'as she thinks of all the benefits that the Empress has conferred upon her.' Her victory is complete and decisive.

CHAPTER II

THE FIGHT FOR THE THRONE

I

AFTER the departure of Williams and Ponia-towski, after the fall of Bestoujef, Catherine found herself severed from all those with whom the chances of her destiny had brought her most in contact since her arrival in Russia. Zahar Tcher-nichef was always in the field; Sergius Saltykof lived at Hamburg in a sort of exile. In April 1759 she lost her daughter. In the following year her mother died at Paris (none too soon, it must be said), and with her the last link was broken that attached her to the country of her birth. But in Russia she had no more isolation

to fear.   Williams had been replaced by Keith,
and Keith, it is true, applied himself with greater
diligence to win the favour of the Grand Duke.
Contrary to his predecessor, he found Peter quite
efficient in the *rôle* that he intended him to play,
a simple *rôle* of reporter and spy.   Peter showed
himself perfect in the part.   His perverse mind
made him find a malicious pleasure in this base
occupation.   Ere long the services that he rendered
to England and Prussia, to which Frederick gave
a word of grateful remembrance in his *History of*
the Seven Years' War, were of public notoriety
at St. Petersburg.   This did not, however, prevent Keith from making himself useful to the
Grand Duchess, and, like Williams, lending her
money.

Poniatowski, too, had been replaced.   In the
spring of 1759 there came to St. Petersburg
Count Schwerin, aide-de-camp of the King of
Prussia, who had been taken prisoner at the
battle of Zorndorf (August 25, 1758).   He was
treated as a distinguished stranger who had come
to pay a visit to the capital.   As a mere matter
of form, two officers were appointed to have him
in charge.   One of these officers had signally
distinguished himself at Zorndorf, where he had
received three wounds without leaving his post.
He had the fatalistic courage of the East.   He
believed in his destiny.   He was right : it was
Gregory Orlof.   There were five brothers in the
Guards.   Tall as his brother Alexis, endowed
like him with herculean strength, Gregory Orlof
excelled them all by the beauty of his calm
regular face.   He was handsomer than Poniatowski, handsomer even than Sergius Saltykof, a

giant with the face of an angel. There was nothing else angelic about him, however. Of small intelligence and no education, living the ordinary life of his companions-at-arms, but living it *à outrance*, passing his time in gambling, drinking, and paying court to brunette and blonde, always ready to pick a quarrel, and to knock down any one who opposed him, ready to run any danger, and to stake his fortune on the cast of the die, the more so as he had nothing to lose, always having the air of being half intoxicated, even when by chance he had taken nothing, insatiable of every sort of pleasure, ready to go blindfolded into any adventure. his whole life a sort of madness ; such was the man who was now to enter into the life of the future Empress, and, still mingling politics and love, to hold for so long the second, if not the first place in her mind and heart. The first place was for ambition. The traits we have indicated do not make precisely a romantic hero, but there was nothing in them to scandalise Catherine. She too, all her life, loved adventures, and consequently she was far from disliking adventurers. The ' headlong recklessness ' that she one day indicated in herself to the Marquis de l'Hôpital, went well with that of Gregory Orlof. More than beauty, more than wit, he possessed a charm which for long was in the eyes of Catherine the most powerful charm of all, which exercised over her a kind of fascination, which at one time attracted her in Patiomkine, and which chained her for years to the uncouth person of this cyclops : ' he had a devil.'

Königsberg, where he had lived in garrison, long kept the legend of his prowess as a *viveur*.

He began to form the same reputation at St. Petersburg, where in 1760 he received the envied post of aide-de-camp of the General Grand Master of Artillery. The post was occupied by Count P. J. Chouvalof, cousin-german of the all-powerful favourite of Elizabeth. This helped to bring Orlof forward. Chouvalof had a mistress, Princess Helen Kourakine, whose beauty was the talk of St. Petersburg. Orlof became the rival of his new chief, and carried the day. This drew all eyes upon him, Catherine's among the rest. But he was near paying dear for his triumph. Chouvalof was not the man to pardon an injury of the sort. The confidence that Orlof had in his lucky star was not at fault : Chouvalof died before he had time to avenge himself, and Catherine continued to interest herself in the adventures of this young man who risked his head in turning that of a fair princess. It happened that he lived just opposite the Winter Palace. This too helped in bringing Orlof and Catherine together.

This officer, so full of charm and assurance, was naturally an influential man in the *milieu* in which he lived. And this *milieu* was to have a main importance for a Grand Duchess of Russia, who was determined 'to follow an independent line.' In her memoirs, Catherine returns again and again to the earnest desire that she professes to have had from the first to conciliate the good will of an element that she feels to be the true and only support of her position in Russia. This element she calls the Russian 'public.' She is for ever concerned about what this 'public' will say or think of her. She tries to win it over to her side. She would fain accustom it to rely on her in case of need, in order that she may rely on it in turn. This is a form of speech which is enough to inspire doubt concerning the authenticity of the document in which we find it. At the time when Catherine is supposed to have written out these confidences, she not merely paid small heed to this element of which she thought so much thirty years before, she had even had time to find out that it did not exist in Russia, at least in this acceptation, and with so well-defined a place of its own. Where could a 'public' of this kind, that is to say, a social collectivity, endowed with will and intelligence, susceptible of thinking and acting in common, have been found in the Russia of that time? Nothing of the kind was to be seen. Above, there was a group of functionaries and of courtiers, religiously subjected to all the degrees of the *tchine* and to all the steps of human baseness, trembling at a look, annihilated by a gesture; below, the people, that is to say, a quantity of muscular forces capable of being put to drudgery, the souls only taken into account in the adding up of units for an inventory; between both, nothing, except the clergy, a considerable power, but little accessible, little manageable, more likely to act *de haut en bas* than *de bas en haut*, in no way to be utilised for political ends. It was not any of these that had supported Elizabeth, that had placed her on the throne. Something there was, nevertheless, that had done so, something which was strong and which could act on occasion, apart from all these : the army.

Catherine loved Gregory Orlof for his beauty,

his courage, his giant's build, his audacity, his recklessness. She loved him also for the four regiments that he and his brothers seemed to hold in the hollow of their hands. He, on his part, did not linger long at the feet of the Princess Kourakine. He was not the man to keep from lifting his eyes higher, especially when they met with such encouraging smiles. He was not the man, either, to make a mystery of his new *amours.* He had published the name of the Princess without caring what the Grand Master of Artillery would say to it; he published the name of the Grand Duchess with equal composure. Peter said nothing: he was otherwise occupied. Elizabeth said nothing: she was dying. Catherine let him act as he pleased: she was not averse to having her name associated in the barracks with that of the fine Orlof, whom the officers adored, and for whom the men would have gone through fire. Later, in 1762, she wrote to Poniatowski, 'Osten remembers seeing Orlof follow me about everywhere and commit a thousand follies; his passion for me was public property.'

She was well pleased to be followed about. After Poniatowski, this violent and headstrong *soudard* must doubtless have seemed to her a little strong in flavour. But she was not Russified for nothing. The taste, the necessity even, of such contrasts was a part of the temperament of this people, which but yesterday had acquired a precocious civilisation, which had become her own people, with whom she little by little assimilated herself, taking their very inmost nature for her own. After a few months passed in the most cunning refinements of the most luxurious ease, Patiomkine threw himself into a *kibitka*, and covered nearly 2000 miles without stopping, without anything to eat but raw onions. Catherine did not travel by *kibitka*, but in love, certainly, she was ready to go from one extreme to another. After Patiomkine, who was a savage, she found charm in Mamonof, whom the Prince de Ligne himself considered well-bred. The sheer brutal passion of the Russian lieutenant gave her a change after the wire-drawn love-making of the Polish diplomatist.

Voltaire, Montesquieu, and Parisian society were not, however, forgotten. It is at this time, in 1762, that she made friends with the afterwards celebrated and troublesome Princess Dachkof. She was the youngest of the three daughters of Count Roman Vorontsof, brother of the vice-chancellor. The eldest, Marie, had married Count Boutourline. The second, Elizabeth, dreamt of marrying the Grand Duke. She was the favourite. The Empress had jestingly named her Madame de Pompadour, and every one at court called her by this name. The third, Catherine, was fifteen years of age when, in 1758, the Grand Duchess met her in the house of Count Michael Vorontsof, her uncle. She did not know a word of Russian, spoke only French, and had read all the books in that language that she could meet with in St. Petersburg. Catherine was immensely taken with her Having married Prince Dachkof shortly after, she followed him to Moscow, and Catherine lost sight of her for two years. In 1761 she returned to St. Petersburg, and passed the summer of

that year in a *datcha* belonging to her uncle
Vorontsof, situated midway between Peterhof,
where the Empress was residing, and Oranienbaum, the usual residence of the Grand Duke
and Duchess during the hot weather. Every
Sunday Catherine went over to Peterhof to see
her son, whom the Empress would not give up.
On the way back she would stop at the Vorontsof *datcha*, and carry off her young friend for
the rest of the day. They discussed philosophy,
history, and literature, and the gravest scientific
and social problems. Perhaps they sometimes
chanced upon gayer subjects ; but with these
two young women, one of whom was scarcely
thirty, and the other not yet twenty, gaiety
was a rare visitor. The Grand Duchess had
grave cares at the time, and the Princess Dachkof
was always a very serious person. Later on,
her society became less agreeable to Catherine,
and ended by becoming absolutely insupportable.
But just then the future Semiramis was very glad
to find some one with whom she could talk of
things of which Orlof understood nothing. It
pleased her, also, to find in the mind of a Russian
some glimmer, however pale, of that Western
culture for which she dreamt of making a home
in the heart of this immense and barbarous
empire. This little person of seventeen, who
had read Voltaire, was a fine opportunity ; the
firstfruits of the propaganda that she wished
to accomplish. And then she was a Russian
grande dame, connected by birth and by marriage
with two influential families. This too had its
importance. Finally, beneath the varnish of an
education similar to her own, as heterogeneous

and as incomplete, beneath the odds and ends
of ideas and the scraps of learning picked up
here and there at the chance of hurried reading,
Catherine discovered in her friend an ardent and
fiery soul, equipped for all hazards. The demon
of madness, which shook the athletic frame of
her new lover, dwelt also in this frail child.
They went hand in hand until the day when the
destiny of one of them was decided.

Neither the acquisition of Orlof nor of this
new friend, however, made up for the loss of
Bestoujef. The statesman trained in affairs, the
man of experience and of wise counsel, called
for a successor. A successor was found, Panine.
Panine was the political scholar of the ex-chancellor. Ten years before, Bestoujef had thought
of him as a possible favourite for Elizabeth.
Panine was then a handsome young man of
twenty-nine, and for some time the Czarina
looked upon him with anything but an indifferent
eye. The Chouvalofs, who considered the place
in question as a sort of patrimony, and who
were in league with the Vorontsofs against the
supremacy of Bestoujef, got him out of the way.
He was sent to Copenhagen, then to Stockholm,
where he played a somewhat important part in
the struggle against French influence. The
change of system, which placed Russia and
France side by side in the same camp, necessitated his recall in 1790. Elizabeth thought of
him for the post of tutor to the Grand Duke
Paul, which had become vacant on the resig-
nation of Behtieief. The Chouvalofs did not
oppose the choice. After Alexander Chouvalof,
after Peter Chouvalof his brother, it was now

Ivan Chouvalof, a cousin, who held the other post, which alone was of consequence. Himself but thirty, he did not fear the competition of Panine, who had aged.

Cold, methodical, with a certain *nonchalance* which became more and more marked, Panine was just the man to act as counterpoise to the stormy temperaments of which Catherine formed the centre. His political ideas drew him naturally to the side of the Grand Duchess, while they drew him away from the Prussian tendencies of the Grand Duke. Like Bestoujef, he remained Austrian in his sympathies. The strange temper of Peter somewhat terrified him, the more so as he had cause to suffer from it himself. There were discussions, naturally, concerning the event, which seemed to draw nearer and nearer, and which began to occupy all minds, from end to end of Europe. Elizabeth was dying, and her death would be, not only at St. Petersburg, the signal of a political crisis of incalculable importance. All the interests concerned in the strife of parties between the great continental powers depended on this near eventuality. After the taking of Colberg (December 1761), a few months more allowed for the combined action of the Russian and Austrian troops, it was the certain, the inevitable, ruin of Frederick. The vanquished of Gross-Jaegersdorf and of Künersdorf had no illusions himself on the point. But it could be equally well predicted that the accession of Peter III. would bring to an end the common campaign against the King of Prussia.

Panine considered the problem, and seemed inclined to solve it, if not absolutely in favour of Catherine's secret ambitions, at least in such a manner as to protect her interests against the hostile intrigues about the bed of the dying Czarina. According to an apparently serious authority, the Vorontsofs had nothing less in view than to procure the divorce of Catherine, and to proclaim the illegitimate birth of the little Paul. After which the heir of Elizabeth would marry the *Freiline* Vorontsof. Happily for Catherine, this too ambitious way of arranging things awoke the rival susceptibilities of the Chouvalofs, who, as a counterblast to the project, went to the extent of plotting that Peter should be sent into Germany, and the little Paul immediately raised to the throne, with Catherine as his guardian. Between these two opposed camps, Panine adopted a middle plan, declaring himself in favour of letting things follow their natural course, save that a salutary influence in the future government of Elizabeth's nephew should be reserved for Catherine, and, through her, for himself. Catherine listened, and said nothing. She had her own ideas. She also talked over things with the Orlofs.

II

Elizabeth died on the 5th of January 1762, without having made any change in her instructions for the succession of Peter. Had she ever had the intention of changing them? The matter is uncertain.

'The wish and expectation of all,' wrote the Baron de Breteuil in October 1760, 'is that she will establish on the throne the little Grand Duke, to whom she seems passionately attached.'

A month later, he recounted the following :—

'The Grand Duke had gone for a couple of days into the country for hunting, and that very day the Empress suddenly ordered that a Russian piece should be played at her theatre, and, contrary to usage, did not invite the foreign ministers and the other persons at the court who were generally present ; so that she went to the play with only the few people who were in immediate attendance on her. The little Duke accompanied her, and the Grand Duchess, having alone been invited, was also present. Scarcely had the performance begun when the Empress complained of the small number of spectators, and she commanded that all her guard should be admitted. The hall was soon filled with soldiers. Then, according to all reports, the Empress took the little Grand Duke on her knees, caressed him in the most marked manner, and, addressing some of these old grenadiers, to whom she owes all her grandeur, she presented the child to them, so to speak, spoke to them of his good qualities and his charms, and seemed to take pleasure in receiving their military compliments. These performances went on almost all through the play, and the Grand Duchess seemed well pleased.'

If we may believe the authority that we have cited above, Panine, while seeming to make common cause with the Chouvalofs, must have played them false at the last moment : a monk had been brought by him to the bedside of Elizabeth, who had induced her to make her peace with Peter   It is more probable that

Elizabeth could not make up her mind, or not in time. She had come to detest her nephew, but she loved her peace of mind above all. Her death, which had been expected for years, left room for the hypothesis of a revolution which would supply the place of her will, weakened as it was by debauch. The Baron de Breteuil wrote :—

When I look at the hate of the nation for the Grand Duke, and the errors of this prince, I am tempted to imagine an entire revolution; but when I observe the base and pusillanimous air of those who are on the point of raising the mask, I see fear and servile obedience come into play with the same tranquillity as at the Empress's usurpation.'

This is precisely what happened. If we may believe Williams, Catherine had planned five years before the part that she was to play by the dying bed of Elizabeth. 'I shall go straight,' she said, 'to the room of my son ; if I meet Alexis Razoumofski I will leave him with my little Paul ; if not, I will take the child into my own room. At the same time I shall send a trusty messenger to summon five officers of the Guard, each of whom will bring fifty soldiers, and I shall send for Bestoujef, Apraksyne, and Lieven. I shall go into the death-chamber, where I shall receive the oath of the captain of the Guard, and I shall take him with me. If I see the least hesitation, I shall lay hands on the Chouvalofs.' She added that she had already had an interview with the hetman Cyril Razoumofski, and that he answered for his regiment, and engaged to

bring with him the Senator Boutourline, Troubetzkoï, and even the vice-chancellor Vorontsof.
She even wrote to Williams · 'The Czar Ivan
the Terrible proposed to fly to England; for
my part I shall not seek refuge with your king,
for I am resolved to reign or to perish.'

Is Williams to be believed? According to
the Abbé Chappe d'Auteroche, it was a quite
different scene that took place at the moment
of the Empress's death. The French historian
represents her throwing herself at her husband's
feet, and declaring her wish to serve him 'as
the first slave of his empire.' Later on,
Catherine was greatly offended by this account
of things, denying it on oath with a singular
vehemence. We may be excused from pro-
nouncing an opinion.

At all events Peter took possession of his
empire quite peaceably. His reign began just
as it had been anticipated on all hands.
Frederick breathed freely again, and might
well feel himself saved by the death of Elizabeth. On the very night of his accession
to the throne, Peter sent couriers to the
different corps of his army, with orders to
suspend hostilities. The troops occupying East
Prussia were to stay their march. Those acting
in concert with the Austrians were to separate
from them. They were all to accept an armistice
if the proposition were made to them by the
Prussian generals. At the same time the
Emperor despatched the chamberlain Goudo-
vitch to Frederick himself with a letter from
his hand giving expression to his friendly intentions. Then followed rapidly public resolutions

and demonstrations announcing a radical change of tendencies and sympathies. Even the French players were dismissed without the smallest consideration. Lastly, in February a declaration addressed to the representatives of France, Spain, and Austria, informed them of what they had to expect under the new rule : Peter turned round upon his allies without ceremony, told them that he had decided to make peace, and advised them to do the same. A scene, picturesquely recounted by the Baron de Breteuil, emphasised, two days after, the last part of this declaration. It was on the 25th of February 1762, at a supper-party given by the chancellor Vorontsof. It lasted from ten in the evening till two in the morning. The Czar, says de Breteuil, 'never ceased all the time to bawl, and drink, and talk nonsense.' Towards the end Peter rose, staggering, and turning towards General Werner and Count Hordt, drank a toast to the King of Prussia. 'Things are different now from what they have been for years past,' he said, 'and we shall see, we shall see!' At the same time he threw confidential smiles and looks at Keith, the English ambassador, whom he called 'his dear friend.' At two o'clock in the morning the company passed into the *salon*. Instead of the usual faro-table there was a great table covered with pipes and tobacco. To pay court to the Emperor, one was obliged to smoke a pipe for hours together, and drink English beer and punch. However, after a long talk with Keith, his Majesty proposed to play at *campi*. During the game, he calls over the Baron de Posse, the Swedish minister, and tries to convince him that the declaration recently issued by Sweden is exactly the same as his own. 'It is only intended,' explains Posse, 'to call the attention of the allies to the difficulties which would be incurred by a prolongation of the war.' 'We must make peace,' declares the Emperor. 'For my part, I will have it.' The game continues. The Baron de Breteuil loses a few ducats to Prince George of Holstein, the uncle of the Czar, whom he had once encountered, in the course of his military career, on a German battle-field. 'Your old antagonist has got the better of you!' cries Peter, laughing. He continues to laugh and repeat the word, like a drunken man. The Baron de Breteuil, a little taken aback, expresses his assurance that neither he nor France will ever have the Prince as adversary again. The Czar makes no reply, but a little while after, seeing Count Almodovar, the Spanish minister, lose in turn, he whispers in the ear of the French envoy, 'Spain will lose.' And he laughs once more. The Baron de Breteuil, choking with rage, endeavours to preserve a cool demeanour, and replies in his most dignified manner, 'I think not, sire.' Upon which he proceeds to point out what might be done with the forces of Spain joined to those of France. The Emperor only replies with mocking 'ha-ha's.' At last the French diplomatist sums up the matter: 'If your Majesty remains steadfast in your alliance, as you have promised and as you are bound to do, both Spain and France are in the best of cases.'

This time Peter can contain himself no longer.

He roars out in a rage: 'I told you two days ago: I will have peace.'

'And we too, sire; but we would have it, as your Majesty would also, honourably, and in agreement with our allies.'

'Just as you please. For my part, I will have peace. . After that, you can do as you like. *Finis coronat opus.* I am a soldier, and I don't joke.' Upon which he turns on his heel.

'Sire,' replies the Baron de Breteuil gravely, 'I will report to the King the declaration that your Majesty is pleased to make to me.'

It is the final rupture. The Chancellor Vorontsof, who is immediately informed of the incident, attributes the fault to his master's drunken condition and his peculiar temper. He offers his excuses. But neither at St. Petersburg nor at Versailles is there any uncertainty as to the bearing of the Emperor's words.

'You will have imagined my indignation,' writes the Duke de Choiseul, 'on hearing of what took place on the 25th of February. I confess I did not expect treatment of this kind, for France is not yet accustomed to having its laws dictated to it by Russia. I do not believe M. Vorontsof can give you any further explanations. It is useless to demand them. We know all there is to know, and the final information that we shall get will be the news of a treaty made between Russia and our enemies.'

As a matter of fact that is exactly what happened two months later. On April 24th Peter signed a treaty of peace with Prussia, in which he inserted a paragraph announcing the speedy conclusion of a defensive and offensive alliance between the two powers. He announces publicly his intention of putting himself, with a body of troops, at the disposition and under the orders of Frederick. It is a project that he has long had in view. In May 1759 the Marquis de l'Hôpital notified to his cabinet :—

'The Grand Duke, finding himself alone with Count Schwerin and Prince Czartoryski, began to praise the King of Prussia, and said in so many words to Count Schwerin that he would think it an honour and glory to make a campaign under the command of the King of Prussia.'

At the same time Peter seemed desirous of seeking a quarrel with Denmark, on account of its German possessions. The Emperor of Russia was ready to stoop to avenge the injuries, real or imaginary, of the Duke of Holstein. A Russian historian has written a book to explain 'the political system,' as he is pleased to call it, of Elizabeth's successor. In his opinion the whole future of Russia would have been at stake if this 'system' had had its way. It seems to us that this is too much honour to Peter III. and his policy. Did he really dream of 'sacrificing the mouth of the Dvina, and cutting himself off from some millions of compatriots, in order that, with the aid of Prussia, he might lay hold of another shore, some hundreds of versts away, seize on the mouth of the Elbe, and extend his dominion over a few thousands of Dano-Germans?' We are inclined to think that he simply wished to express his admiration for Frederick, and astonish the Germans with his general's uniform. He continued to play at soldiers; only, having the choice before him, he was no longer content with foot-soldiers in paste.

In the interior he proclaimed himself an earnest reformer. Ukase followed ukase, one decreeing the secularisation of the estates of the clergy, another the emancipation of the nobility, another the suppression of the 'secret chancellor-ship,' or political police organisation. What are we to think of this precipitate legislation? Was Peter really and truly a liberal? A contemporary, Prince Michael Chtcherbatof, explained after his own fashion the ukase on the nobility. One evening when he wished to escape the vigilance of his mistress, Peter called aside his secretary of state, Dimitri Volkof, and thus addressed him: 'I have told Mlle. Vorontsof that I shall spend part of the night working with you on a project of the greatest importance. You must therefore let me have a ukase to-morrow which will be the talk of the court and the town.' Volkof bowed; next day Peter was satisfied, and the nobility as well. It is probable that the new Emperor, while influenced to some extent by his surroundings, and applying, without reflection, the ideas that they gave him, was obedient, in especial, to the instinct of meddling with every-thing which we find in most children, and which in him was increased by his naturally restless spirit. It amused him to overturn the constitu-tion of his empire with a signature, and to see about him the frightened looks of those whom these rapid changes alarmed. They were his little jokes. Perhaps, too, he thought to imitate Frederick. He enjoyed himself vastly, and felt himself in a fair way to make a great sovereign.

Was he really in danger of alienating the affection of his subjects, or of shaking the foundations of his throne, by these measures abroad and at home? We cannot believe it. His subjects had seen so many contradictory measures! The clergy was certainly wounded to the quick, but it said nothing. The nobility had had reason to be satisfied, but it too had nothing to say. The senate offered to the Emperor a statue of gold, which he refused. Later on, much was said about the symptoms of disorganisation which had begun to manifest themselves throughout the machinery of government before the event which brought the new reign to an end. Such observations are always made after the event. Meanwhile Peter reigned tranquilly, despite his eccentricities. Biron before him had been more eccentric still. The machinery of government in Russia resembled the massive sledge that had brought Catherine as far as Moscow: it was proof against blows.

Peter was guilty of two capital faults—in making one malcontent and in exasperating another. The malcontent was the army. Not that it was so averse as people have imagined to changing sides, and fighting with the Prussians against the Austrians after having fought with the Austrians against the Prussians. The hatred of the peaked helmet, attributed to the soldiers commanded in 1762 by a Tchernichef or a Roumiantsof, seems to us a quite modern invention. The peaked helmet did not exist, and, German for German, the warriors of Maria Theresa were no less so than those of Frederick. Peter wished to introduce into his army the

Prussian discipline; it is that which his army could not forgive. It had a discipline of its own. For a slight infraction, one of those grenadiers whom Elizabeth cherished so dearly, and with such good reason, could be sentenced to 3000, 4000, or even 5000 blows of the stick, without protesting against the sentence. If, sometimes, he did protest against this frightful torture, he went back to the ranks without a murmur. But it seemed to him intolerable that he should be made to go all over a manœuvre again because of a fault in the *ensemble*. Then Peter spoke of changing the uniforms: that was a second offence. Finally, he spoke of suppressing the Guards, as his grandfather had suppressed the *Strelitz*. This was to lay hands on the Holy of Holies. For nearly half a century the Guards had been the most solid and stable thing in the empire. The new Czar began by dismissing the bodyguards, those whose under-officers the late Empress had invited to dinner. He replaced them by a Holstein regiment. Prince George of Holstein was named Commander-in-Chief of the Russian army, and placed at the head of the horse-guards, who had always had the sovereign himself as their Colonel. It was too much to be endured. It seems to us that the almost unanimous testimony of contemporaries in regard to the hostile public feeling evoked by the new Emperor refers entirely to these military reforms, and to the effect which they produced in the ranks of the army. We know already what the word 'public' meant in Russia.

The exasperated malcontent was Catherine. In this respect a positive madness seemed to have come over Peter. On January 15, 1762, the Baron de Breteuil wrote to the Duc de Choiseul—

'The Empress is in the cruellest state and treated with the most marked contempt. I have told you how she endeavoured to fortify herself with philosophy, and how little this food consorts with her disposition. I now know, for certain, that she is already much put out by the way in which the Emperor treats her, and by the airs of Mlle. de Vorontsof. I should not be surprised, knowing her courage and violence, if this were to drive her to some extremity. I know that some of her friends are doing their best to pacify her, but they would risk everything for her, if she required it.'

In the month of April, when he took up his residence in the new palace which had just been finished, Peter occupied one of the wings, and assigned to his wife apartments at the other extremity. Close to him was lodged Elizabeth Vorontsof. From a certain point of view this arrangement was quite agreeable to Catherine; it gave her more liberty, and she needed it in every way : she was once more *enceinte*, and, this time, without the slightest possibility of assigning the paternity to the Emperor. It was none the less a visible sign of the contemptuous treatment which the Baron de Breteuil speaks of, and the official recognition, so to speak, of a state of things difficult to tolerate. Peter constantly subjected her to the most gross and offensive treatment, the most paltry and cruel bickerings. One day, as he was supping with his mistress, he sent for Count Hordt, who was with the Empress. The Swede, not daring to say to Catherine where

he was wanted, declined the invitation. Thereupon Peter arrived himself, announcing brutally
to the Count that they were waiting for him at
the Vorontsof's, and that he must make up his
mind to come. Another day, having discovered
that the Empress was very fond of fruit, he
ordered that none should be served at table.
From time to time he had fits of jealousy.
Catherine, according to the general custom of
the time, even among young and pretty women,
took snuff. She acquired the habit at an early
age, and clung to it all her life. Sergius Galitzine
relates that she had to give up snuff-taking, by
the Emperor's command, because she had once
asked his (Sergius's) father for a pinch of snuff.
The scene is well known in which the Emperor
apostrophised the Empress in public, and flung at
her head a gross insult. It was the 21st of June
1762, at a dinner of four hundred people, the
dignitaries of the three first orders and the foreign
ministers, on the occasion of the ratification of
the treaty of peace with Prussia. The Empress
was seated in her usual place in the middle of
the table. The Emperor, having on his right
the Baron von Goltz, was seated at one end.
Before drinking the health of Frederick, the
Emperor proposed that of the imperial family.
Scarcely had the Empress set down her glass,
when he sent his aide-de-camp, Goudowitch, to
know why she had not risen to do honour to the
toast. She replied that as the imperial family
consisted only of the Emperor, herself, and her
son, she had not thought it necessary. Peter
immediately sent back Goudowitch, with orders
to tell the Empress that she was a fool (*doura*),

and that she ought to know that the two Princes
of Holstein, his uncles, formed part of the imperial family.   And, fearing no doubt that Goudowitch would not execute his commission faithfully,
he himself shouted ' *Doura!* ' across the table,
addressing the compliment to the one for whom
it was intended.   Every one heard the word.
Tears started from Catherine's eyes.

These were but insults.   Peter had the folly
of adding threats.   The same day, the *Freiline*
Vorontsof received the order of St. Catherine,
which was habitually reserved to princesses of
the blood-royal.   Catherine herself had only had
it after having been officially designated as the
fiancée of the future Emperor.   It even appears
that on leaving the table, drunk as usual, Peter
gave the order to Prince Bariatinski to arrest the
Empress, and only the entreaties of Prince
George of Holstein persuaded him to revoke his
decision.   But it was matter of general belief
that, urged on by the Vorontsofs, he would pro-
ceed to this extremity.   Catherine would be shut
up in a convent, Paul thrown into prison, and
the favourite legally married.   She had certainly
gained an absolute hold over him.   She was
just the mistress for this imperial puppet, half
German corporal.   She was not pretty; 'ugly,
common, and stupid,' says Masson.   The German Scherer, who has only praises for Peter,
admits that he gave evidence, in his choice of a
companion, of deplorable taste—the only fault, in
his eyes, that is to be found in him.   She was
worthless and without education.   'She swore
like a trooper, squinted, and spat while talking.'
It seems that she sometimes beat the Emperor,

but she got drunk with him, which was some compensation. It is reported that at the very moment of the revolution, which hurled down Peter and his mistress, the manifesto destined to remove Catherine from the throne, and to set up the Vorontsof in her place, was made out, and ready to be published to the world.

Thus did Catherine find herself face to face with a dilemma, of which both ways indicated a terrible risk to run, with this difference, that there was nothing to gain on one side and not much to lose on the other. She made her choice in consequence.

III

The history of the conspiracy of 1762, which cost the throne and the life of Peter III., has yet to be written, and, up to the present, sufficiently authentic and definite documents for the historian are lacking. Rulhière seems to be utterly mistaken in regard to the part played by Panine and the Princess Dachkof in bringing about this event. According to him they did little or nothing. Nevertheless, according to him, it is the Princess Dachkof who began, by sacrificing her virtue in order to win over Panine, who was himself little disposed to run the risk. It must be added that the scruples of the Princess were owing mainly to her belief that a very near relationship existed between her and the man whose homage she at first repulsed. She thought she was his daughter. An obscure intermediary, the Piedmontese Odard, afterwards secretary to Catherine, persuaded her out of this notion, and after that the two lovers were soon in agreement. Unhappily they were not from the first in agreement with Catherine as to the end towards which their efforts were to tend. The Princess's reading, the residence of Panine at Stockholm, had imbued them both with republican ideas. They would not give the power to Catherine save on certain conditions. Catherine declined any sort of compromise, and, having the Orlofs under her hand, seemed disposed to go without the services which were offered her at such a price. They therefore decided to work independently towards the dislodgment of Peter, waiting on the event to see how he should be replaced. It was an instance of the 'parallel action,' of which recent events have given rise to further instances. Princess Dachkof and Panine recruited partisans among the high officers of the army, stooping sometimes to the very soldiers. The Orlofs worked among the soldiers, and made several tentatives among the chiefs. Sometimes they met one another in the barracks, and, not being mutually acquainted, looked upon one another with suspicion. At length Catherine succeeded in uniting the two intrigues, and took the direction of the movement into her own hands.

Such is the account of Rulhière. Convincing as it has seemed to-day to the most intelligent writers, it is easy to find in it grave objections. The portrait that Diderot, who afterwards knew the Princess Dachkof at Paris, has left of this beauty, is one :—

'The Princess is by no means beautiful ; she is small ; her forehead is high and broad, she has fat puffy cheeks, eyes neither large nor small, a little deeply set in their sockets, black eyes and eyelashes, a flat nose, a large mouth, thick lips, bad teeth, a round, straight throat of the national shape, the chest convex, no figure, promptitude in her movements, few graces, nothing imposing.'

She seems, certainly, to have exercised a certain influence, due perhaps to the vivacity of her character, on the indolent spirit of the future minister of Catherine ; that she can have had the power to rid him not only of his indolence, but also of his habitual prudence, to the point of implicating him in an enterprise of which he was well able to appreciate all the danger, seems to us more than doubtful. That on her side Catherine should have put her interests, her destiny and that of her son, her ambition, and her very life, into the hands of this conspiratress of eighteen, is what we find the greatest difficulty in admitting as possible. The Princess, too, has told us in her memoirs the manner in which her first advances were received. It was a little before the death of Elizabeth. One winter evening, towards midnight, the Grand Duchess, who had already gone to bed, saw her friend appear, trembling with fright or cold, and entreating her to confide in her, in view of the dangers which surrounded her. She desired to know what was the plan of the future Empress, and what instructions she had to give her. Catherine first of all did her best to keep this intrepid adventuress from catching cold. She made her lie down by her side, covered her up with the bedclothes, and then gently advised her to return to her own bed and not be frightened. She had no plan, and she put her trust in Providence.

In reality no one, among those who were most concerned in foreseeing the great event, had any suspicion of its approach, or saw it coming. Who could pay any attention to the obscure and unmethodical machinations of a few hare-brained creatures? According to one of the versions that we owe to the Princess Dachkof, the very conspirators themselves had no better view of things: 'The affair was well forward before she, or the Empress, or any one at all, was aware of it. Three hours before the revolution there was not a soul who expected it in less than three years.'

At all events it seems that, up to the last moment, there was no settled plan, nor even any very definite idea, on the part of any one, as to the course to be followed and the methods to be used in attaining the end in view. How was Peter to be dethroned and Catherine set in his place? No one knew. According to Odard's confidences to Béranger, several attempts were made, without success, to seize the Emperor. As far as one can judge, they went forward at hazard. The Princess Dachkof, so much is probable, spoke to some officers. There was, it is certain, a whole propaganda, a work of corrupting and tampering, carried on in the barracks by the brothers Orlof on a wide scale. Money was not lacking, even before the tentative finally made upon the Baron de Breteuil. At the beginning of March, Gregory Orlof occupied the post of paying officer to the artillery. The grand master of artillery, the luckless lover of the Princess Kourakine, had just died, and had been succeeded by a former chamberlain of the young court, who had been removed from his post by Elizabeth on account of his excessive devotion to Catherine—the Frenchman Villebois. Villebois was the son of a page of Peter I., who had afterwards been made vice-admiral. It was written that a Frenchman once again should play an important part in the *coup d'état* destined to give a new ruler to Russia, and that La Chétardie should have a successor. It is probable, indeed, that the choice of Gregory Orlof was due to the personal intervention of the new grand master, inspired, no doubt, by Catherine herself. Nothing seemed to point out the young officer as a suitable person for such a post of confidence. One might as well have put the cash-box on deposit in the cave of Ali-Baba. The second in command under Villebois, Lieutenant-General Pournour, made the observation. He was informed that Orlof was protected by the Empress, and he bowed. The paying officer made heavy demands upon the treasury. In this way not less than ninety-nine soldiers in each regiment of the Guard had been gained over—the Ismaïlofski (the first before which Elizabeth had presented herself on the day of the *coup d'état*), the Siemienofski, the Preobrajenski, and the regiment of horse guards in which served the famous Patiomkine.

Catherine was sometimes induced to give direct and personal aid to those who were recruiting in her interests. She seems, nevertheless, to have shown much restraint and discretion in the matter. One of the grenadiers won over by Alexis Orlof, the grenadier Strolof, required a sign from the Empress. He was promised that if he would be in the Czarina's way in the course of her promenade in the park of the imperial palace, he should have this sign : her Majesty would give him her hand to kiss. Catherine lent herself readily to the plan, by which she ran no sort of risk. 'Everybody kisses my hand,' she said, later on, to Chrapowicki. But the brave soldier was moved to the depths of his soul. He shed tears as he bent over the imperial hand, and asked no further conviction.

The last to be convinced, in this conspiracy, would seem to have been Catherine herself. In the account that she is supposed to have written of this period of her life, she states that she refused to lend an ear to the proposals that were made to her from the time of Elizabeth's death, until, after having publicly insulted her, Peter carried his spite and extravagance to the point of wishing to have her arrested. The incident, as we know, happened on the 21st of June, that is to say, only a few weeks before the *coup d'état*. But even then, and up to the time of the *coup d'état* itself, no active part is known to have been taken by the future Empress in the operations of her friends. Her part, up to the last moment, would seem to have been a part of attitude and bearing alone. In this respect she was admirable. The art with which she always continued to take the opposite side to her husband, and tone down whatever was offensive in his conduct by some counterpart exaggeration of behaviour, places her among the finest political actresses of all time. The death of Elizabeth, and the complication of ceremonies which arose from the clashing of the rites of the Greek Church with the court etiquette over the mortal remains of the Empress, provided a fresh occasion for the new Emperor to display the singularity and churlishness of his disposition. He did not fail to take it, showing himself indecorous to excess. Catherine protested, and won the admiration and sympathy of all by her manifestations of respect and filial piety.

'No one,' wrote the Baron de Breteuil, 'has been more assiduous in carrying out the late Empress's funeral rites, which, according to the Greek Church, are numerous and most superstitious, and at which she must certainly laugh in her sleeve, but the clergy and the people believe her to be deeply affected, and are highly delighted.'

There is a portrait of her in the morning dress which she always wore at this time. She observed carefully all the religious ceremonies, fasts, *jours maigres*, holidays, everything for which Peter affected the most absolute contempt. At a solemn mass, sung in the chapel of the palace, on the occasion of Trinity Sunday, the Austrian ambassador was amazed to see the Emperor walking unceremoniously about the holy edifice, and talking aloud during the service with the gentlemen and ladies of the court, while the Empress, motionless in her place, appeared buried in her prayers.

Peter, growing more and more violent as time went on, forgot himself to the extent of inflicting manual correction upon the members of his immediate retinue, upon high dignitaries, upon his most devoted followers, in public, before the assembled court. Narychkine, Mielgounof, Volkof, had in turn to suffer these indignities. Catherine was sweetness itself. All who came near her united in praise of her affability, her evenness of temper, her good graces. To the brutalities of the Emperor, of which she was herself one of the victims, she gently opposed the most dignified deportment, well made to inspire sympathy, without allowing sympathy to degenerate into pity and disesteem. At the famous banquet where the Emperor flung at her the word 'Fool!' she let some tears be seen, just enough to touch the hearts of those who witnessed the painful scene; then, turning immediately to Count Strogonof, who was standing behind her chair, she begged him to tell her something merry, to make her laugh and distract people's attention.

At one moment she carried her science of dissimulation so far as to become amiable and considerate for Peter himself. The diplomatic correspondence notifies an unexpected reconciliation of husband and wife. The Empress appeared, smiling and gracious, at the Emperor's suppers, in the midst of orgies of beer and tobacco. She endured stoically the odour of pipes, the heavy German drunkenness, the low talk of drinkers. It was the critical moment. Catherine, as we have said, was *enceinte*. She had need to hide the fact from all eyes, and especially from the eyes of the Emperor. There is a story that on the day when she was taken with the pangs of childbirth, her faithful *valet de chambre*, Chkourine, set fire to a house belonging to him in one of the suburbs of the city, in order to attract the curious in that direction. Peter ran off there, naturally, to enjoy the sight, and distribute insults and blows of his cane. His favourites followed. Catherine gave birth, on the 23rd April, to a son, who took the name of Bobrinski, and became the founder of one of the most important families in Russia. We shall meet him again later on. It was at this time that, a courtier complimenting the Empress on looking so well, and bringing such a ray of beauty into the company, she could not resist saying: 'You have no idea how much it sometimes costs me to look well.'

But where was all this to lead? She little knew, in all probability. A day would come, no doubt, when the subterranean labour of her friends would come to the light of day, bringing with it an explosion; when the extravagances of her husband would come to a crisis: then it would be time for her to act. Then she would act. Meanwhile, as she had said to Princess Dachkof, she put her trust in Providence. According to Frederick, it was the best she could have done. 'She could not yet carry anything through,' he said afterwards, recalling these times; 'she threw herself into the arms of those who were ready to save her.' That ability in the conduct of affairs, that sureness of vision, that prudence and dexterity needed to pull through an enterprise of this sort, were never specially in her line. It was in her temperament that her true superiority was to be found, by that that she really shone. It was on this account that she had always to rely principally, as she did all her life, on that superior and mysterious force that she invoked in speaking to the Princess Dachkof, and whose might Frederick himself did not deny, irreverently calling it 'His Sacred Majesty Chance.' To abandon herself to Orlof, as she did now, or to Patiomkine, as she did later, was really, properly speaking, nothing else. Chance brought good luck with Orlof, good luck, and perhaps genius, with Patiomkine, disaster with Zoubof. But Catherine still remained great. For the moment, chance gave her the victory. Chance did not, however, act alone; but rather with the aid of the man most interested in bringing the enterprise to nought. 'He let himself be dethroned as a child lets himself be sent to bed,' said Frederick, speaking of Peter III.

CHAPTER III

TIIE VICTORY

1

PETER left St. Petersburg June 24th for Oranienbaum. On the 22nd there was a supper at which 500 guests sat down, and there were fireworks after the supper in honour of the peace with Prussia. On the 23rd the feasting still continued, and it continued afterwards at Oranienbaum with a smaller number of guests. The sojourn of the Emperor in his summer residence was to be of short duration. Peter intended shortly to rejoin his army in Pomerania and put to flight the Danes, until he had the chance of making his name glorious on some vaster battle-field, whither his new ally should summon him. He meant to embark at the end of July. The fleet, reduced by sickness, was not really in condition to set sail. Peter was not at a loss. He signed a ukase ordering the sick sailors to get well.

These warlike projects caused some anxiety to his friends, beginning with Frederick himself. His Prussian Majesty's envoys, the Baron von Goltz and Count Schwerin, had not failed to remonstrate with him on the subject. Was it prudent for the Emperor to leave his capital and his empire before allowing himself time to establish himself upon his throne, before even having been crowned? Frederick insisted personally on this last point. Before undertaking any enterprise, he should go to Moscow and assume the diadem of the Czar. In a country like Russia this question of form was of immense importance. Peter would listen to nothing. 'One is sure of the Russians when one knows how to take them,' he said. He imagined that he had this knowledge.

He imagined also that he had his eye upon the· possible conspirators. The two Orlofs had been pointed out to him. One of their friends, Lieutenant Perfilef, put himself at the disposal of the Czar, and undertook to spy on the five brothers, and play them into his hands. It was he himself who played into their hands. The

M

Orlofs were distrustful of him, and at the last moment made merry over the confident traitor.

On June 29th, Catherine, whom Peter had had the imprudence to leave behind at St. Petersburg, had herself to take up her summer quarters. She received orders to go to Peterhof. At Oranienbaum it was Elizabeth Vorontsof who reigned. Paul remained at St. Petersburg under the care of Panine. Peter nevertheless counted on seeing his wife before setting out on the proposed campaign. He had put off the date of his departure in order to celebrate the 10th of July (29th June), his feast-day. He meant to celebrate it at Peterhof. On the morning of the 9th he set out for the palace, where a grand dinner was to be given in his honour by the Empress on the following day. Peter travelled slowly, taking a large following after him, among which were seventeen ladies. He did not arrive at Peterhof till two o'clock. A surprise was awaiting him; the château was empty. Peter found only a few servants overcome with terror.

'And the Empress?'

'Gone!'

'Where?'

No one knew, or no one would answer. A peasant approached and handed a paper to the Emperor. It was a letter from Bressan, the former French valet of Peter, whom he had appointed to the supervision of the manufacture of Gobelins. Bressan wrote that the Empress had arrived at St. Petersburg that morning, and had been proclaimed sole and absolute sovereign. Peter could not believe his eyes. He rushed like a madman through the empty rooms, hunted in every corner, and all through the gardens, calling the Empress again and again. The crowd of frightened courtiers followed him in his useless search. They had at last to give in to the evidence of their own eyes.

What had happened? No one has ever quite known. The uncertainties and contradictions which have already embarrassed us in the course of our narrative confront us once more at this juncture. The narrative of Princess Dachkof seems in many respects dubious, and that of Catherine does not bear examination. On the night of the 8th or 9th July Catherine's friend appears to have been awakened by one of the Orlofs, with the news of the arrest of one of the conspirators, Captain Passek. It meant the discovery of the plot and the certain ruin of all who had taken part in it. Princess Dachkof did not hesitate. She gave orders to give the immediate alarm to the Ismaïlofski regiment, that of which they were most certain; to prepare it to receive the Empress; and at the same time to send for her to Peterhof. It was done. There was, nevertheless, a certain hesitation on the part of the Orlofs. The youngest brother, Theodore, came back a few hours afterwards to submit their objections to the Princess. Was it not too soon to venture on so bold a stroke? She declared angrily that they had wasted too much time already. He bowed to her will, and all obeyed. That is the friend's version. Catherine's is quite different. A few years afterwards she was greatly wroth with Ivan Chouvalof, 'the basest and most cowardly of men,' who has dared to write to Voltaire 'that a girl of nineteen had

changed the government of Russia.' Most assuredly, she declares, the Orlofs had something
else to do than to put themselves at the command of a little scatter-brain. To the last
moment, on the contrary 'she was kept from
knowing the most essential part of this affair.'
Everything was done under the 'quite personal'
direction of Catherine, and of Catherine alone,
in consequence of plans which had been made
and agreed upon 'six months before,' between
her and the heads of the conspiracy. Six months
before! Is this really true? Has not Catherine
herself said elsewhere that she paid no heed to
the proposals for the dethronement of her husband till after she had been publicly insulted
by him—that is to say, only *three weeks* before
the 9th of July?

It is all very uncertain. Quarrels between
jealous women usually are. Moreover, both may
have spoken in good faith, recalling as they did,
so long afterwards, memories blurred with mists
of emotion, and attributing to themselves an
imaginary part in the events that they both
imagined they had conducted, and by which they
were both most likely conducted themselves. It
is probable that the arrest of Passek, due, as it
seems, to a mere accident, hastened things on,
and decided the conspirators to risk everything
in order to save their lives, which they saw to be
in danger. It is certain that, on the 9th of July,
at five o'clock in the morning, Alexis Orlof presented himself suddenly at Peterhof, and brought
the Empress back to St. Petersburg.

Catherine was sound asleep—it is she who
gives us this detail—when the young officer

entered her room. Nothing had yet been decided on, and she was not prepared for anything. To understand the scene which followed, according to her own story of it, one must have come in contact with primitive natures like that of this Orlof. One meets many like them to-day in Russia. The thought of such folk being utterly without any complication, their expression of this thought is always simple. The art of preparation is unknown to them, and all the fine shades. They say exactly what they have to say, going straight to the point. They say in the same manner and with the same tone the most commonplace or the most startling of things. They speak always in monochord. If the moon were to fall from the sky, a peasant near Moscow would say to you, 'The moon has fallen,' in the same tone as he would tell you that his cow had had a calf. Alexis Orlof simply woke the Empress and said to her: 'It is time to get up. Everything is ready for your proclamation.'

She asked for explanations. He said, 'Passek is arrested. You must come.' That was all. She dressed herself hurriedly, without 'making a toilette,' and jumped into the coach that had brought Orlof. One of her women, the Charogrodskaïa, took her place by her side, Orlof mounted in front, the faithful Chkourine behind, and the vehicle set out at headlong speed for St. Petersburg. On the way they met Michel, the French *coiffeur* of her Majesty, who was as usual on his way to wait upon her. He was taken along.

There were nearly 20 miles to cover, and the

horses, which had already done the distance one way, were scarcely able to start on the return journey. No one had thought of organising a relay. This negligence was near costing them dear. Two horses from a passing peasant's cart perhaps saved Catherine, and won for her a crown. Five versts outside the town they met Gregory Orlof and Prince Bariatinski, in a state of great anxiety; they changed from the one coach to the other, and arrived at last before the barracks of the Ismaïlofski regiment.

'Thus,' writes Rulhière, 'to reign despotically over the vastest empire in the world, arrived Catherine, between six and seven in the morning, having set out on the word of a soldier, brought by peasants, conducted by her lover, and accompanied by her lady's maid and her *coiffeur.*'

Only a dozen men were there. In reality, nothing had been seriously prepared, notwithstanding what Alexis Orlof had said. Drums were beaten. Soldiers half dressed and half asleep came tumbling out. They were told to shout 'Long live the Empress!' They looked forward to a distribution of *vodka*, and shouted whatever was told them. Two of them were sent for a priest, whom they brought back between them. The priest also did whatever he was told. He raised the cross, mumbled a form of oath, the soldiers all bowed down: it was done, the Empress was proclaimed.

'The throne of Russia is neither hereditary nor elective,' said the Neapolitan Caraccioli; 'it is *occupative.*'

The proclamation made no mention of Paul. It declared Catherine sole and absolute and aristocratic sovereign (*samodierjsamodierjitsa*). This was not at all what Panine had intended. But where was Panine at this hour, and who troubled about Panine?

'A pack,' says Herzen, 'of oligarchs, strangers, pandours, and minions, brought by night an unknown, a child, a German, raised her to the throne, worshipped her, and distributed kicks and blows in her name to all who had anything to say in objection.'

Of the other regiments of the Guard, one only, the Preobrajenski, made some show of resistance. Simon Vorontsof, a brother of the favourite, who commanded a company in it, would not betray a cause which might pass for that of his sister. He was besides, as he proved afterwards, a man of duty and honour. He harangued his men; Major Voieïkof supported him, and the regiment marched resolutely against the mutineers who followed Catherine. The two little armies met before the church of Our Lady of Kasan. Catherine had on her side the superiority of numbers, but it was only that of a crowd in disorder. The Preobrajenski regiment, on the contrary, marshalled by its officers, and drawn up in rank, presented an imposing front of battle; it might yet decide the issue of the day.

But the fortune of Catherine declared itself. At the moment when loyalists and rebels came to a standstill within a few paces from one another, ready to come to blows, one of the colleagues of Simon Vorontsof, who marched in the ranks, cried suddenly: '*Oura!* Long live the Empress!' It was a train of powder.

The whole regiment took up the cry and disbanded in an instant, the soldiers threw themselves into the arms of their comrades, and then, falling on their knees, they asked pardon of the Empress for not having greeted her at once, accusing their officers. Voieikof and Vorontsof broke their swords. They were arrested. Catherine afterwards pardoned them, but she never forgot. Vorontsof had to quit the army, where his merits and his brilliant services brought him nothing but vexation. Appointed ambassador at London, he lived in a sort of honourable exile.

Every one now crowded into the church of Our Lady of Kasan, where Catherine betook herself to receive the oaths of fidelity of her new subjects. Panine soon made his appearance. It is said that in the coach with him was the little Paul, in his nightcap. The child may thus have been present at his own downfall, for it was really his downfall, at least provisionally, which was being consummated. After the revered temple it was the Winter Palace, the scene of so many of Catherine's past humiliations, that saw her surrounded with a crowd, hastening to do homage. The senate and the synod came forward among the rest. These two great bodies had already made it their habit to march behind the regiments of the Guard. Another personage came on the scene whom Catherine had not at all expected to see—the chancellor Vorontsof. He was still unconscious of what was going forward, and *naïvely* demanded of the Empress why she had left Peterhof. For answer, she made sign that he was to be brought along. He was told to go into the church and take the oath. He went there.

Lastly, elbowing her way through the crowd, all out of breath, agitated, and somewhat disappointed, arrived the pretended organiser of all this triumph—the Princess Dachkof. Her coach had not been able to get as far as the steps of the palace, but, according to her account, the heroes of the day, the officers and soldiers who surrounded the entrance, raised her on their shoulders and brought her in. Her dress and her coiffure had to suffer, but her self-esteem found a compensation for the mortifications which were soon to begin for her. For her interview with the Empress was briefer and less solemn than she had hoped for. It was not the hour for tender effusions, nor for grand ceremonies. There was serious business to be done. First of all, a serious form had to be given to what had just been improvised in a burst of youthful energy and victorious boldness. A manifesto was necessary. It was an obscure employé from the chancellor's office, Tieplof, who was appointed to draw it up. Why not Panine? There are various stories current on this subject. Did the tutor of the little Paul actually think it *apropos*, even at this moment, and had he the courage, to stand up for his favourite idea and his pupil? According to one version, the officers of the Ismaïlofski regiment were opposed to the signature of a reversal, binding Catherine not to reign after the end of Paul's minority. According to another version, the reversal dictated by Panine, and imposed by him upon the Empress, had been signed and deposited in the archives of the

Senate, but the Orlofs, by one account, the chancellor Vorontsof, by another, had afterwards withdrawn the document and handed it over to Catherine. The story is very improbable. Panine was not the man to believe in compromises of this kind, and to delude himself as to the worth of such a guarantee. He knew the history of his country. The Empress Anne had risen to the throne under the security of a veritable constitutional charter. Six weeks afterwards nothing more was heard of it. The future minister might have had other reasons for not taking part in the drawing up of the manifesto.

What Tieplof wrote was sent to press and read to the people, who cried, ' Long live the Empress!' as they had heard the soldiers cry. Catherine reviewed the troops, who hailed her once again; and the new reign had been established : not a drop of blood had been shed. There were a few isolated scenes of disorder. The house of Prince George of Holstein was attacked and pillaged, and he and his wife were somewhat roughly handled, the rings of the Princess being torn off by the soldiers. Some shops were broken into, and the soldiers demanded wine. One wine-merchant lost 4000 roubles' worth. The indemnities claimed by the victims of these excesses amounted to 24,000 roubles, not a very serious amount. When the evening was come, and the intoxication of the moment had worn off, and Catherine and her companions, once more in the Winter Palace, proceeded to review the situation, a certain anxiety began to be felt. If, from one point of view, everything in regard to the establishment

of the throne had been done, from another, everything had yet to be done. All would count for
nothing if Peter were to make a resistance.

Was it within his power to do so ? The answer
left no room for doubt, and perhaps Panine was
just then considering it. Peter had with him
about 1500 Holsteiners, an excellent body of
men, and ready, according to all appearance, to
fight for him to the last, especially as they
would be fighting for themselves at the same
time. At the head of this little army was the
first soldier of Russia, and one of the first of the
epoch—Field-Marshal Münich. Recalled by the
new Emperor from Siberia, he would never desert
his benefactor. Now Catherine herself had at
her command only the four regiments that had
proclaimed her. The main body of the Russian
force was in Pomerania, as yet belonging to no
one, or rather belonging to the Emperor, and at
his command. If Peter made a resistance, if he
gained time, if he made the most of the name
and fame of his victorious marshal, would not
this Pomeranian army obey his orders, and come
to the rescue ? He was the Emperor, and he
was about to open a new campaign, a prospect
generally agreeable to the soldier, especially after
a series of brilliant successes. Up to the present
he had only given offence to the Guards, of whose
privileges all the rest of the army was jealous.
The Orlofs, on their side, had not used their
influence beyond this point. The problem was
formidable.

But where was the Emperor at this moment,
and what was he thinking about and doing?

II

After having satisfied himself that the Empress was not where he had expected to find her, Peter could not at once admit the truth, or grasp the whole extent, of his misfortune. The man in whom he placed his confidence, Perfilef, had not forewarned him. The hapless Perfilef had passed the night playing at cards with Gregory Orlof, thinking to have him thus under his eye. Peter resolved to send for information. He had plenty of people about him. The chancellor Vorontsof, Prince Troubetzkoï, Alexander Chouvalof, offered to go to St. Petersburg. None of them returned. But a Holsteiner, returning from the town, where he had been spending a twenty-four hours' leave of absence, confirmed the bad news. It was now three o'clock. Peter made another resolution : he summoned Volkof, and ordered him to draw up several manifestoes, by way of beginning a campaign on paper. Nevertheless, on the advice of Münich, he decided to send one of his aides-de-camp, Count Devierre, to Kronstadt, in order to make sure of this important position. An hour afterwards, he remembered that he was a soldier, put on his field-day uniform, and sent for the Holstein troops that had remained behind at Oranienbaum. His intention was to fortify himself at Peterhof, and hold his own against the insurrection. The Holsteiners arrived at eight, but Peter had changed his mind. Münich could not answer for putting Peterhof in condition to stand a siege. He would have preferred to go to Kronstadt instead of sending there. He had his plan. Suddenly Peter wheeled round, and agreed with his field-marshal. But by this time it was night. They set out, nevertheless; but, one would have thought, on a pleasure-party. A yacht and a galley with oars took on board the Emperor's *cortège*, masculine and feminine. They arrived in sight of Kronstadt at one o'clock in the morning.

'Who goes there?' cried a sentinel from the top of the ramparts.

'The Emperor.'

'There is no Emperor. Keep off!'

Count Devierre had been outstripped by an envoy of Catherine, Admiral Talitsine.

Münich was not yet disheartened. He and Goudowitch entreated Peter to disembark in spite of all. They would never dare fire upon them; of that they were certain. But Peter was down in the hold, trembling in every limb. He had only had to do with cardboard fortresses. The women uttered piercing shrieks. The vessels were turned about.

Then Münich proposed another plan: to go on to the port of Reval, embark on a warship, and make their way to Pomerania, where Peter could take command of his army.

'Do this, sire,' said the old warrior, 'and six weeks afterwards St. Petersburg and Russia will again be at your feet. I answer for it with my head.'

But Peter had exhausted his whole stock of energy. He thought only of getting back to Oranienbaum, and entering into negotiations. They returned to Oranienbaum. There too they met with unexpected news. The Empress had left for St. Petersburg at the head of her four regiments, and was marching upon Peter and his Holsteiners.

It was a triumphal march. Catherine led the troops on horseback wearing the uniform of the grenadiers of the Preobrajenski regiment. A crown of oak-leaves adorned her cap, with its sable fur, and her long hair floated in the wind. By her side, dressed in the same uniform, galloped Princess Dachkof. The soldiers were in ecstasies. They had unanimously thrown aside the uniforms into which they had been put by Peter, tearing them to pieces or selling them to the second-hand dealers ; and they had returned to their old garb, which Peter I. had imported from Germany, but which passed already as national. They burned to measure arms with the Holsteiners.

They had not this satisfaction. After a night's march, at five o'clock in the morning, a messenger bearing a flag of truce arrived from Peter. It was Prince Alexander Galitzine. The Emperor offered to divide the power with the Empress. Catherine disdained to answer. An hour afterward, she received the act of abdication of her husband. She halted at Peterhof, whither Peter was brought. Panine, who had been deputed to notify to him the final orders of the Czarina, found him in the most pitiful state. Peter endeavoured to kiss his hand, entreating not to be separated from his mistress. He cried like a whipt child. The favourite crawled to the knees of Catherine's envoy ; she too begged to be allowed to stay by her lover. They were separated none the less. Mlle. Vorontsof was

sent to Moscow. Peter was sent provisionally
to a house situated at Ropcha, 'a very lonely but
a very agreeable spot,' Catherine declares, nearly
twenty miles from Peterhof, where he was to
remain until suitable accommodation had been
found for him in the fortress of Schlüsselburg, the
Russian Bastille.

On the following day, July 14, Catherine made
a solemn entry into St. Petersburg. She had
only remained a few hours at Peterhof. Something, however, had happened, besides the downfall of Peter. Princess Dachkof had made a
discovery, of which she speaks sadly enough in
her memoirs, and which, by the surprise it caused
her, proves that, for an organiser of plots, she
was somewhat simple. On entering the Empress's *salon* at the dinner-hour she saw a man
stretched at full length on a sofa. It was Gregory
Orlof. He had before him a heap of sealed papers
which he was nonchalantly proceeding to open.

'What are you doing?' cried the Princess,
recognising, by the aspect familiar to her in her
uncle's house, documents belonging to the chancellor's office. 'No one has a right to touch
them, except the Empress and those whom she
specially appoints.'

'Exactly,' replied Orlof, without changing his
position, and with the same air of disdainful
indifference. '*She* told me to look through this.'
He seemed very much bored by his task, and
resolved to get it over as quickly as possible.

The Princess was thunderstruck. Her astonishment was not at an end. Three covers were
laid on a table at the other end of the room.
The Empress, arriving immediately, asked her

friend to seat herself beside her. The third place
was for the young lieutenant. But he made no
move The Empress then had the table moved
over by the divan. She and the Princess sat
down opposite to the young man, who still lay at
full length on the sofa. He was, it appeared,
wounded in the leg.

Thus was disclosed the situation which he was
to occupy in connection with the new sovereign.
It was the inauguration of *favouritism*.

III

Some further ordeals still awaited Catherine at
St. Petersburg. The very night after her return,
there was a great noise outside the palace. The
soldiers of the Ismailofski regiment had left their
barracks, and demanded to see the Empress, to
assure themselves that she had not been carried
off She had to get up from bed, and once
again put on her grenadier's uniform, in order
to reassure them.

'I cannot and would not,' she writes some
months later to Poniatowski, 'tell you all the
obstacles there are to your coming here. . . . My
situation is such that I have to be extremely
careful, and the least soldier of the Guards who
sees me says to himself: "See the work of my
hands." I am frightened to death at the letters
you write me.'

She held her own admirably, however, with
the difficulties and dangers of the situation.
Neither in the preparation nor the execution
of the *coup d'état* had she shown very great
forethought or capacity, qualities, certainly, de-

sirable in a leader ; but she had shown courage, coolness, resoluteness, and especially the art of doing things with effect. These means of action she still employed. All the eye-witnesses of the events which were then taking place at St. Petersburg are unanimous in praise of her calmness, her affable and yet imposing air, and the smiling majesty of her mien and bearing. She was already showing herself 'imperturbable.'

She did not neglect, either, the means she had long ago chosen for the subjection of wills and the conquest of devotions : she manifested herself from the first as an ostentatious Empress, splendidly rewarding those who served her, generous to profusion. During the first few months of her reign, it is a veritable Pactolus that streams forth upon those who have wrought for her her fortune. Up to November 16, 1762, the amount of indemnities paid, apart from payment in kind, in land, and in peasants, comes to 795,622 roubles, or nearly four million francs at the then rate of reckoning. And these sums are for the most part but instalments. Thus Gregory Orlof has received only 3000 roubles out of the 50,000 assigned to him. The resources of the Treasury do not admit of more at the present. Princess Dachkof figures on the list of payments to the amount of 25,000 roubles. A sum of 225,850 roubles has been appropriated to the remittance of a half-year's pay, by which the staff of the Guards' regiments are the gainers. The soldiers are not so well off. They have had plenty to drink on the day of the 12th July. On this head the expense amounts to 41,000 roubles, or more than 200,000 francs. But, not long after the great event, a consider-

N

able number of these Praetorians are in want, and Catherine does nothing for them. It is true that she is no longer in need of them.

The absent are not forgotten. One of Catherine's first cares was to send an express messenger to the ex-chancellor Bestoujef, announcing her accession to the throne, and inviting him to rejoin her in the capital. The bearer of this good news, chosen by Catherine, was a certain Nicholas Ivanovitch Kalyshkine, who, in February 1758, being then a sergeant in a regiment of the Guards, had been intrusted with the surveillance of the jeweller Bernardi, implicated in the Bestoujef case, and had aided in the exchange of correspondence between the Grand Duchess and the prisoners. That, too, Catherine remembered. She was nevertheless raising false hopes in her former associate in politics. Bestoujef hastened to her at once, and was received with open arms. Catherine was very glad to have at hand a man of his experience and authority. She paraded his name and his past services, and often had recourse to his counsels. But he no doubt anticipated recovering his place as omnipotent minister, indeed an influence even greater than he had had under Elizabeth. In this he was greatly mistaken.

There were a number of similar disappointments. Field-Marshal Münich, who had hastened to make his submission, had a very considerable one. Catherine did not appear to cherish any ill-will against him on account of the assistance, useless, it is true, that he had rendered to Peter. He had only done his duty. He said it handsomely enough, and she seemed to lend ear

to it in like manner. But she did with him as she
did with Bestoujef. She got rid of him politely.
She judged, to use the expression of a modern
statesman, that a new situation needed new men.

Another to be disenchanted was Princess
Dachkof. She had conceived of the reign of
Catherine as a sort of transformation scene, in
which she would continue day by day to sway
the destinies of the empire, prancing on a noble
steed at the head of a column of grenadiers.
She had acquired a taste for a uniform, for intrigue, for parade. She imagined herself to be
neither esteemed and rewarded according to her
merits, nor utilised according to her capacities.
We shall come across her again later on, with
her dreams, her pretensions, and all the follies
that poisoned her own life, and gave no little
trouble to her imperial friend. We shall also
come across Bestoujef and Münich.

Catherine was very near making another malcontent in the person of an obscure friend, of
whom we have already spoken. Princess Dachkof was not the only one to claim a principal
share in the event of the 12th July. Four days
after the *coup d'état*, General Betzky was announced to the Empress. He had been employed in making some distributions of money to
the soldiers gained over by the Orlofs. He had
received an order and a few thousand roubles.
Catherine imagined that he had come to thank
her. He fell on his knees, and, in that position, he entreated the Empress to state before
witnesses to whom she owed her crown.

'To God and to my subjects' choice,' said
Catherine simply.

On hearing these words, Betzky rose, and with a tragic gesture took off the ribbon of his order.

'What are you doing?'

'I am no more worthy to bear these insignia, the reward of my services, since my services are disowned by the Empress. I imagined myself to have been the sole workman of her grandeur. Was it not I who raised the Guards? Was it not I who scattered the gold? The Empress denies it. I am the most unhappy of men.'

The Empress turned it off with a joke.

'You gave me the crown, Betzky, I admit. Therefore I would receive it from your hands alone. It is you to whom I confide the care of rendering it as beautiful as possible. I put at your disposal all the jewellers of my empire.'

Betzky took the joke seriously. He looked after the jewellers who had to prepare the crown against the day of coronation, and was satisfied. So, at least, the Princess Dachkof tells the story, in which she may well have put some amount of invention.

In general, however, as we have said, Catherine was as generous to her friends as she was magnanimous to her enemies. The new reign began well. The enthusiasm with which it had been received in the capital found an echo in the remotest provinces. Suddenly a dark cloud came across this radiant dawn. On July 18, as she was retiring from the senate, where she had read a new manifesto setting forth the description, somewhat coloured, of the means whereby she had risen to the throne, Catherine was about to prepare to appear before the court, when a man rushed into her dressing-room, covered with sweat and dust, his clothes all in disorder. It was Alexis Orlof. He had ridden full speed from Ropcha to announce to the Empress the death of Peter III.

IV

How had this come about? It is still a mystery. More than in any other country in Europe, it yet remains for history in Russia to get at the true sense of the official accounts of great events of state. The walls of palaces built of granite are thick, tongues are silent. Peter had resigned himself to his fate with surprising facility. He had confined his complaints and demands to three things, that he might have his mistress, his monkey, and his violin. He passed his time in drinking and smoking. On the 18th of July he was found dead. That is almost all that we know with certainty.

That his death was a violent one is almost certain. At the time no one doubted it. Writing to the Duc de Choiseul, the French *chargé- d'affaires*, Béranger stated that he had by him 'everything that could justify the generally received opinion.' He had not seen the body of the sovereign, exposed in public with the usual ceremony, for the diplomatic corps had not been invited to see it, and Béranger knew that those who found their way there were noted. But he had sent a trustworthy man, whose report went to confirm his suspicions. The body of the unfortunate sovereign was quite black, and 'extra-vasated blood oozed through the pores, and even showed through the gloves which covered the hands.' Those who thought it their duty to kiss the corpse on the mouth, according to the custom of the country, came back with their lips swollen.

There is here a certain amount of what is imaginary, though in a diplomatic document. But the fact itself is supported by the strongest presumptions. As for the mode of assassination, since it seems that one must admit the hypothesis, suppositions have varied equally. Some have spoken of poisoning by Burgundy, Peter's favourite wine, others of strangling. The most part have suggested Alexis Orlof as the author, inspirer, or even executor, *propria manu*, of the deed. One version, however, which is not without authority, brings forward quite different data. It sets Orlof completely aside. It is not he but Tieplof who has done, or at least arranged it all. On his injunction, a Swedish officer in the service of Russia, Svanovitz (?), strangled Peter with a musket-strap. The crime took place, not on the 18th, but the 15th, of July. It is not Orlof, it is Prince Bariatinski, who carried the news to St. Petersburg.

Orlof or Tieplof, the question may seem of secondary or trifling importance. It is not so. If Tieplof was the instigator of the crime, it is Catherine who was the supreme instigator. For how can we imagine that he would act without her consent? With Orlof it would be quite different. He and his brother Gregory were then, and were for some time to be, the masters, to a certain point, of the situation that they had brought about, masters also in how they chose to follow up the game in which their lives were at stake. They had not consulted Catherine over the *coup d'état*; they may well not have consulted her this time.

'The Empress was quite ignorant of this crime,' declared Frederick, twenty years afterwards, talking with the Comte de Ségur, 'and she heard of it with a despair which was not feigned, for she justly foresaw the judgment that everybody passes upon her to-day.'

'Everybody' was perhaps too much to say. But the great majority certainly held the opinion which Castéra, Masson, Helbig, and others have echoed. In a journal of the period, printed at Leipzig, the death of Peter was compared with that of King Edward of England, murdered in prison by order of his wife Isabella (1327). Later on, there was a certain change of opinion, to which the memoirs of Princess Dachkof contributed not a little. On the death of Catherine Paul is said to have discovered in the papers of the Empress a letter of Alexis Orlof, written immediately after the event, and referring definitely to himself as the author of the crime. Bloodthirstiness, terror, and remorse all expressed themselves in it. The Emperor lifted his eyes to heaven and said, 'Thanks be to God!' But the Princess Dachkof, who relates the scene, did not witness it.

Among modern writers there is still some conflict of opinions and conjectures. Catherine herself, it must be confessed, did much to heighten the obscurity of this terrible enigma, by enveloping the event in all the darkness within the power of an absolute sovereign. If she has been wronged, it is perhaps she herself who, to a certain extent, provoked the calumny by proscribing the truth. Her severity in putting down all public discussion of the tragic incident went to the extent of attacking the work of Rulhière, who nevertheless has pronounced no opinion on the question of her share in the murder. Despite her science of attitudes, that which she saw fit to assume at the moment of the catastrophe was not perhaps the best calculated to disarm public malignity, though it testified to the strength of her character, and her resources as an actress. In a council hastily summoned, it was decided that the news should be kept secret for twenty-four hours. The Empress thereupon appeared before the court without betraying the slightest trace of emotion. It was only on the following day, a manifesto having brought to the knowledge of the senate the news of the dreadful ending, that Catherine put on the air of one who has but just heard what has happened : she wept copiously before her immediate retinue, and did not appear in public.

One last word on the subject of this question which can never be fathomed : neither Orlof, nor Tieplof, nor any one, was prosecuted on account of the drama of Ropcha. Does not this throw the responsibility on the sovereign, on whatever hypothesis ? There must have been at all events consent on her part, consent to what had been done, if not to the doing of it. And this leaves one spot of blood on the hands which had just seized the imperial sceptre. Perhaps there were others. But perhaps human greatness cannot reach certain heights without these soils, which bring it down to the common level of humanity. And Catherine was great. How, by what means, and despite what defects, we shall now endeavour to show. Not having undertaken to write the history of her life, we shall here quit the narrative, in the course of which we have tried to indicate the origins and beginnings of her strange career. This preliminary investigation has seemed to us necessary for the proper placing and showing up of what is the real object of our study, that is to say, the portrait of a woman and a sovereign who, in both characters, has had few rivals in the history of the world, and the aspect of a reign which has been, up to the present, unequalled in the history of a great nation. We have endeavoured to show how Catherine became what she was; we shall now endeavour to say what she was.

PART II

THE EMPRESS

BOOK I

THE WOMAN

CHAPTER I

APPEARANCE—CHARACTER—TEMPERAMENT

I

'To tell the truth, I have never fancied myself extremely beautiful, but I had the gift of pleasing, and that, I think, was my greatest gift.' So Catherine herself defines the particular kind of attraction that nature had given her in outward appearance. Thus, having passed all her life in hearing herself compared to all the Cleopatras of history, she did not admit the justice of the comparison. Not that she underrated its worth. 'Believe me,' she wrote to Grimm, 'there can never be too much of beauty, and I have always placed a very high estimation on it, though I have never been very beautiful.' Did she deliberately depreciate her charms, through a modest ignorance or an artifice of refined coquetry? One is tempted to believe it, on hearing the almost unanimous opinion of her contemporaries. The 'Semiramis of the North' flashed across the latter half of the eighteenth century, and over the very threshold of the nineteenth, as a marvellous incarnation, not only of power, grandeur, and triumphant success, but also of adorable and adored femininity. In the eyes of all, or of nearly all, she was not only imposing, majestic, terrible, but also seductive, beautiful among the beautiful, queen by right of beauty as by right of genius, Pallas and Venus Victrix.

Well, it seems that her contemporaries saw the marvellous Czarina in a sort of mirage. The illusion was so complete that it extended to the most apparent and the most insignificant details. Thus, the greater part of those who came into her presence speak of her lofty stature, by which she dominated a crowd. Now, as a matter of fact, she was under the middle height, short almost, with a precocious tendency to grow stout. The very colour of her eyes has given rise to absurd contradictions. Some found them brown, others blue, and Rulhière has tried to harmonise both accounts by making them brown with a shade of blue in some lights. Here is his whole portrait—a portrait which belongs to the period a little before Catherine's accession to the throne, at the age of thirty-seven. No portrait of an earlier date has come down to us with anything like so much detail: Poniatowski's is only four or five years earlier in date, and is a lover's portrait.

'Her figure,' writes Rulhière, 'is noble and agreeable, her bearing proud; her person and her demeanour full of grace. Her air is that of a sovereign. All her features indicate character. Her neck is long, her head stands out well; the union of these two parts is of remarkable beauty, alike in the profile and in the movements of the head ; and she is not unmindful of her beauty in this respect. Her forehead is large and open, her nose almost aquiline ; her mouth is fresh, and embellished by her teeth ; her chin a little large, and inclined to fleshiness. Her hair is chestnut in colour, and of the greatest beauty; her eyebrows brown, her eyes brown and very beautiful—in certain lights there seem to be shades of blue ; and her skin is of dazzling whiteness. Pride is the main characteristic of her physiognomy. The amiability and good-nature which are also to be seen there seem, to a penetrating eye, merely the effect of an extreme desire to make a pleasing impression.'

Rulhière is neither a lover nor an enthusiast. Compare, however, with this sketch the sketch done in pencil about this time by a Russian artist, Tchemessof. There is a story that this portrait was made at the desire of Patiomkine, whom Catherine began to favour just after, or perhaps just before, the revolution of July. Catherine was very pleased with it, and took the artist into her service as secretary to her cabinet. And yet what an Empress this Tchemessof shows us, and how unlike all that we see of other painters, sculptors, and memoir-writers, from Benner to Lampi, from Rulhière to the Prince de Ligne ! The face is agreeable indeed, if you will, and intelligent, but so little ideal, but—dare one say it ?—so common. The costume perhaps has something to do with this, a strange mourning attire with the hair oddly dressed, covering the forehead down to the eye-brows, and overtopping the head with a pair of bats'-wings. But the hard, smiling face, the

heavy, half-masculine features, stand out with a
brutal frankness.   You would say a German
vivandière turned into a nun.   Cleopatra, never!

Was Tchemessof a deceiver, and did Catherine,
in seeing herself in the portrait, merely show
that total ignorance of art which she afterwards
confessed with such candour to Falconet?   It
may be, to a certain point.   We have nevertheless a sort of duplicate of the Russian artist's
sketch in a written portrait done some years
later by Richardson, who seems to have had a
mind and eyes of his own, not to be taken in by
any kind of illusion.   This is how he notes his
impressions :—

'The Empress of Russia is under the middle
height, graceful and well-proportioned, but in-
clining to be stout.   She has a good colour, and
nevertheless endeavours to improve it with
rouge, after the manner of all the women of this
country.   Her mouth is well-shaped, with good
teeth ; her blue eyes have a scrutinising expression—something not so pronounced as an in-
quisitive look, nor so ugly as a defiant look.
The features are in general regular and agreeable.   The general effect is such, that one would
do an injustice in attributing to it a masculine
air, and something less than justice in calling it
entirely feminine.'

This is not exactly in the tone of the *naïf* and
all but gross realism of Tchemessof.   A common
trait, however, appears in both, and it is what
would seem to have been the dominant trait of
the model, and, from the point of view of plastic
beauty, to have considerably diminished, if not
destroyed, its charm : that *mannish* expression,

namely, which is emphasised in both, and which we find, through all the magic of colours, in the work of even the least conscientious of artists. The portrait that was the delight of Voltaire, and is still to be seen at Ferney—even that betrays something of it. Catherine was nevertheless observant in the matter, and down to the very last. A wrinkle that she discovered near the root of the nose in the portrait painted by Lampi, not long before her death, seeming to her to give a hard expression to her face, brought both picture and painter into trouble. Lampi nevertheless, and quite justly, had the reputation of not saying the truth too cruelly to his models. He effaced the wrinkle, and the all but septuagenarian Empress took the air of a young nymph. History does not tell us if she was satisfied this time.

'What do you think I look like?' asked Catherine of the Prince de Ligne, on his first visit to St. Petersburg; 'long, lanky, eyes like stars, and a big hoop' This was in 1780. The Empress was fifty. This is what the Prince de Ligne thought of her: 'She still looked well. One saw that she had been beautiful rather than pretty: the majesty of her forehead was tempered by her pleasant eyes and smile, but the forehead was everything. It needed no Lavater to read there, as in a book, genius, justice, courage, depth, equanimity, sweetness, calm, and decision: the breadth of the forehead indicated memory and imagination; there was room for everything. Her chin, somewhat pointed, was not absolutely prominent, but it was anything but retiring, and had a certain nobility of aspect. The oval,

o

notwithstanding, was not well designed, though excessively pleasing, for frankness and gaiety dwelt on the lips.   Her fine bust had been acquired somewhat at the expense of her waist, once so terribly thin ; but people generally grow fat in Russia.   If she had not so tightly drawn back her hair, which should have come down more around her face, she would have looked much better.   One never noticed that she was short.'

Again an enthusiast, but the Comte de Ségur, who piqued himself on being less so, in his quality of diplomatist, noted at the same time almost identically the same traits.   'The whiteness and brilliance of her complexion,' he says, 'were the charms that she kept the longest.' But Castéra explains in his own way her triumph over the 'irreparable outrage': 'In the last years of her reign she used a great deal of rouge.'   It is just this that Catherine would never confess to.   We read in one of her letters to Grimm, dated 1783 :—

'Thank you for the pots of rouge with which you advise me to brighten my complexion ; but when I tried to use it, I found that it was so crude in colour that it made me look frightful. So you will excuse me if I cannot imitate or adopt this pretty fashion, notwithstanding my great liking for your Paris fashions.'

The most authoritative, the least impressive, testimony, from the plastic point of view, is perhaps that of Mlle. Vigée-Lebrun, who, unfortunately, never saw Catherine in her best days. She had nothing to praise in the conduct of the sovereign, so far a guarantee of her sincerity.

She could not induce the Empress to pose to her. Her brush, later on, did no more than evoke certain recollections. Pen in hand, she retraced them thus :—

' I was at first extremely surprised to find that she was short; I had expected her to be mighty in stature, as high as her renown. She was very stout, but she had still a handsome face, admirably framed in by her white hair, raised up on her head. Genius sat on her large high forehead ; her eyes were soft and clear, her nose quite Grecian, her complexion bright, her physiognomy very mobile. I said she was short; yet on her reception days, her head held high, her eagle glance, the composure that comes of the habit of command, all in her had such majesty that she seemed to me the queen of the world. She wore on these occasions the insignia of three orders, and her costume was simple and dignified. It consisted in a tunic of muslin embroidered with gold, the ample sleeves folded across in the Asiatic style. Above this tunic was a dolman of red velvet with very short sleeves. The bonnet that framed in her white hair was not decked with ribbons, but with diamonds of the greatest beauty.'

Catherine had early adopted the habit of holding her head very high in public, and she kept it all her life. Aided by her prestige, this gave her an effect of height that deceived even observers like Richardson. The art of *mise en scène*, in which she was incomparable, has remained a tradition at the court of Russia. A court lady at Vienna once gave us her impressions of the arrival of the Emperor Nicholas in that

capital.   When she saw him enter the castle,
in all the splendour of his uniform, his virile
beauty, and that air of majesty that shone in
his whole person, upright, lofty in stature, a
head taller than the princes, aides-de-camp, and
chamberlains, she felt that here was a demigod.
In the upper gallery, where she was placed, she
could not turn away her eyes from the sight.
Suddenly, she saw that the swarm of courtiers
had retired, the doors were closed.   Only the
imperial family and a few of the private retinue
remained.   But the Emperor—where was he?
There, sunk into a seat, his tall form doubled
in upon itself, the muscles of his face released
from constraint, settling into an expression of
unspeakable anguish; unrecognisable, only the
half of himself, as if fallen from the height of
grandeur to the depth of misery: the demigod
was but a handful of suffering human flesh.   This
was in 1850.   Nicholas was then already stricken
by the first attacks of the disease that under-
mined the last years of his life, and prematurely
ended it.   Withdrawn from the eyes of the crowd,
he bowed beneath its weight.   Before the public,
by an heroic effort of will, he became once more
the splendid Emperor of the past.   Perhaps it was
so with Catherine in the last years of her reign.

The Princess of Saxe-Coburg, who saw her
for the first time in 1795, begins her account of
the meeting unpleasantly enough, saying that
she always fancied a sorceress must look much as
did the old Empress.   But the sequel shows that
her idea of a sorceress was by no means disagreeable.   She praises in particular the ' singularly
fine complexion ' retained by the Empress, and

says that in general she seemed to find in her 'the personification of robust old age, though abroad there is much talk of her maladies.'

Catherine, nevertheless, had never very good health. She suffered much from headaches, accompanied by colics. This did not prevent her from laughing at physic and physicians to the very last. It was quite an affair to make her swallow a potion. One day when her doctor, Rogerson, had succeeded in making her take some pills, he was so delighted as to forget himself, and clapped her familiarly on the shoulder, crying, 'Bravo, madame!' She was not in the least offended.

From 1722 she was obliged to use glasses to read. Her hearing, though very sharp, was affected by an odd peculiarity: each of her ears heard sounds in a different way, not merely in loudness, but in tone. This no doubt was the reason why she could never appreciate music, hard as she tried to acquire the taste. Her sense of harmony was completely lacking.

It was pretended that when the scarves in which she was accustomed to wrap up her head at night came to be washed, they were seen to emit sparks. The same phenomenon occurred with her bedclothes. Such fables only serve to indicate her actual physical influence over the minds of her contemporaries, marvelling just then over the mysterious discoveries of Franklin.

II

'I assure you,' she writes in 1774 to Grimm, 'that I have not the defects you impute to me, because I do not find in myself the qualities that you give me.   I am perhaps, good-natured, ordinarily, but, by nature, I am constrained to will terribly what I will, and there you have what I am worth.'

Observe, however, that if, as a general thing, she is persevering in the exercise and in the invariable tension of this natural energy, having always willed, according to her expression, 'that the good of the empire should be accomplished,' and having willed it with extraordinary force, in small things she is inconstancy itself.   She wills everything strongly, but she changes her mind with a no less surprising facility, as her idea of what is 'good' varies.   In this respect she is a woman, from head to foot.   In 1767 she devotes herself to her *Instruction* for the new laws that she would give to Russia.   This work, in which she has pillaged Montesquieu and Beccaria, is in her eyes destined to open a new era in the history of Russia.   And she wills, ardently, passionately, that it should be put into action.   Difficulties, however, arise ; un-looked-for delays interpose themselves.   Where-upon, all at once, she loses interest in the thing. In 1775 she excogitates *Rules* for the administra-tion of her provinces.   And she writes : 'My last rules of the 7th November contain 250 quarto pages of print, and I swear to you that it is the best thing I have ever done, and that, in comparison, I look upon the *Instruction* as so much nonsense.'   And she is dying with desire to show this new masterpiece to her con-fidant.   Less than a year afterwards it is finished. Grimm has not had sight of the document, and as he insists on being favoured with it, she loses patience : 'Why is he so anxious to read anything so little amusing? It is very good, very fine, perhaps, but quite tedious.' At the end of a month she has forgotten all about it.

She has the same way with men as with things : sudden, passionate infatuations, of an unexampled impetuosity, followed by disenchantments and by an equally rapid subsidence into the most complete indifference. The greater part of the able men whom she drew to Russia, Diderot among the rest, experienced it in turn. After having passed twenty years of her reign in adorning different residences which have been successively preferred and preferable in her eyes, she takes a fancy, all of a sudden, in 1786, to a site near St. Petersburg, which has no advantages in itself. She summons the Russian architect Starof, of the Academy of St. Petersburg, to build a palace there in all haste ; and she writes to Grimm : 'All my country houses are as hovels in comparison with Pella, which is rising like a phœnix.'

Not being wanting, by any means, either in common sense or in acuteness, she comes to find out, late enough, what we have just noted. 'Two days ago,' she writes in 1781, 'I made the discovery that I am *a beginner* by profession, and that up to now I have finished nothing of all that I have begun.' And a year afterwards : 'For all that, I only want the time to finish; it is like my laws, my regulations : everything is begun, nothing finished.' She has her illusions, however, and she adds : 'If I live ten years longer, all will be finished to perfection' Two

years and more having passed, she ends by
perceiving that time has nothing to do with the
matter. 'Never have I so completely realised
that I am a very accumulation of broken ends,'
she declares, not without a certain melancholy.
To which she adds, that she is 'as stupid as a
goose,' and that she is convinced Prince Patiomkine had much more notion of good management
than she.

She would not be a woman if it did not sometimes happen to her not to know very well what
she wanted, or even not know it at all, while she
was very much in want of something. *Apropos*
of a certain Wagnière, who was secretary to
Voltaire, whose services she desired for herself,
and whom, after all, she did not know what to
do with, she writes to her *souffre-douleur* :—

'A truce to your excuses .   and to mine,
for not knowing exactly, now as often, what I
wanted, nor what I did not want, and for having
consequently written for and against. . . . If you
will, I will found a professorship, in addition to
the one you counsel, on the science of indecision,
more natural to me than people think.'

It is to be observed that a disposition of this
kind is not made to give a firm and well-balanced
direction to the affairs of an empire. And, indeed, nothing of the kind is to be found in the
part that Catherine played in history. If this
part was a large one, it was—as she well knew
herself—because she had to do with a new people,
at the first stage of its career, the stage of expansion. In this stage a people has no need
of being directed ; for the most part, it is not
even susceptible of direction. It is an 'impelled

force' which follows its own impulsion. In obeying it, it is in no danger of going astray. The sole misfortune of which it is capable is that of falling asleep. It would be vain and useless to take such a nation by the hand, and lead it into the way that it knows so well how to find by itself. It suffices to give it a shaking, and start it forward from time to time. That is what Catherine understood in the most wonderful way. Her action was that of a stimulant and a propeller of prodigious vigour.

In this respect she bears comparison with the greatest men of history. Her soul is like a spring, always at full tension, always vibrating, of a temper which resists every test. In the month of August 1765 she is unwell, and is keeping her bed. Rumours are spread that she is *enceinte*, and that an abortion is to be procured. Nevertheless she has arranged for some great manoeuvres, 'a camp,' as it was called then, for the end of the month, and she has announced that she will be present. She is present. The last day, during the 'battle,' she remains on horseback for five hours, having to direct the manoeuvres and to send orders, by the intermediary of her aide-de-camp, to Marshal Boutourline and to General Prince Galitzine, who command the two wings of the army. The aide-de-camp, glittering in a cuirass of gold studded with jewels, is Gregory Orlof. Some months later, riots having broken out in the capital, she comes in the middle of the night from Tzarskoïe-Sielo to St. Petersburg with Orlof, Passek, and a few other trusty friends, mounts on horseback, and traverses the streets

to make sure that her orders have been properly
carried out, and proper precautions taken.   Even
now she has not fully recovered from the more
or less mysterious crisis that she has passed
through.   She can take no nourishment.   She,
however, thinks well to appear cheerful and in
good health.   Festivity follows festivity;   the
French play comes to Tzarskoïe.

Physical or moral dejection, lassitude, or discouragement, are things equally unknown to her.
Her force of resistance seems to increase in proportion to the demand upon it.   In 1791, when
things look dark about her, when she has to face
Sweden and Turkey, and is in danger of a
rupture with England, she has, or affects to have,
the most tranquil serenity, the most contagious
good humour.   She laughs and jests; advises those
about her to give up English liquors in good
time, and get accustomed to the national drinks.

And what ' go '; what ardour, for ever youthful ;
what impetuousness, never relaxed !

' Courage !   Forward !   That is the motto with
which I have passed through good years and bad
years alike, and now I have passed through
forty, all told, and what is the present evil compared with the past ? '

That is her habitual tone.   The force of will
that she has at command allows her both to control the outward expression of her feelings, and
even to abstract herself when she will from these
feelings when they become troublesome, intense
as they may be, for she is far from being indifferent, or hard to move, or naturally calm.
Sang-froid, for instance, is not at all a part of her
disposition.   In May 1790, on the eve of a sea-

fight with Sweden, she passes whole nights without sleep, puts every one about her on pins and needles, gets a *rougeur* on her cheek, which she attributes to the acuteness of her emotions, and behaves in such a way that every one, including her Prime Minister, Besborodko, bursts into tears. No sooner has she known the issue of the battle than her peace of mind is restored, and no matter what bad news may follow, she is gay and light-hearted again. Every moment she is passing through some fever or other. She falls ill with anxiety, and has colics. One day Chrapowicki, her factotum, finds her lying on a sofa, complaining of pains in the region of the heart. ' It is the bad weather, no doubt,' says he, ' that indisposes your Majesty.' ' No,' replies she, ' it is Otchakof ; the fortress will be taken to-day or to-morrow ; I have often such presentiments.' These presentiments often prove deceptive, as in the present case, for Otchakof was not taken till two months after. On hearing the news of the death of Louis XVI., she receives such a shock that she is obliged to take to her bed. It is true that, this time, she makes no attempt to master or to dissimulate her emotion, which, however, is not inspired only by a sentiment of political solidarity, for the fibres of her heart are extremely excitable. She has not merely ' sensibility,' after the fashion of the day ; she is sincerely accessible to sympathy and pity.

' I forgot to drink, eat, and sleep,' she writes in 1776, announcing the death of her daughter-in-law, ' and I know not how I kept up my strength. There were moments when my very heart was torn by the suffering I saw about me.'

This does not hinder her from adding to the letter, which is lengthy, a host of details concerning current affairs, with the usual jokes, a little heavy, which serve to season her familiar correspondence. After giving herself up to her impressions, she returns to herself, and she explains it all :—

'On Friday I seemed to turn to stone. . . . I who am so given to weeping, saw death without a tear. I said to myself : "If thou weep, the others will sob ; if thou sob, the others will faint, and every one will lose their head and their· wits."'

She never lost her head, and, she declares in one of her letters, she never fainted. Whenever she has to play a part, to take an attitude, and, by her example, to impose it upon others, she is always ready. In August 1790 she thinks seriously of accompanying the army reserve to Finland. 'Had it been needful,' she said afterwards, 'I should have left my bones in the last battalion. I have never known fear.'

With our present-day notions, it does not seem a very signal proof of courage that she gave in 1768, in being the first, or almost the first, in her capital and in her empire, to be inoculated. For the time it was a great event, and an act of heroism celebrated by all her contemporaries. One need but read the notes written on the subject by the inoculator himself, the Englishman Dimsdale, expressly brought over from London, to realise the idea that the profession itself still cherished in regard to the danger of the operation. We cut open or trepan a man to-day with much less concern. Catherine bared her arm to the lancet on the 26th October 1768. A week afterwards she had her son inoculated. On the 22nd of November the members of the legislative commission, and all the chief dignitaries, assembled in the church of Our Lady of Kasan, where a decree of the senate was read, commanding public prayers for the occasion; after which they went in a body to present their compliments and thanks to her Majesty. A boy of seven, named Markof, who had been inoculated first of all, in order to use the lymph found on him, was ennobled in return for it, and received the surname of Ospiennyï (*Ospa* = smallpox). Catherine took a liking to him, and had him brought up under her eyes. The family of this name, now occupying a high position in Russia, owes its fortune to this ancestor. Dr. Dimsdale received the title of baron, the honorary charge of the physicians in ordinary to her Majesty, the rank of Chancellor of State, and a pension of £500 sterling. It was certainly much ado about nothing; but some years later, in 1772, the Abbé Galiani announced, as still an important piece of news, the inoculation of the son of the Prince of San Angelo Imperiali at Naples, the first that had taken place in that city. In 1768 Voltaire himself found much to admire in an Empress who had been inoculated 'with less ceremony than a nun who takes a bath.' Catherine is perhaps the one who thought least of her bravery. Before the deputations that came to compliment her, she thought it well to take a serious air, declaring 'that she had done no more than her duty, for a shepherd is bound to give his life for his sheep.' But, writing a few days afterwards to General Braun, the Governor of Livonia, she laughs at those who are lost in admiration of her courage : 'As for courage, I think every little urchin in the streets of London has just as much.'

III

Certainly, she possesses a happy equilibrium of faculties, an excellent moral health. It is this which renders her easy to get on with, though she has perhaps less indulgence and benignity than she would credit herself with, but still is in no wise given to wrangling, nor excessively hard to please, nor unreasonably severe. Outside official ceremonies, in regard to which she is very particular, giving to them the greatest possible lustre, she is full of charm in her intercourse with others. She has an easy simplicity which puts every one at ease, and which allows her to maintain her own rank, and to keep others in their proper place, without her appearing to give the matter a thought. On the birth of her grandson, Alexander, she falls to regretting that there are no more fairies 'to endow little children with all one would like them to have,' and she writes to Grimm : 'For my part, I would give them nice presents, and I would whisper in their ear · "Ladies, be natural, only be natural, and experience will do pretty well all the rest."' She is *bon enfant*, and puts on a familiar manner. She hits her secretary in the ribs with a roll of paper, and tells him : 'Some day I will kill you like that.' In corresponding with her master of the horse, M. Eck, she writes : 'Monsieur mon voisin.'

The Prince de Ligne recounts an episode of the tour in the Crimea, when she took it into her head to be thee'd and thou'd by every one, and to *tutoyer* them in return. This whim often returned to her. 'You cannot conceive,' she writes to Grimm, 'how I love to be *tutoyée*; I wish it were done all over Europe.' Then hear her account of her relations with Mme. Todi, a famous *prima donna*, whose talent she could not appreciate, but whom she was willing to pay very liberally. This was at Tzarskoïe-Sielo :—

'Mme. Todi is here, and she is always about with her husband. Very often we meet face to face, always however without coming in collision. I say to her: "Good-morning or good-evening, Mme. Todi, how do you do?" She kisses my hands, and I her cheek; our dogs smell one another; she takes hers under her arm, I call mine, and we both go on our way. When she sings, I listen and applaud, and we both say that we get on very well together.'

She carries her condescension in the matter of sociability to great lengths. If any one ventures to criticise her choice of friends and lovers, she replies: 'Before being what I am I was thirty-three years what others are, and it is not quite twenty years that I have been what they are not. And that teaches one how to live.' On the other hand she makes merry at the expense of the great: 'Do you know why I dread Kings' visits? Because they are generally tiresome, insipid people, and you have to be stiff and formal with them. These persons of renown pay much respect to my unaffected ways, and I would show them all my wit; sometimes I show it by listening to them, and as I love to chatter, the silence bores me.'

Her proverbial munificence is not only in ostentation. Grimm often distributed large sums for her anonymously. And she puts a charming grace and delicacy in some of her gifts. 'Your Royal Highness,' she writes to the Comte d'Artois, who is leaving Russia, 'wishes, doubtless, to make some small presents to the people who have done you service during your stay here. But, as you know, I have forbidden all commerce and communication with your unhappy France, and you will seek in vain to buy any trinkets in the city; there are none in Russia save in my cabinet; and I hope your Highness will accept these from his affectionate friend Catherine.'

What she lacks, in this as in so many things, is moderation. She is well aware of it herself, and admits: 'I know not how to give; I give too much or not enough.' One would say that her destiny, in raising her to such a height, has taken from her the sense of proportions. She is either prodigal or miserly. When she has exhausted her resources by her excessive expenditure and liberalities she has 'a heart of stone' for the most worthy, the most just, demands upon her. She gives a third of his pension to Prince Viazemski on his retirement. He has served her for thirty years, and she has appreciated his services, but he has ceased to please her. The poor man dies of vexation.

With those who please her, as long as they have that good fortune, she knows no stint. In 1781, when Count Branicki married a niece of Patiomkine, she gave 500,000 roubles as a marriage portion to the bride, and the same amount to her husband, to pay his debts. One day she amused herself with imagining how the principal people at her court might meet their end. Ivan Tchernichef would die of rage, Countess Roumiantsof of having shuffled the cards too much, Mme. Vsievolodsky of an excess of sighs; and so forth. She herself would die— of complaisance.

It is not only complaisance, there is in her an instinctive generosity which comes out in more than one way. With those whom she honours with her confidence she has none of that facile change of front so common to her sex. She is incapable of suspicion. One of the foreign artists whom she had commissioned to make considerable purchases for her gallery at the Hermitage, Reiffenstein—the 'divine' Reiffen-stein, as she called him—fancied his honesty suspected. Grimm, who acted as intermediary, became anxious about it.

'Begone with your notes and accounts, both of you!' wrote the Empress to the latter. 'I never suspected either of you in my life. Why do you trouble me with stingy, useless things of that sort?'

She added: 'No one about me has insinuated anything against *le divin.*' Grimm could well believe her, for she was absolutely averse to this kind of insinuation, so much favoured in courts. In general, any one did but do a bad turn for himself by saying evil of others. Patiomkine himself experienced this in trying to shake the credit of Prince Viazemski.

If there was need, however, to serve or defend

her friends, she was ready to do anything, in total forgetfulness of her rank. She learns, for instance, that Mme. Ribas, the wife of an Italian adventurer whom she has made Admiral, is in childbed. She jumps into the first carriage that she finds at the gate of the palace, enters like a whirlwind into the room of her friend, turns up her sleeves, and puts on an apron. 'Now there are two of us,' she says to the midwife; 'let us do our best.' It often happens that advantage is taken of this well-known characteristic. 'They know I am good to bother,' she says. Is she simply 'good,' in reality? Yes, in her way, which assuredly is not the way of everybody. The absolute mistress of forty millions of men is not 'everybody.' Mme. Vigée-Lebrun dreamed of painting the portrait of the great sovereign. 'Take,' said some one, 'the map of the empire of Russia for canvas, the darkness of ignorance for background, the spoils of Poland for drapery, human blood for colouring, the monuments of her reign for the cartoon, and for the shadow six months of her son's reign.' There is some truth in this sombre picture, but it wants shading. At the moment of the terrible uprising of Pougatchef, sharp as was Catherine in the repression of a revolt which put her empire to the stake, she bids General Panine use no more than the indispensable severity. After the capture of the rebel, she does her best to succour the victims of this terrible civil war. Yet, in Poland, the conduct of her generals is for the most part atrocious, and she never interferes. She even compliments Souvarof after the massacre which accompanies the taking of Warsaw. And in this empire of hers, 'from which

·the light now comes,' the knout still bears sway, the stick still falls on the bleeding shoulders of the serf. She lets knout and stick do their work. How is this to be understood?

It is needful first of all to realise the conception —a well-reasoned and elaborated conception—of the position of the sovereign and of the exigencies of that position, which obtained in the mind of this autocratic ruler. We cannot make war without dead or wounded, nor can we subdue a people jealous of its liberty without stifling its resistance in blood. Having resolved on the annexation of Poland—rightly or wrongly, need not be discussed here—it was necessary to accept all the consequences of the enterprise. This Catherine did, taking upon herself, calmly and frankly, the entire responsibility of the affair. Calmly, for, in these matters, reasons of state alone influence her ; they take the place of conscience, and even of feeling. Frankly, for she is not a hypocrite. An actress ever, and of the first order, by reason of her position, which is nothing but a part to play. It is in this sense that the French envoy Durand could say of her : ' My experience is quite useless ; the woman is more false than our women are tricky. I can say no more.' But she was never a hypocrite by preference, for the pleasure of deceiving, like so many ; nor by need of deceiving herself. ' She was too proud to deceive,' said the Prince de Ligne.

In what she did, or suffered to be done, in Poland, she has had many imitators, beginning with the pious Maria Theresa herself. Only Maria Theresa mingled her tears with the blood that she shed. 'She is always crying and stealing,' said Frederick. Catherine keeps dry-eyed.

Catherine, too, followed a different principle of government. A sovereign, however absolute, cannot be everywhere at once. Souvarof has orders to take Warsaw. He takes it. How? That is his affair, not that of any one else. The principle is contestable, but we have not to discuss political theories in a study of character.

Finally, Catherine is a Russian sovereign, and the Russia of the eighteenth century, without going further, is a country where European ideas in regard to justice and sentiment are quite out of place, where both moral and physical sensibility seem to obey different laws. In 1766, during the Empress's stay at Peterhof, a sudden alarum one night startles her Majesty and all about her. There is great excitement and confusion. It turns out that a lackey, who has been making love to one of the waiting-maids of Catherine, has caused all this fright. He is brought to trial, and condemned to receive a hundred and one strokes of the knout, which is practically equivalent to a sentence of death, to have his nose slit, to be branded on the forehead with a hot iron, and to end his days in Siberia, if he recovers. No one has anything to say against the sentence. It is after such traits, and on the scale of notions, sentiments, and sensations, apparently proper to the surroundings in which they have root, that we require to judge a sovereign who, politically speaking, could certainly not claim the title of 'most gracious.'

Apart from politics, Catherine is an adored

and adorable sovereign. Those about her have nothing but praise for her dealings. Her servants are spoilt children. The story of the chimney-sweep is well known. Always an early riser, in order to work more quietly in the silence of the early hours, the Empress sometimes lights her own fire, so as not to disturb any one. One morning, as she sets the faggots in a blaze, she hears piercing cries from the chimney, followed by a volley of abuse. She understands, quickly puts out the fire, and humbly proffers her excuses to the poor little chimney-sweep whom she had nearly roasted alive. There are thousands of similar stories told of her. One day, the Countess Bruce enters the Empress's bedroom and finds her Majesty alone, half-dressed, with her arms folded in the attitude of one who is waiting patiently because she is obliged to wait. Seeing her surprise, Catherine explains the case—

'What do you think? my waiting-maids have all deserted me. I had been trying on a dress which fitted so badly that I lost my temper; so they left me like this . . . and I am waiting till they have cooled down.'

One day she sends Grimm an almost indecipherable letter, and thus excuses herself—

'My *valets de chambre* give me two new pens a day, but when they are worn out I never venture to ask for more, but I turn and turn them again as best I can.'

One evening, after ringing in vain for some time, she goes into the anteroom and finds these same *valets de chambre* absorbed in a game of cards. She offers one of them to take his place so that she can finish the game for him, while he can do an urgent errand for her. She catches some servants in the act of making off with provisions intended for her table. 'Let this be the last time,' she says, with severity; then she adds: 'And now, be off quickly, or the *maréchal de la cour* will catch you.' She sees in the courtyard of the palace an old woman running after a fowl, and soon the valets are running after the old woman, anxious to show their zeal under the eyes of the Empress. For this fowl is a fowl 'belonging to her Majesty's treasure,' and the woman is the grandmother of a court scullion; a double crime. Catherine, after making inquiries, orders a fowl to be given every day to the poor old soul, but a fowl ready trussed.

She keeps by her, despite her infirmities, an old German nurse, whom she watches over with the greatest care. 'I feared her,' she writes to Grimm, announcing her death, 'as I dread fire, or the visits of kings and great people. Whenever she saw me, she would seize me by the head, and kiss me again and again till she half stifled me. And she always smelt of tobacco, which her respected husband used largely.'

Nevertheless, she is far from being patient, for naturally she is quick-tempered, too quick-tempered. Her fits of rage are one of her most noticeable defects. Grimm compares her to Etna, and she delights in the comparison. She calls the volcano 'my cousin,' and frequently asks for news of it. For she knows her defect, and it is this that enables her to combat it effectually. If she gives way to the first paroxysm of anger, she immediately recovers command of herself. If it is in her private room, she turns up her sleeves with a gesture to which she is accustomed, and begins to walk to and fro, drinking glass after glass of water. Never does she give an order or a signature in one of these passing fits of rage. In her speech she gives way sometimes to undignified expressions, as in her sallies against Gustave III. during the war with Sweden. '*Canaille*' in French and '*Bestie*' in German are too often part of her vocabulary. She always, however, regrets what she has done or said, and, in course of time, so strictly does she watch over and restrain herself, she attains to a bearing which makes this weakness of her character or temperament seem almost incredible.

'She said to me slowly,' writes the Prince de Ligne, 'that she had been extremely quick-tempered, which one could scarcely believe. . . . Her three bows *à la Russe* are made always in the same way in entering a room, one to the left, one to the right, and one in the middle. Everything in her was measured, methodical. . . . She loves to repeat ' J'ai de l'imperturbabilité,' taking a quarter of an hour to say the word.'

Senac de Meilhan, who visited Russia in 1750, confirms these characteristics. In one of his letters, dated from St. Petersburg, he speaks of the inexpressible impression of tranquillity and serenity with which the appearance of Catherine before the court is always accompanied. She does not affect the rigidity of a statue. She looks round her with eyes that seem to see everything. She speaks slowly, not as if seeking for words, but as if choosing quietly those that suit her.

Nevertheless, to the end of her life, Catherine kept to her habit of pinning her serviette under her chin on sitting down to table 'She could not otherwise,' as she frankly avows, 'eat an egg, without dropping half of it on her collerette.'

IV

Her temperament is particularly lively, sanguine, and impetuous. This appears, we know well, in more than one aspect of her private life. To this we shall have to return. Let us say here that the shamelessness of her morals, which it would be idle to try to attenuate, does not seem to have its root in any constitutional vice. She is neither hysterical nor tainted with nymphomania. It is a sensual woman who, being Empress, gives free course to her senses, imperially. What she does in this order of things is done as she does everything else, quietly, imperturbably—we might almost say methodically. She gives way to no bewilderments of imagination, to no disorder of nerves. Love with her is but the natural function of a physical and moral organism endowed with exceptional energy, and it has the same imperious character, the same lasting power, as the other phenomena of her life. She is still amorous at sixty-seven !

Her other tastes are those of a person well-balanced, both mentally and physically. She loves the arts, and the society of intelligent and learned people. She loves nature. Gardening, 'plantomania' as she calls it, is one of her favourite occupations. Note that though she adores flowers, she cannot endure too strong perfumes, that of musk in particular. Every day, at a fixed hour, which a bell announces to the winged population, she appears at a window of the palace and throws out crumbs to the thousands of birds that are accustomed to come to her to be fed Elizabeth used to feed frogs, which were expressly kept in the park : one sees the difference, the morbid, extravagant note. In Catherine there is nothing of the kind. She likes birds, dogs, who play a considerable part in her private life, horses too ; she likes animals in general, but she prefers those which are more generally liked. All that is very simple, very natural, very normal.

Elizabeth led an irregular life, turning night into day, never having a fixed hour for anything. Catherine is regularity itself; always early to bed, up with the dawn, fitting in her occupations as well as her pleasures with a programme that she has made out beforehand, and that she carries out without deviation. Elizabeth used to get drunk ; Catherine is sober, eating little, only drinking a mouthful of wine at her principal meal, never taking supper. In public and in private, save for the mysteries of the alcove, she is perfectly correct in demeanour, never allowing an impropriety in conversation. And in this there is no hypocrisy, for she shows, and indeed shows off, her lovers.

In order to find something unnatural, abnormal, in her, some have laid emphasis on her supposed indifference to family feeling. The point is susceptible of controversy. She despised and detested her husband, if she did not kill him or let him be killed ; and she was not tender towards

her son, if she did not think of disinheriting him.'
Still it must be remembered what this husband
and this son really were, both to her and to
Russia.   She never saw again her only brother,
never having allowed him to come and see her,
though she only survived him by three years.
That was a matter of policy.   She found that
there were Germans enough in Russia, herself
among the number.   With her, it is certain, the
head always ruled the heart, and, though German,
she was by no means sentimental.   But she was,
as we shall see, a delightful grandmother, and she
was passionately fond of children.

Her shameless sensuality thus seems an isolated phenomenon, without connection with any
other in her temperament.   Perhaps this is only
in appearance ; perhaps we should seek a certain
connection, if not the relation of cause to effect,
between this side of her nature and another that
we are about to look into, that is to say, the
intellectual culture of one who loved to call
herself the pupil of Voltaire.   If, indeed, there
is method in this madness of the senses, which
she does not lose even in middle age, there
is also a certain lofty cynicism, a certain tranquil assurance, which a physiological peculiarity,
anomaly if you will, is not sufficient to explain.
The philosophical spirit of the eighteenth century
has passed over it, and not only the spirit of the
age of Brantôme.

v

Catherine is a great temperament, not a great
intellect.   She herself did not pretend to 'a
creative mind.'   Nevertheless she prides herself

on her originality. 'All my life,' she writes to Mme. de Bielke, 'I never could tolerate imitation, and, to put it bluntly, I am as much of an original as the most determined Englishman.' But it is in her tastes, her habits, her modes of action, that is to say in her temperament rather than in her mind, that we must look for this personal note. There is not a single new idea in her *Instruction* for the laws, written at the age of thirty-six, in the full vigour of her intellectual faculties. It is the second-rate work of a student of rhetoric, who has been given as a task the analysis of Montesquieu and Beccaria, and who has done creditably, but without showing any great talent. This work, nevertheless, gives her enormous trouble. At the end of March 1765 she has been toiling at it for two months, at the rate of three hours a day. Her best hours, in the morning, are given up to this work. By the middle of June she has covered sixty-four pages, and she feels that she has made a considerable effort. She is quite worn out. 'I have emptied my sack,' she writes, 'and, after this, I shall not write another word for the rest of my life.' We have all known these vows, and, too, this impression of weariness at the end of the first long effort. But having regard to the actual result, this author's trouble is almost laughable. The sack, too, that she had emptied, or thought she had emptied, was easy to replace, for it was not hers. She found plenty more in turn.

Had she then nothing of her own? Yes, much good sense, to begin with, joined, singularly enough, to a great wealth of imagination. She passed the thirty-four years of her reign in building castles in the air, magnificent buildings, founded on nothing, and evaporating in space at the least breath. But the day came when one stone, a single stone, was placed in the soil, as if by miracle, at the angle of the fantastic edifice. It was Catherine who had planted it there. The Russian people, this good people which has not yet come to realise itself, nor to dispute with those who govern it, did the rest. It brought its sweat and blood, and, like the Egyptian colossi, where the effort of thousands of unknown existences is superposed, the edifice rose and assumed tangible form. The conquest of the Taurida was thus accomplished. This was one of Catherine's· dreams, put in action and translated into a novel of adventures by Patiomkine. But the corner-stone appeared suddenly in a port of the Black Sea, and the Crimea of to-day was then created.

Nevertheless Catherine fascinated, and even dazzled, by her qualities of mind the most part of those to whom she gave the chance of judging ; men of a superior order of intellect, such as Diderot, for example. It was an effect of mirage, it seems to us, the artificial product of a kind of fascination in which there were many elements ; a superior force of will, the supreme art of *mise en scène* that we know already, and a third element, surprising, unlooked for, well-nigh incredible in this German of the North—a heat and fire which are extraordinary, overpowering, which seem as if ·they must be Southern by birth. Judging by the reports of her way of talking, the flow and colour of words which crowd from her lips, the absolute volubility which she manifests at every turn, Catherine is a true Southern. 'She loved to chatter,' she said, and Grimm despaired of being able to preserve for posterity any idea of what her conversation was.

'One must have seen, at those moments, this singular head, made up of genius and of grace, to form an idea of the fire that swayed her, the shafts that she let fly, the sallies that pressed, jostling, so to speak, and tumbling on one another, like the limpid waters of a natural waterfall. Had it only been in my power to take down literally these conversations, the world would have possessed a precious and perhaps unique fragment of the history of the human mind. The imagination and the judgment were equally impressed by this profound and rapid sweep of vision, whose immense reach passed like a flash. And how could one seize, on the sudden wing, all these fine, fugitive traits of light ?'

What Grimm dared not attempt, Catherine has essayed to do herself. In 1780, the day after a conversation which had astonished Count Ivan Tchernichef, she sent him, at his request, a literal report of it. This fragment has been preserved, and it is curious. Must we confess that it is somewhat deceptive? It reminds us of an observation that an old *savant*, who had reached the extreme limits of human existence, and who was an *enfant terrible* on occasion, made before us one day to a politician afflicted with the mania of publishing, in the least official of quarters, speeches that the House had not always heard : 'Excuse me, sir, I see at every moment, in what you have given me to read, the words : Sensation, prolonged applause, uproar. But though

I have looked for it, I can see nothing extra-ordinary in all you say.'

It is a somewhat similar impression that we receive on reading the famous report. We look in vain for the brilliant sayings, the sallies of wit, the sparks of genius, of which Grimm tells us.

To begin with, there is a quotation from the *Plaideurs* of Racine, 'Ma foi, sur l'avenir bien fou qui se fiera,' serving as motto to flights of political prophesying, in which 'the eagle eye' is nowhere to be seen.

'I predict that France, Austria, Prussia, and Russia will clash together for a time, will do one another grievous hurt, and aid one another in turn, and will all four arrive at the highest pitch of glory.'

This resembles the deliverance of an extra-lucid somnambulist, unless one chooses to see in it a vision of the wars of Europe. But did Catherine foresee the Revolution, as some have alleged? We do not see it, unless indeed it be in this phrase: 'Buffon has predicted that one day a comet will hook on to our globe and carry it with it. I fancy that its course will be from west to east.' But this is the veriest style of fortune-telling, and Mlle. Lenormand would not have expressed it better. The mistakes of the King of France could not but strike the penetrating mind of the Czarina. Two years before she said to Count Tchernichef: 'I do not like to see Marie-Antoinette *laugh so much, and laugh at everything.* It is true that she is a woman, and very much a woman; I am too, somewhat; in her place and her circumstances I should be afraid that some one would say: He who laughs last laughs best.' The saying is expressive, and has a wide bearing. In this she saw true, thanks to her good sense and to her sense of the part of government, which none of her rivals in modern history possessed in the same degree. With talents of a superior order —and both Frederick and Napoleon were probably her inferiors in this respect—Catherine had more flexibility, was more fruitful in resources, had a more delicate sense of touch. She was an incomparable *virtuoso* in the art of ruling.

But to return to the report of her conversation, or rather of her monologue. She hits on an unhappy phrase in reference to England : 'England! Fanaticism built it, fanaticism supports it, fanaticism will destroy it.' We ask ourselves what this may mean, and what could have suggested it. It is really nothing but an actuality of the moment, in the manner of our present day journalists. We are in 1780, and London has just been the scene of a popular movement against the Catholics, provoked by the ambitious and unscrupulous Lord Gordon. To the traditional cry of 'No Popery!' a band of twenty thousand fanatics has marched upon Westminster, and the members of Parliament have themselves been somewhat violently treated. In this passing crisis Catherine discovers an historic law.

Then follow some philosophical considerations : 'One may have wit, talent, morals, virtue, reason, as much as you will; but not glory, success, fortune, and especially favour.'

That is not very new, nor very profound, nor even very true. For talented and virtuous people have had to suffer on account of their talent and their virtue as often, or oftener, than rich people on account of their money-bags. Here is what seems to be a less commonplace turn of thought :—

'To gain a victory is nothing; land is some-thing; money everything. The rich have an astonishing power over humankind, since kings themselves end by respecting those who have made money.'

This reflection might have been inspired in an intelligence trained in the school of modern materialism by the enormous fortunes of which this century has seen the accumulation. Yet the house of Rothschild was not yet born. But was not the father of Alexander of Macedon disturbed by just such thoughts?

As for the piece as a whole, we can see nothing astonishing about it except the import-ance that Catherine herself, and not Tchernichef alone, seems to have attached to it. It is true that one side, and no doubt the most attractive, of the conversation is lost for us. The words are there; but the accent, the impetuous flow of speech, the well-modulated voice, had not these a success of their own, the true orator's success?

'In your words, divine Princess, there is neither method nor order. There is that sove-reign and *incomprehensible* spirit with which you are dowered.' Thus did Field-Marshal Münich express himself in a letter addressed to the Empress a few months after her accession. The eloquence of Catherine had, for him also, its enigmatic side.

CHAPTER II

IDEAS AND PRINCIPLES

I

WITH the temperament that we have seen, Catherine could not well be a woman with principles, at least immutable principles, nor with formulated ideas. Her fixed ideas, which she has often had, were so only for the moment; they were comets, not the guiding stars of her life.

One point, however, on which she never varies, is the national character, essentially Russian, that she impresses on her government, and that she seeks to extend to the entire development, political, intellectual, and moral, of the Slavonic people, over whose destinies she, a German princess, has been called to preside. Not only the administrative and legislative acts of her reign, but her slightest sayings and doings bear the trace of this constant preoccupation. Falconet had hard work not to invest Peter I. with the national Russian costume that the Czar was so emphatic in forbidding throughout his empire. Catherine would have had this trait in the history of the great reformer forgotten. She would have imposed, not merely upon the present, but upon the past, of her adopted country, a whole host of things contrary to the fact, but conformable to the idea that it had pleased her to give herself and others in regard to this land of vast horizons, so tempting to flights of fancy. She

Q

would have rewritten in her own way the whole history of the old Muscovite fatherland. In 1790 Sénac de Meilhan offered himself as historiographer of the empire : she hesitated to accept the offer. Would he be willing to lay aside the *prejudices* 'that most strangers have against Russia' ?—to the point of believing, for example, 'that before Peter the Great the empire had neither laws nor administration.' Now, 'it is true that the troubles which followed on the death of the Czar Ivan Vassilevitch had put back Russia from forty to fifty years, but before this time it was on the level of the rest of Europe . . . the Grand Dukes of Russia took a prominent part in the affairs of Europe, and were allied and connected with all the sovereign houses of our hemisphere.'

After this the poor Sénac despaired of being able to cope with his task. But here too Catherine was convinced. She wrote to Grimm : 'No history furnishes better or greater men than ours. I am passionately fond of this history.' She meant, besides, to have a good space given to her own reign, 'for we live in an age in which, far from hiding the lustre of things and actions, it is essential to sustain people's minds.' Would Sénac consent to be 'directed' in this respect ?

Here again we observe a trace of the huge proportions which the vast empire, so strangely become her own property, had little by little attained in the Czarina's mind ; and we see one fixed star the more in her firmament. This hyperbolic idea of grandeur, applied to all the constituent elements of the national inheritance, to the past as to the present of Russia, to its extent as to its population, to its material power as to its moral worth, to its preponderance in the Slavonic world as to its European position, is one of those which never left Catherine, and never lost its hold upon her. She seems dazzled, hallucinated, and as if hypnotised before this collossal conception. High as was the opinion that she had, and that she wished others to have of herself, of the merits of her government, and of the great events which marked it, she did not hesitate to make herself small by comparison : 'All that I can do for Russia is but a drop of water in the sea.'

Russia is the sea, the ocean with its unsounded depths, its borders lost to sight in the immensity of space. It is for that that she has been willing to submerge in it her own past, and the very remembrance of her German fatherland. Nevertheless, it is she who writes, in 1782, complaining to Grimm of the conduct of the Sultan Abdul-Hamid : '*Das ist unmöglich dass ich mir sollte auft die Nase spielen lassen.* You know that a German will never suffer that.' But her mind is essentially mobile, and, as she confesses, she does not always know what she wants, or even what she says, especially when she chats with her confidant, pen in hand, in her moments of most complete unbending, after the fatigues of her formidable task. But she has conscientiously applied to herself her Russophilist programme, and she has become Russian from head to foot, not only on the surface and by an artifice, but sincerely and profoundly, in her mind and flesh, in her most formal language, her most familiar motion, her most private thought. The following lines were probably seen by no one till after **her** death.

'Never has the universe produced a creature more manly, more solid, more frank, more human, more benevolent, more generous, more obliging, than the Scythian (Scythian and Russian are synonymous in her eyes). No man equals him in regularity of features, in beauty of face, in fineness of complexion, build, and stature; having for the most part well-nourished, or nervous and muscular, limbs, a thick beard, long and bushy hair; naturally averse to all ruse and artifice, to which his probity and uprightness are utterly alien. There is not on the earth a horse-soldier or foot-soldier, or sailor, or manager to equal him. No one is tenderer to his children and his kinsmen. He has an inborn deference for his parents and superiors. He is prompt and exact in obedience, always faithful.'

This is quite a rhapsody! And no doubt there is something in it of personal recollection, too flatteringly recalled. In course of time, however, something more immaterial, purer and more profound, found its way into the love of Russia that the love of certain Russians gave to Catherine.

We must not forget, among the ideas to which she remained faithful, what has been called the great idea of her reign : the Greek project. We shall see that she has had it in view from 1762, and that she still has it in view on the eve of her death. It was a beautiful dream, beautiful and fantastic. The resurrection of Greece, the enfranchisement of the Yougo-Slavs, mingled with other equally dazzling, but less disinterested

visions : Constantinople opening its gates to
Christianity, represented by a Russian army ;
the crescent replaced on the dome of St. Sophia
by the double Greek cross, crowned by the two-
headed imperial eagle. It is on this account
that the second son of Paul is named Constantine,
and not Peter or Ivan ; it is on this account
that there is a Greek nurse and a Greek servant,
who was afterwards to become an important personage, Count Kourouta. There was also a corps
of Greek cadets, a Greek district-government at
Kherson, newly founded, and under the charge of
Eugene, a Bulgarian. Medals were struck, on which
were seen symbolic and suggestive images : on
one side the Empress, on the other Constantinople
in flames, a minaret crumbling into the sea, and
the cross resplendent in the clouds. The journal
of Chrapowicki is not less edifying on the subject.
On August 17, 1787, he considers a secret project of Patiomkine for the capture of Bakou and
Derbent. Capital for that could be made out of
the troubles in Persia, and, by means of other
connections, a province could be formed to be
called Albania, which would serve as provisional
appointment for the Grand Duke Constantine.
On April 21, 1788, Moldavia and Wallachia
are discussed : these provinces should remain
independent, in order to serve as nucleus to
the future 'Dacia,' that is to say, the future
monarchy of Greece. On October 9, 1789, the
i's are dotted. The Greeks need to be 'stirred
up' : Constantine may take charge of that. He
has a future before him. In thirty years he will
have got from Sebastopol to Constantinople.

II

In 1769 the cause of liberty has no more enthusiastic defender in Europe than the Empress of Russia.

'To the brave Corsicans, defenders of liberty and of their country, and, in particular, to General Paoli: Gentlemen! All Europe has for many years seen you oppose oppression, defend and redeem the country from an unjust usurpation, and fight for liberty. It is the duty of every human creature to aid and support all who manifest sentiments so noble, so great, and so natural.'

The letter is from the hand of Catherine, and is signed 'Your sincere friends, the inhabitants of the North Pole (*sic*).' A sum of money is added, which passes in the eyes of the brave Corsicans as the result of a subscription. This, doubtless, is in order to spare them the humiliation of being subventioned by an absolute monarch, and also to make them believe that there is, in the neighbourhood of the 'North Pole,' a respectable number of people capable of sympathising with the cause they defend.

In 1781 Catherine comes forward on behalf of Necker. His famous *Compte rendu*, which is practically an act of accusation against the administration of royal finances, that is to say against royalty itself, enchants and delights her. She does not doubt that heaven has destined the able Genevese for the salvation of France.

Certainly she has not much love, just then,

either for France or for the turn that things are taking there; but in her hostile feelings the court holds as large, if not larger, a place than the people, and the old *régime* foundering under the rising flood of social claims has no part in her favour. This is the impression we receive from her correspondence with her son and her daughter-in-law, during the visit of their Imperial Highnesses, in 1782, to Paris. Here is a specimen. It is Catherine who writes :—

'May God bless her most Christian Majesty, her shows, her balls and her plays, her rouge and her beards, well or ill adjusted. I am not sorry that this annoys you and makes you anxious to return. But, how is it that, with its passion for the play, Paris is no better off than we? I know the reason; it is because every one leaves the good show for the bad; that in tragedy they have nothing but what is atrocious; that plays are written by those who know neither how to make comedies for laughter nor tragedies for tears; that comedy, instead of bringing laughter, brings tears; that nothing is in its proper place; that colours even have only abject and indecent names. All that encourages no sort of talent, but·spoils it.'

A frivolous and corrupt court, in the midst of a society which its evil example has brought to the verge of a fatal precipice, that is the idea Catherine seems to hold, at this time, in regard to the country of her 'dear master,' who himself has given colour to her opinions, in denying at every opportunity his kinship with the pitiable 'Vandals.' Her dominant idea, however, is a feeling of indifference in regard to men and things there.

For a long time, up to the very verge of the revolutionary crisis, the events and agitations, in this far country, seem to her without any general importance; she does not perceive their bearing. Nor, whatever may have been said to the contrary, does she see the approach of the tempest. On April 19, 1788, she writes to Grimm: 'I do not share the belief of those who imagine that we are on the eve of a great revolution.' Hearing, in the course of her tour through the Crimea, of the resolution of Louis XVI. to convoke an 'Assembly of Notables,' she sees in it only an imitation of her own legislative commission. She invites Lafayette to visit her at Kief. To open her eyes on what is being prepared by the Lafayettes, it needs the thunderclap of the taking of the Bastille. Then she begins to understand what is in the air, and the *Gazette de St.- Pétersbourg,* which had been silent on the Assembly of the States and the Tennis-court Oath, breaks out in indignant protestations: 'Our hand shakes with horror,' etc. The rest of the article may be imagined. Soon the constituents are compared by the officious journal to 'a drunken mob,' as their successors are to be compared to 'cannibals.'

From this moment Catherine's ideas underwent a rapid change, and it is curious to follow, in her correspondence and her confidential conversation, the progress of this evolution. In June 1790 Grimm, who has not yet had time to perceive the change which is coming over the Empress's mind, asks for her portrait on behalf of Bailly, offering in exchange that of the revolutionary hero of the day. Catherine replies—

'Listen : I cannot accede to your request, and it is as little suitable for the mayor who has dis-monarchised France to have the portrait of the most aristocratic Empress in Europe, as it would be for her to send it to the dismonarchising mayor; it would be to place both the dis-monarchising mayor and the *aristocratissime* Empress in contradiction with themselves and their functions, past, present, and future.'

And two days after—

'I repeat that you are not to give to the dis-monarchising mayor the portrait of the greatest aristocrat in Europe; I would have nothing to do with Jean Marcel, who will be strung up *à la lanterne* some day soon.'

Here is a complete throwing overboard of republicanism. It is not so with regard to philo-sophy, to which the Empress still clings. She endeavours to find out how far it is responsible for the present events—

TO GRIMM.

'*June 25, 1790.*

'The National Assembly should burn all the best French authors, and all that has carried their language over Europe, for all that declares against the abominable mess that they have made. . . . As for the people and its opinion, that is of no great consequence!'

It is this last phrase especially which shows the antagonism, now only capable of increase, be-tween the spirit of Catherine and of the Revolu-tion. It is the part, more and more prominent, played by the people in the events of which Paris has become the theatre that shocks and offends the sovereign. There was a time when, in this

respect also, she had other ideas.   At the outset
of her reign, in gathering together her legislative
commission, she did nothing less, in reality, than
summon it from the mass of her subjects.   But it
is then, too, that, coming for the first time in
contact with the popular element, she began little
by little to change her mind in regard to it.
Perhaps she was unwise in generalising from her
impressions, but she had no other points of
comparison.   She could but form her opinion on
what was before her eyes, and this opinion
became a profound contempt.   In 1787, as her
secretary, Chrapowicki, points out to her the enormous number of peasants who crowd to see her
and pay homage to her in a certain country town,
she replies with a shrug of the shoulders : ' They
would come just the same to see a bear.'   It is
the same spirit to which she gives utterance two
years after, when, referring to the composition of
the political clubs in France, she says : ' How can
shoemakers have anything to do with affairs?   A
shoemaker only knows how to make shoes.'

Soon philosophy in turn is abandoned.   Catherine still speaks with respect of ' good French
authors,' but she makes her choice, and, Voltaire
excepted, she throws overboard all those of the
eighteenth century.   Diderot, d'Alembert, and
Montesquieu himself, are sacrificed at one blow—

TO GRIMM.

' *Sept.* 12, 1790.

' I must tell you the truth, the tone with you now is
that of mere intemperance ; this is not the tone to
make France illustrious. . . . What will the French do
with their best writers, *who almost all lived under Louis*

XIV.? All—Voltaire himself—are royalists; they preach order and tranquillity, and all that is opposed to the system of this hydra with twelve hundred heads.'

The National Assembly is referred to more and more bitterly. On August 7th, 1790, Chrapowicki notes in his journal: 'Said in presence of her Majesty, speaking of France: "It is a metaphysical country; every member of the assembly is a king, and every citizen is an animal." Received with approbation.' At the same time Catherine writes to Grimm—

' Sept. 27, 1790.

'In bed I reflected over things, and, among others, I thought that one reason why the Mathieu de Montmorencys, the Noailles, etc., are so ill-taught and so base in spirit that they are among the first promoters of the decree abolishing the nobility . . . is that the schools of the Jesuits have been abolished among you: whatever you may say, those scamps looked well after the morals and tastes of the young people, and whatever is best in France came out of their schools.'

'Jan. 13, 1791.

'One never knows if you are living in the midst of the murders, carnage, and uproar of the den of thieves who have seized upon the government of France, and who will soon turn it into Gaul as it was in the time of Caesar. But Caesar put them down! When will this Caesar come? Oh, come he will, you need not doubt.

' May 23, 1791.

'The best of possible constitutions is worth nothing when it makes more people unhappy than happy, when brave and honest folk have to drudge, and only the rogues are in clover, because their pockets are filled, and nobody punishes them.'

, Observe,, however, with what moderation

Catherine is still capable, at this period, of discussing one of the revolutionary principles most repugnant to her. Her letter of June 30th, 1791, to the Prince de Ligne may be given in evidence—

'I think that the Academies ought to offer a first prize for the question: What do honour and worth, synonyms dear to heroic ears, become in the mind of an active citizen under a jealous and suspicious government, which proscribes all distinction, while nature itself has given to the intelligent man a pre-eminence over the fool, and courage is founded on the sentiment of the force of the body or of the head? Second prize for the question: Are honour and worth really needful? And if so, surely one should not restrain the desire of emulation, and clog it with an insupportable enemy, equality.'

But soon she is carried away by more violent feelings—

'*Sept.* 1, 1791.

'If the French Revolution takes in Europe, there will come another Gengis or Tamerlane to restore it to reason: that is what I prophesy, and be sure it will come true, but it will not be in my time, nor, I hope, in that of M. Alexandre.'

When the news of the death of Louis XVI. reaches her, Catherine, as we have mentioned, is cut to the heart; she betakes herself to bed, in a sort of fever, and she cries to her confidant—

'*Feb.* 1, 1793.

'The very name of France should be exterminated! Equality is a monster. It would fain be king!'

This time the holocaust is complete. Voltaire

is sacrificed with the rest. And in the words and writing of the Empress there are almost savage calls to vengeance, the most extravagant projects of repression—

Feb. 15, 1794.
'I propose that all the Protestant powers should embrace the Greek religion, to save themselves from the irreligious, immoral, anarchical, abominable, and diabolical plague, enemy of God and of thrones ; it is the sole apostolic and truly Christian religion—an oak with wide-spreading roots.'

Thus, after Caesar, she calls for Tamerlane and his exterminating sword; after the Jesuits, a long-bearded pope, who will bring the lost peoples into the safe fold of the Orthodox Church. Is the Caesar for whom she calls, he whom France and Europe have indeed felt? Yes and no. This Caesar she did not at first perceive. In 1791 she is evidently dreaming of some officer of justice coming from without—some Brunswick. It is only later on that her point of view changes, becomes clearer, and then, it must be admitted, she comes very near the truth—touches it almost. Catherine sees Napoleon before he has appeared; she points to him, describes his characteristics—
'If France is to come out of this alive,' she writes, February 11, 1794, 'she will be more vigorous than ever; she will be meek and obedient as a lamb; but it will need a man both great and bold, a man above his contemporaries, and perhaps above the age. Is he born? Is he not? Will he come? All depends on that. If he is found, he will arrest the last downfall, and

that will be arrested whenever he is found, in France or elsewhere.'

The men of the Revolution who preceded Napoleon all shared in the indignation of the Empress, and in the severity of her judgments. Lafayette is now called 'the big booby.' Mirabeau is at first better treated. The praises showered on his tardy loyalism in the *Gazette de St.-Pétersbourg* show that the relations of the tribune with the Russian Legation at Paris were not unknown, nor yet the services that were looked for from him. But, after his death, Catherine's personal opinion is emphatically expressed in her letters to Grimm—

'Mirabeau was the colossus or monster of our time; in any other he would have been avoided, detected, imprisoned, hanged, or broken on the wheel.'

And three days afterwards—

'I do not like the honours paid to Mirabeau, and I do not understand the why or wherefore, unless it be to encourage wickedness and all the vices. Mirabeau merits the esteem of Sodom and Gomorrha.'

She retracts, too, her admiration for Necker—

'I agree with the views of M. F. on Malet du Pan and on that bad and foolish Necker: to me they are not merely hateful, but mere bores and chatterboxes.'

She is not more tender towards the Duke of Orleans—

'I hope that no Bourbon will ever again bear the name of Orleans, after the horror that I feel towards the last who bore it.'

As for the Abbé Siegés, she settles his account

at once : 'I subscribe to the hanging of the Abbé Siegés.'

It is but just to say that the Revolutionaries give her back her own. Volney returns the gold medal which the Empress has formerly bestowed on him. Sylvain Maréchal, in his *Jugement Dernier des Rois*, depicts the Empress in grotesque hand-to-hand conflict with the Pope, who throws his tiara at her head, after which she is swallowed up with all her accomplices by a volcano that opens under her feet. The *Moniteur* is not always amiable towards her.

Nevertheless, it must be noted that, for a long time, Catherine, while severely condemning the revolutionary movement, does not, in Russia or elsewhere, set on foot against it any act of direct repression. She remains a passive, and in some sort disinterested, spectator of passing events. Her whole attitude seems to say that all these things have no concern for her; that, whatever may happen, she has nothing to fear for herself or for the empire. At bottom, she is probably convinced of it to the last. Only it happens that the combinations, or we might better say the improvisations, of her policy come to impose upon her convictions. The precise epoch when she decides to abandon her inaction sufficiently indicates her reasons for doing so : it 'is the moment when, having settled affairs with Turkey and Sweden, she judges the hour come to interfere in Poland, and to put her hand to the master-work of her reign. The French Revolution then appears in her eyes as one of those propitious 'conjunctions' which, with conjectures and circumstances, make up, for her, the whole of politics. A dialogue with her secretary Chrapowicki, December 14, 1791, gives clear utterance to her view in this respect—

'I am doing all I can to get the courts of Berlin and Vienna to concern themselves with French affairs.'

'They are not very active.'

'No. The court of Berlin goes forward, but that of Vienna remains behind. They do not see my point. Am I wrong? There are reasons that one cannot say openly. I wish them to become concerned in the French affairs in order to leave me elbow-room. I have many undertakings to be achieved. I would have them occupied so that they may leave my way clear.'

And immediately Catherine sets the tocsin ringing. Up to the present she has been content to publish in Paris, through her minister Simoline (in August 1790) a ukase commanding all her subjects to quit France, in order that more of them should not think to imitate the example of the young Count Alexander Strogonof, who, with his tutor, had joined a revolutionary club. But it had not occurred to her to interdict in her empire the incendiary publications coming from the banks of the Seine. Russia remained the sole country in Europe open to the circulation of the papers printed at Paris. One number of the *Moniteur* had been confiscated, because it enlarged somewhat too explicitly on the score of the Grand Duke and different personages of the court. From that day Catherine examined every number before authorising the distribution. She soon came across one where she herself, in her turn, was very hardly treated : she was described as 'the Messalina of the North.' 'That concerns no one but myself,' she said proudly, and ordered its distribution. She tolerated the presence in St. Petersburg of the brother of Marat, who, while condemning the sanguinary furies of the other, did not conceal his republican views. Tutor in the house of Count Saltykof, he often comes to court with his pupil. It is only in 1792 that he changes his name, and takes that of Boudri. Then, in truth, all around him changes : the Empress embarks in the anti-revolutionary campaign, at first without much enthusiasm, purely as a political manœuvre, but more and more sincerely, and more and more passionately too, entering little by little into the part she has wished to play, and adopting as her own those ideas, sentiments, and instincts. Not content with attacking the revolutionary spirit in France and among the French, she pursues it in Russia, among the Russians themselves, which is really doing it more honour than it deserves. In regard to France she draws up, in 1792, a memorandum on the means of restoring the monarchy. It must be said that she does not manifest much common-sense in the project. She imagines that a force of ten thousand men, marching from end to end of the country, would suffice to the task. The cost would only be £500,000, which could be borrowed at Genoa. France, once handed back to its king, would return the amount. In regard to the Frenchmen imbued with the revolutionary spirit, who might be found in her dominions, she concocts the famous ukase of February 3, 1793, which constrains them under threat of immediate expulsion, to take an oath, of which the terms could not have been' better imagined by a tribunal of inquisitors. Nor does she treat her subjects with more indulgence. To ward them off from the contagion. of Jacobinism, she has recourse to means which she could not have sufficiently scorned at the commencement of her reign. Learning the choice that had been made of Prozorofski for the post of Governor of Moscow, Patiomkine writes to his imperial friend—

'You have taken out of your arsenal the most ancient piece of artillery, which will certainly shoot in the direction in which you set it, for it has no motion of its own; but beware lest it covers with blood for ever the name of your Majesty.'

Prozorofski and his collaborators of Moscow and St. Petersburg, Arharof, Chechkofski, and Pestel, seemed, in the vigorous phrase of a Russian writer, 'to have risen into the light of day out of the torture-chambers of the *Preobrajenski Prikaz*, already lost in the night of oblivion.' The trial of the Muscovite publicist, Novikof, condemned to fifteen years' imprisonment for carrying on certain publications to which the Empress herself had formerly contributed, inaugurates a *régime* which justifies only too well the apprehensions of Patiomkine. Catherine bears a grudge even against the high French cravats, covering the chin, which the dandies of St. Petersburg, Prince Borys Galitzine at their head, persist in wearing.

We have endeavoured to present the notions inspired in Catherine by the great political and social upheaval of the end of the eighteenth century. These notions, it is evident, were narrow. Catherine could not see that, under all its deplorable errors, its culpable mistakes, the movement that she sought to repress contained something noble, lofty, and generous. Perhaps mere intelligence could not suffice for the comprehension of these things. What was wanted was a certain personal elevation of sentiment, which Catherine never possessed. In trying to fight with the Revolution, she seized her chance of stifling the last vestiges of national independence on the banks of the Vistula: that was a matter of policy, and we may waive our judgment respecting it. But, the fight once at end in Poland, she was neither touched as a woman, nor impressed as a sovereign, by what made the glory of the expiring republic and its rehabilitation before posterity, by the last resistance of the vanquished, by the hero who personified all its useless effort and its tragic destiny. Having summoned to St. Petersburg as a common malefactor the vanquished soldier whom Michelet named 'the last Knight of the West and the first Citizen of the East,' whom Napoleon afterwards, at the height of his power, would have called to his aid, and who, in his Swiss shelter, was not to be dazzled by Napoleon, Catherine was not even curious to see him. She was content to abuse him. 'Kostiouchko'— she did not even know how to spell his name— 'has been brought here; he is seen to be in every way a mere fool, quite beneath contempt. That is how she judges the man. 'Ma pauvre bête de Kostiouchka,' we read in another letter.

That is all the pity she can spare to the soldier
who had fallen on the field of Macieiowice, the
soldier in whose wounds the very soul of a great
and noble people seemed to pass in one last cry
of agony.

Paul I., on reaching the throne, is said to have
visited the ex-dictator in his prison, and, bending
low before him, desired his pardon for his mother.
Perhaps it is only a legend, and if so, so much
the worse for the son of Catherine. At all events
he set the prisoner free. Catherine had never
thought of doing it.

We once heard a German, who to-day occupies
a high position at Vienna, declare that, being
cosmopolitan in his tastes, he liked every nation-
ality equally, except one, and that his own ; for,
said he, along with many good qualities, it had
one defect which he disliked above all others, it
did not know how to be generous.

In one sense, and from this point of view, just
or not, Catherine remained German. She knew
how to give, sometimes even how to pardon, but
she was utterly inaccessible to certain sentiments
that awaken naturally in all true hearts at the
sight of weakness, suffering, and misfortune.
Her ideas, as we know them, did not allow her
to appreciate a certain type of simple grandeur.
Her own simplicity was all made of show and
convention. She was always playing a part
when she showed herself under this aspect. She
was willing to come down from Olympus, and
she even took pleasure in it, but Olympus and
all its train must be not far off. This is why, in
1782, she refused the honour of receiving
Franklin. 'I do not care for him,' she said.

She did not understand him. In 1795 she did not understand Kosciuszko.

Is it true that she ever echoed the one among all the kings her contemporaries whom she professed the most to scorn, Louis XV., by repeating in her way the famous saying 'After me the deluge'? '*Poslie mienia hot trava nie rosti* (After me the grass may cease to grow)' she is said to have said at the end of her life. It may well be. But to arrive at that point, she had need to abjure all that made the true glory of her reign, all to which she owes to-day that immortality of which she had the sublime thirst.

BOOK II

THE SOVEREIGN

CHAPTER I

THE ART OF RULING

1

I love the fallow land,' wrote Catherine. 'I have said it a thousand times, I am good for nothing out of Russia.' She thus proved the extreme lucidity of mind which permitted her, at least occasionally, to achieve this *tour de force*— a just appreciation of her own merits. Prince Henry of Prussia, sent to St. Petersburg, as an act of gratitude, by his brother, and there studying the sovereign with a German's resolution to get to the bottom of things, said one day to the Comte de Ségur—

'She (Catherine) is made to shine, she is immortalised during her lifetime; otherwise, she would no doubt shine much less; but in her country she is more intelligent than all those about her. It is easy to be great on such a throne.'

Catherine did not fail to recognise one of the elements, and perhaps the most essential, of all her successes—luck. 'I have had nothing but good luck,' she said frankly enough. How indeed could she fail to see in the path of her life this indispensable factor of all prosperity? In 1770 she copied with her own hand a note from her improvised admiral, the commandant-in-chief of her naval forces in the Levant, Alexis Orlof, who, though he had never till then seen a ship or a sailor, knew enough at the end of a week to see that those with whom he had been told to conquer 'were not worth a pinch of salt.' 'My hair stands on end as I think of these things,' wrote Orlof. 'If we had to do with any but Turks, there would soon be an end of the fleet.' It is this fleet and its admiral that won the victory of Tchesmé, shattering to atoms one of the finest fleets that Turkey had ever sent to sea. And in 1781 Catherine had already sent to Grimm the following *résumé* of the history of her reign, set forth by her new secretary and factotum, Besborodko, in the fantastic form of an inventory :—

Governments instituted according to the new form, ...	29
Towns built, ...	144
Treaties made, ...	30
Victories won, ...	78
Notable edicts, decreeing laws, . . .	88
Edicts on behalf of the people, . . .	123
Total,	492

Four hundred and ninety-two active measures! This astonishing piece of book-keeping, which betrays so naïvely all that there was of romantic, extravagant, childish, and very feminine, in the extraordinary genius that swayed Russia, and in some sort Europe, during thirty-four years,

will no doubt make the reader smile.   It corresponds, however, truly enough, to a sum-total
of great things accomplished under her direct
inspiration.

And all that, was it not really due to her good
luck?   No indeed! Prince Henry of Prussia is
too severe, Catherine too modest, and we have
proved it already in speaking of the character of
the great sovereign.   With such a character one
generally puts something more than chance and
success in the balance of human destinies, over
which one is called to preside.   Catherine put
there, to begin with, remarkable qualities of
tenue.   On July 3, 1764, the envoy of Frederick,
Comte de Solms, wrote to his master—

'On the part of the nation discontent and
commotion, and much courage and firmness, at
least in appearance, on the part of the Empress.
She left here (Livonia) with an air of the greatest
serenity and the most composed countenance,
though, only two days before, there had been a
mutiny in the army.'

In another circumstance, the Prince de Ligne
has noted—

' I was the only one to see that the last declaration on part of Turkey gave her only a quarter
of an hour's reflection on the instability of human
things, and the uncertainty of success and glory.
She left the room with the same air of serenity
that she had before her courier had gone.'

Imposing on all the world, her friends as well
as her enemies, by this attitude, Catherine can
never be imposed upon by man or thing, and is
never put out of countenance.   In 1788, at the
moment when the Swedish war broke out, there

was a terrible lack of men, both in the army and in the government, but especially in the army. The Count of Anhalt presents himself, backed by his European reputation as a soldier, and offers his services. He is received with open arms. But he demands the rank of general-in-chief, and the supreme command. Catherine refuses. The German condottiere, surprised and indignant, declares that he will go and plant cabbages. 'Look after them well,' replies the Empress calmly.

To increase the prestige that she already has, she does not disdain, from time to time, to have recourse to certain artifices, to certain effects of pose and arrangement. The Comte de Ségur, on presenting his credentials, perceives 'something theatrical' in the behaviour of the Empress; but this 'something' has such an effect upon the new-comer that he forgets the formal speech he has prepared beforehand, and is obliged to improvise another. One of his predecessors, yet more overcome, was unable, if we may believe Catherine, to get beyond the words, 'The King my master,' which he repeated three times in succession. At the third repetition Catherine put an end to his misery by saying that she well knew the good-will of his master towards her. But she looked upon him, from that moment, as a fool, though he had the reputation in Paris of being a man of ready wit. She was indulgent only to her servants. It should be said that she had the right to be exigent in regard to those who had to speak before her, for, as the Prince de Ligne has observed, she had 'the art of listening.' 'Such was her presence of mind,' he tells us, 'that she seemed to be listening, even when she was thinking of something else.' The Prince de Ligne adds that nevertheless his own Empress, Maria Theresa, had 'more charm and magic,' Catherine manifests more authority. And she is careful to keep this side of her sovereign prestige intact. One day, at an official dinner, having to express some discontent with the envoy of a foreign power, she makes one of those scenes of which Napoleon, later on, was so fond. In the midst of her tirade she hears her secretary, Chrapowicki, observing in an undertone how much it is to be regretted that the *matouchka* loses her temper in this way. She stops short, changes the conversation, behaves most amiably to the end of dinner ; but on rising from table she goes straight to the interrupter : ' How dare you criticise in public what I say!' Her voice trembles with wrath, and the cup of coffee that she holds in her hand is in danger of falling to the ground. She puts down the cup without emptying it, and dismisses the unfortunate secretary. He thinks himself lost, and goes home expecting, at the very least, an order to set out for Siberia. A messenger comes to summon him before her Majesty. Catherine is still much excited, and overwhelms him with reproaches. He falls on his knees. 'Come,' says the Empress, presenting him with a snuff-box set with diamonds, 'keep this, and when you have any observations to make in public on what I say or do, hold your tongue and take a pinch of snuff. The reminder may be of use to me.'

With such command over herself, it is certain that she must exercise great command over others. It is indeed enormous, and all the traits of her character, of her temperament, and of her mind, serve to strengthen it. Her attitude impresses and fascinates, her energy, her fire, her youthful 'go,' her confidence, her audacity, her *verve*, her way of presenting things to others as they present themselves to her, that is to say, on the brightest side, her scorn of danger and difficulty, made up of a good half of ignorance and a good third of adventurous infatuation, her day-dreams, that sort of gorgeous hallucination in which she lives, and through which the sense of real things comes to her; all that aids her in driving forward good and bad, wise and foolish alike, driving them forward as a horseman does his horse, now carressed and now flogged, spurred, shaken, and in some sort borne along by the effort of a will which increases tenfold the play of the muscles. Read the correspondence of the sovereign with her generals in the first Turkish war, Galitzine and Roumiantsof. Galitzine is utterly incompetent, Roumiantsof is an accomplished soldier: she scarcely notices the difference They must both march; they must both beat the Turks; it is impossible that they should not do that. The Turks, what are they? A herd, not an army. And then, 'Europe is observing us.' One seems to hear Napoleon beside the Pyramids. She thanks Roumiantsof for a Turkish poignard that he has sent her, but the capture of two 'hospodars' would please her better. Nor is that enough: 'I beg you to be good enough to send me the Vizier himself, and, if God wills, his Highness the Sultan himself.' She will do all to render the victory easy: 'She is setting fire to the Turkish empire at all four corners.' She sends word to her Minister of War, so that he may hold himself in readiness: 'Monsieur, monsieur, I want plenty of cannons. .... What am I to do if the cannons are dear?' One would take her for a fine lady ordering a further supply of dresses from a good maker. She adds: 'I have now an army at Cuban, an army acting against the Turks, an army against the brainless Poles; I am about to collar the Swedes, and I have three more *soumatohi* (brawls) *in petto*, that I dare not avow. Send me, if you can without attracting notice, a map of the Mediterranean and the Archipelago, and then pray God: God will arrange all.'

But now, in September 1771, one of the lieutenants of Roumiantsof, General Essen, is defeated under the walls of Giourgi. It is nothing. 'Where there has been water, there is water still,' says the Russian proverb. The Russian proverb is right. 'God favours us, but sometimes he punishes us in order that we may not become too proud.' We must go ahead, and all will be well. Roumiantsof goes ahead, he leaves the right. bank of the Danube. Victory! cries Catherine. Quick, a pen, to send the good news to Voltaire, that the good news may spread through all Europe! Alas! in obeying his sovereign, Roumiantsof has attempted too much. He is obliged to beat a retreat. He excuses himself on account of the state of the army. He imagines that he has enemies about the Empress who have purposely left him without enough food and ammunition. 'He does not know what he is saying!' Catherine has never heard that he had enemies capable of doing him a mischief with her. That would be impossible. 'She has no people about her to whisper in her ear. . . . She will have none of such folk. . . . She judges those capable of doing well by what they do.' No doubt Roumiantsof's army is weak. Especially (a little cut in passing) as it must have suffered in the marches and counter-marches from one bank of the Danube to the other. But the Empress cannot forget the inscription engraved on the obelisk commemorating the victory won by Roumiantsof at Kagoul: it declares that he had only 17,000 men under his command. With his skill and energy he can renew this feat of arms; provided always that he does not allow himself to be discouraged. Forward! Forward!

II

This correspondence discovers yet another superiority in Catherine : her skill in the management of men. In that she is simply marvellous. She employs all the resources of a trained diplomatist, of a subtle psychologist, and of a woman who knows the art of fascination; she employs them together or apart, she handles them with unequalled *maestria*. If it is true that she sometimes takes her lovers for generals and statesmen, it is no less true that she treats on occasion her generals and statesmen as lovers. When the sovereign can do nothing, the Circe intervenes. If it avails nothing to command, to threaten, or to punish, she becomes coaxing and wheedling. Towards the soldiers that she sends to death, bidding them only win for her victory, she has delicate

attentions, flattering forethought, adorable little
ways.   After the battle of Kinburn (October
1787), having to send quantities of ribbon to the
heroes of the day, she arranges them with her
own hands, in a basket of flowers, which she
sends to Patiomkine.   In September 1789 she
sends to Prince von Nassau-Siegen, the new
commander of the fleet, two warm dressing-gowns,
'like those I sent last year to Marshal Prince
Patiomkine before Otchakof, and which were of
great service to him, as he himself assured me.'
She flatters the literary ambitions of the Comte
de Ségur in absolutely insisting on putting his
Coriolanus on the stage, and, in the course of the
performance, she seizes both his hands to make
him applaud himself.   She even gives out that she
knows the piece by heart, reciting aloud a dozen
lines, where, it is true, she has caught a political
allusion that she wishes to emphasise.

Should fortune smile upon the efforts she has
thus provoked and stimulated, she is profusely
grateful : honours, pensions, gifts of money, of
peasants, of land, rain upon the artisans of her
glory.   But she does not abandon those who have
had the misfortune to be unlucky.   In June
1790 Prince von Nassau-Siegen is ingloriously
defeated.   She immediately writes to him—

'I hope you know me well enough to be sure
that the gossip of the town, which has apparently
reached you, will have no effect upon me.   I know
perfectly your zeal; I do it justice; I most sincerely share your mortification; I am distressed
to hear that it has even affected your health. . . .
Mon Dieu, who is there, then, that has not had
great reverses in his life?   Have not the greatest

captains had their unlucky days. The late King of Prussia was really only great after a great reverse. . . . Remember, Prince, your successes in the South and North, rise above these untoward events, and go forward against the enemy, instead of asking me to appoint another commander for the fleet. I cannot do so now without giving occasion to your enemies. I lay too great store by the services you have rendered me not to support you, especially at a time when you are suffering, as you tell me, in body and mind.'

She supports him, in fact, against all. As, in his endeavour to retire from the position, he appeals to the unfavourable state of affairs, she replies that it will be cruel of him towards her if he cannot remedy them. ' I have always liked to take an interest in the affairs of those who looked after mine.' And, as the clamour of court and town still continue against the defeated general, she writes to him again—

'You acted upon a plan approved by me and upon my orders, and, coming from the supreme authority, they could not have been submitted to any further opinion, since, as long as I live, I shall never allow what I have ordered and approved of in regard to service to be called in question by a living soul; nor does any one here attempt to do so. You are right, and you must be right, since I say that you are right. That is an "aristocratic" reason, no doubt; but it can be no otherwise without turning everything upside down.'

And it is always thus. In 1794 General Igelström, having been surprised at Warsaw by a popular outbreak, is suspended from office; but, one day, as those about the Empress are intent ·· upon running him down, she raises her voice: 'Silence, gentlemen; do not forget that he served me for thirty years, and that I owe to him the peace with Sweden.'

A fragment of conversation with Count Nicolas Roumiantsof, the son of the hero of the first Turkish war, which is reported to us by Gretch, shows, on the other hand, the multiplicity of means which she has at her command, and which she uses to obtain the aid of those whose devotion is likely to be useful to her. She asks the Count if he thinks it easy to govern men. 'I think there is nothing more difficult,' replies Roumiantsof. 'Come now, you have only to observe three principles: the first is to act so that people fancy they are doing of their own accord what you make them do.' 'That is quite enough,' interrupts Roumiantsof. Admiral Tchitchagof relates that his brother, who was gentleman of the bedchamber, had one day the misfortune to be late in arriving. The Empress observed it, and did not fail to comment on this negligence, but it was in the form of eulogies heaped on the father of Tchitchagof, who, for fifty years, never once failed to be at his post. Those who were present imagined that the young man was receiving the most extraordinary signs of imperial favour, until he confessed to them afterwards that he had never been so miserable and confused. 'I make it a point to praise aloud, and to complain quietly,' said Catherine.

And is it not easy to imagine the effect that a word from her lips, a gesture of her hand, the slightest mark of satisfaction or of dissatisfaction, coming from her, would have over the simple and impressionable people with whom she was for the most part brought in contact? Tchitchagof relates that a General Vorontsof, Commandant of the Post of Revel, whom he had known well, was struck by an attack of apoplexy, of which he died, at the mere idea of having incurred the sovereign's displeasure. A non-commissioned officer named Stepan Chiraï, sent to the Empress by Souvarof with the news of the taking of a fortress, returned with the Cross of St. Vladimir of the fourth class, which the Empress herself had pinned on his chest. Thirty years later the Emperor Nicholas, on the day of his coronation, thought to advance him a class. He returned the new cross: he could not make up his mind to give up the one that he had received from the hands of the *matouchka*!

III

Catherine's art of ruling was not, however, without its shortcomings, some of which were due to the mere fact of her sex, whose dependences and weaknesses she was powerless to overcome. 'Ah!' she cried one day, 'if heaven had only granted me breeches instead of petticoats, I could do anything. It is with eyes and arms that one rules, and a woman has only ears.' The petticoats were not solely responsible for her difficulties. We have already referred to a defect which bore heavily upon the conduct of affairs during her reign : this great leader of men, who knew so well how to make use of them, did not know how to choose them. Her judgment, usually so accurate and penetrating, her lucidity, great as it was, deserted her on this point.   She could not see in others either the qualities or the defects that she discovered and analysed in herself with so extraordinary a clearness of sight.   There was here a gap in her intelligence, due probably, in part at least, to the influence of her temperament.   It seems that her vision of men in general was disturbed, in this respect, by the breath of passion which influenced all her life.   The general, the statesman, of whom she had need, she seemed to see only through the male whom she liked or disliked.   What she looked for first, in the face of any functionary whatever, was the romantic side, the more or less attractive exterior.   That she took Patiomkine for an able man may be excused; he was perhaps a madman, but he had the madness of genius.   He belonged to the category of men who are called forces of nature.   And this force, let loose upon immensity in this 'fallow land' for which Catherine felt that she had been born, had its value.   But after Patiomkine came Zoubof. He was a mere puppet: Catherine took him for a man of genius.

The contrary also happened to her.   Roumiantsof having presented before her one of his lieutenants, General Weissmann, whom he judged capable of taking his place in case of need, Catherine conversed with him on three occasions, and, having turned him this way and that, 'came to the conclusion that he was an absolute fool.' The wretched man shortly afterwards rushed upon his death in the battle of Koutchouk-Kajnardji.   In the opinion of all competent to judge, he was beyond compare as a soldier,

and valiant among the valiant. One historian
has called him 'the Achilles of the Russian
army.'

These mistakes of judgment were frequent.
But Catherine did more than this, and worse.
With the obstinacy which characterised her, and
the infatuation that her successes gave her, she
came little by little to translate this capital defect
into a *parti pris*, to formulate it as a system ; one
man was worth another, in her eyes, so long as
he was docile and prompt to obey. She had in
this respect maxims which might well disconcert
her admirers.

'Tell me,' she wrote to Grimm, 'if ever
sovereign has more absolutely chosen his ministers according to the voice of public opinion
than Louis XVI.? And we have seen what
happened. According to me, no country has a
dearth of men. Don't try to look all round about
you, try to use what you have at hand. It is
always said of us that we have a dearth of men ;
yet in spite of all, things come right. Peter I.
had the same, and knew not how to read or write ;
well, did not things succeed? *Ergo*, there is no
such thing as a dearth of men ; there is a multi-
tude, but you must make them move : all will go
well if you have this other to make them move.
What does your coachman do, *souffre-douleur*,
when you are boxed up in your coach? A good
heart goes everywhere ; because this or that is
narrow and limited, the master is not.'

And again : 'Assuredly men of worth are
never lacking, for it is affairs which make men
and men which make affairs ; I have never tried
to look for them, and I have always found close

at hand the men who have served me, and I have for the most part been well served.'

This does not hinder her from one day making this reflection, which she puts in a letter to the Prince de Ligne—

'Ah, Prince, who knows better than I do that there are clerks who are ignorant that a maritime town has a port?'

And this other—

'It is not ideas which are wanting; it is in the execution, it is in the application, that things often go awry.'

This does not prevent her, in 1774, from being on the point of going to Moscow herself in order to put down Pougatchef; for, since the death of Bibikof, she knows not who can cope with him. She summons a council: Gregory Orlof declares that he has slept badly and has not an idea in his head; Razoumofski and Galitzine are silent; Patiomkine is for the man whom she chooses; Panine alone has the courage to give advice, and his advice is that the Empress should appeal to his brother, General Panine, whose services she has long neglected, thinking that another would do equally well in his place. The peril being urgent, she submits, sacrifices her *amour-propre*, and Panine saves the crown and the empire. In 1788, after the first encounter with the Swedes, she court-martials three captains of frigates; the next day she writes to Patiomkine: 'They deserve the gallows, but there is nobody else to put in their place, unless he falls from the sky.'

With the multiplicity of her enterprises, and with her ideas on this point, which are but the expression of her caprices, she uses up a terrible number of men. Her maxim that 'affairs make men' leads her to multiply to excess the number of functionaries. According to one testimony, if the two capitals and a few other larger towns are left out of the question, there is one functionary to every ten inhabitants in the provinces. And her idea that one man is worth as much as another causes her, for a mere nothing, for a word that offends her, for a cast of countenance that she finds unpleasing, or even without motive, for the pleasure of change and the delight of having to do with some one new, as she avows naïvely in a letter to Grimm, to set aside, disgraced or merely cashiered, one or another of her most devoted servants. In 1788 Roumiantsof, the greatest warrior whom Russia produced before Souvarof, is still alive, and well able to take the command, and Alexis Orlof, the hero of Tchesmé, is burning to renew his old exploits. He has had a certain apprenticeship to the trade, which he entered into in 1770, and a name that the enthusiasm of Catherine herself has surrounded with such an aureole, that his reputation is worth in itself a fleet or an army. But both the one and the other, Roumiantsof and Orlof, have long been sacrificed to Patiomkine, and Catherine is reduced to seeking generals and admirals in England, in Holland, in Germany. At last she finds Nassau-Siegen, who, after having enchanted her by his matador airs and stage costumes, ere long costs her a fleet, and the shame of a disaster without precedent in the history of the young Russian navy.

The extravagant optimism, which is part of the character of Catherine, and which colleagues like Nassau and Patiomkine assiduously encourage, has also to be observed. The story of the scene-painting on canvas, which, during the visit to the Crimea, is said to have represented the absent villages, has been disproved. It is not so very far from the truth, on the testimony even of those who have contested its reality. The Prince de Ligne is among these; he observes, nevertheless, that Catherine, never going on foot, could see no more than what was shown her, and imagined frequently that a town was built and inhabited, 'when this town had no streets, the streets no houses, and the houses no roofs, doors, or windows.' The Comte de Langeron, who was afterwards governor of these very provinces, and whose memoirs have not the slightest trace of retrospective hostility, goes even further. A proclamation of the governor of Harkof, Vassili Tchertkof, issued at the same time to announce to the inhabitants the coming of the sovereign, and to instruct them in their duties on this solemn occasion, is equally characteristic in the same way. It is severely ordered that the inhabitants are to dress themselves in their best clothes when her Majesty is expected to pass by. The girls are to have their hair carefully combed out and adorned with flowers. They are also to strew flowers on the Empress's path, and all the population is to 'express its delight by appropriate gestures and attitudes.' The houses on the route are to be repainted, the roofs repaired, the doors and windows decked with festoons, and, as far as possible, with rugs

pleasing to the eye. It is forbidden for any one
to get drunk, or to present to her Majesty the
smallest request ; this under penalty of the knout
and hard labour. The local magistrates will see
to it in addition that the passage of the sovereign
does not raise the price of food. Prince Chtcherbatof relates that at Moscow all the beggars had
been put outside, so that the Empress should not
see them. 'The Empress has looked, but not
seen (*vidiela i ne vidala*),' he adds, with an un-
translatable play on words. This is how she
came to be convinced that 'there were no hungry
people in Russia.' She gives that assurance one
day to Grimm !

But the conquest and the arrangement of the
Tauric peninsula were, in the hands of Patiomkine, nothing but a colossal *féerie* mounted by
that prodigious improvisatore and disappearing
with him. It was difficult to decide, on seeing
him at work, which to admire the most : his
extraordinary activity and the fertility of his
imagination, or the incredible *naïveté* with which
both Catherine and himself take their creation,
part madness, part fancy, part childish mystifica-
tion, absolutely *au sérieux*. A desert is to be
transformed into a cultivated and well-populated
land, inhabited by industry and the arts, and
this is to be done in a few years, as if by magic.
Patiomkine sets to work. He plants forests in
the Steppes, imports the seeds of all known
vegetables, trains vines, cultivates mulberry-trees
for silk-worms, builds manufactories, theatres,
palaces, barracks, and cathedrals. He covers the
peninsula with magnificent towns. The history
of these towns is astounding. The examples

which America offers to-day to our astonishment,
in the same order of instantaneous improvisations, are outdone.   In 1784 a site is wanted
for the capital of the province, which is to be
named 'Iekatierinoslaf' — glory of Catherine.
Two months after the site has been marked out,
there is already a project for a university, open
not only to natives, but also to the strangers
who are expected to flock from all the corners
of Europe.   Soon an army of workmen appears
on the right bank of the Dnieper, at the spot
chosen, not far from a humble Tartar village
called Kaïdak; Lieutenant Sinielnikof, who has
charge of them, receives 200,000 roubles for the
first cost, and the work commences.   The town
is to extend along the river about 25 versts, and
to cover 300 square versts with streets 200 feet
wide.   There is to be a park, with a botanical
garden, fish-pond, and different other embellish-
ments.   In the middle is to be the palace of the
Prince of Taurida, Patiomkine the magnificent.
Around are the buildings apportioned to the
different services of the administration ; then
come the dwellings of the workmen employed in
building the town, the workshops, the manufactories, the houses of the coming population.
Twelve large factories, one of them for silk
fabrics, are planned, and the funds for establishing them partly collected.   A town-hall in the
style of the old basilicas, a great bazaar in the
style of the Propylaeum, a Bourse, a theatre, a
Conservatoire of music, finally a cathedral on the
model of St. Peter's, but *larger*, will be erected
in various parts of the city, suitably chosen.   The
materials are ready, Patiomkine declares.   In

addition, professors are already summoned for the university and the conservatoire. The celebrated Sarti is to direct the latter. For the chair of history in the university a Frenchman named Guyenne is appointed, a soldier by profession. But these details must not be looked into too closely. An observatory too is thought of, and a sort of Quartier Latin for the students.

Such are the plans; now see the results. The palace of Patiomkine is built of conservatories, one for pine-apples, another for laurels and orange-trees, others again for pomegranates, dates, etc. The silk factory is also built. It costs 240,000 roubles, and works for two years, after which various reasons, the principal of which is a scarcity of material, bring it to an end. The silk-worm industry, for which a manager has been brought from abroad at a considerable salary, produces a maximum of *twenty pounds* of silk a year! The remainder of the great city exists only in fancy. But Iekatierinoslaf had, all the same, a chance of becoming in time a little provincial town. Kherson, of which Joseph II. laid the first stone in 1787, saying that after him Catherine had laid the last, did not even arrive at this modest result. In other parts of the empire the rapid erection of administrative or industrial centres ran similar risks. In 1787 the poet Dierjavine, accompanying the governor of Petrosavodsk in a journey undertaken for the inauguration of a town which had been appointed chief town of the district, never reached the goal, he tells us: the town existed only on paper!

Nevertheless the Crimea was conquered and began to be populated.

'Such, in Russia,' said the Comte de Ségur, 'is the double magic of absolute power and of passive obedience, that nobody murmurs, even though in want of everything, and things go on, although nothing has been prepared or looked after in advance.'

'Things went on,' in fact, from one end to the other of Catherine's reign, and 'passive obedience,' no doubt, had a large share in it. The adventure of Sutherland, the English banker at St. Petersburg, is well known. One day the chief of police, Ryleief, presents himself, and, with all sorts of excuses, communicates to him an order of the sovereign which concerns him, an order which he cannot but deplore, despite his respect for the will of her Majesty, but which it is out of his power not to execute. In a word, he has been ordered to *stuff* the unfortunate banker. Conceive of the poor man's fright! Happily the mistake is discovered in time. The Empress had spoken of stuffing a favourite dog that she had lost, and the English name had put Ryleief on the wrong track. The English Dr. Dimsdale relates, in the notes he has left on his residence in Russia, that having wished to take the lymph for inoculating the Empress from a child belong ing to poor *moujiks*, the mother opposed it: according to the general belief, it meant the death of the child. But the father intervened · 'If the Empress ordered us to cut off both the child's legs, should we not do it?' Dimsdale adds nevertheless another characteristic. The sick child was placed in an overheated room, in a fetid atmosphere, the opening of a window, according to the parents, meaning certain death.

But Dimsdale produced a rouble : he could open as much as he liked.

The anecdote reveals another agent, universal and all-powerful, which the ways of the country put in the hands of Catherine. She did not fail to use it. She used it vigorously and to excess, after her usual style. She gave much, and let even more be taken. The waste of money in every branch of the administration was enormous. One day Catherine, in the midst of a violent headache, could not suppress a smile : ' She did not wonder that she was suffering so much, for she had seen in the accounts that she used a *poud* (over thirty pounds) of powder every day for her hair !' This detail enables one to judge of the rest. But the accounts that Harris sent to the English court, with the detail of 'tens of thousands of pounds sterling' used by his French colleagues in corrupting the functionaries of the Empress, were not less fanciful. The Baron de Breteuil was the sole French minister at this epoch who was empowered to employ in this manner a considerable sum, to the extent of a million of francs; and he never made use of the permission. His successors had something to do to obtain a few ten thousand pounds intended for the buying over of certain influences or certain secret documents. And these attempts, considered even at Versailles as useless or dangerous, had not as a rule any success during the reign of Catherine. A functionary of the Empress, who had, or appeared to have, a great fancy for a fine coach made in Paris, thought better of it before he had received the present, and informed the sovereign, who dictated to him herself an ironically-polite letter of refusal   After the Baron de Breteuil, in the long series of agents representing the French policy who succeeded him at St. Petersburg, the Comte de Ségur was the only one who succeeded in exercising any particular influence, and money, which he would have found it very difficult to raise, had no share in this.

From 1762 to the death of Catherine, there was only one great corrupting influence in her empire—and that was herself.   It is certain that she used it mainly for the good of the empire, as she conceived it, and that she found in it the resources for the accomplishment of great things. It is not less certain that morality had to suffer for it, and that the influence of ideas and customs thus implanted in the national genius, was destined to exercise on its later development a long and untoward action.

We shall now endeavour to pass rapidly in review the results obtained by means of all these resources as they were wielded in the hands of the sovereign.

CHAPTER II

HOME POLICY

I

HAPPY is the nation without a history: from 1775 the Russian people counted, in point of view of the home policy, among the happy nations.   After the great effort which she had to make in putting down the revolt of Pougatchef, Catherine found herself at first fatigued, then disenchanted, and finally absorbed by her foreign policy, by the conquest of the Crimea, the second Turkish war, the second and third division of Poland, and the anti-revolutionary campaign. Up to 1775 she asserted, and had need to assert, her exuberant activity in every direction. She had first to defend her throne against a series of more or less threatening attempts. A series of repressive measures, more or less calculated to add to her glory, corresponded with them.

In October 1762 a certain Peter Hrouchtchof was accused, with the brothers Simon, Ivan, and Peter Gourief, of having plotted for the re-establishment on the throne of Ivan of Brunswick, shut up since 1741 in prison. Having been condemned, together with his accomplices, to transportation to the government of Oremburg, Hrouchtchof took part in 1772 in the revolt of the exiles in Siberia, under the leadership of the famous Beniowski. He succeeded in escaping, after a series of romantic adventures, reached the west of Europe by way of America, and served in the French army in the rank of captain.

This conspiracy, true or false, for the reality of the criminal intentions imputed to the accused seems not to have been clearly established, has often been confused with another later event, in which the Princess Dachkof was compromised. In May 1763, during Catherine's visit to Moscow on the occasion of her coronation, fresh arrests for high treason were commanded by the Empress. But the unhappy Ivan, languishing in his prison, was not the cause this time. It was quite another affair. There had been a rumour that Catherine intended to marry Gregory Orlof. Some of those who had taken the most active part in the elevation of the new Czarina, Fedor Hitrovo at their head, judged the interests of the empire endangered by this real or imaginary project. They formed a plot to hinder the Empress from carrying it out, or, in case of her persisting, to kill the favourite. Hitrovo, the first to be arrested, named as accomplices, Panine, Hliebof, Tieplof, Passek, the greater part of the heroes of the 12th of July, and the Princess Dachkof. He afterwards contradicted his assertions, and declared that he had only had to do with more obscure friends, the two brothers Roslavlef and Lasounski. Princess Dachkof, on being examined, declared proudly that she knew nothing in the matter, but that, if she had known anything, she would have kept silence just the same. Moreover, if the Empress wished to bring her head to the scaffold, after she had helped to set the crown on hers, she was prepared! The affair had no very serious consequences. Hitrovo alone was exiled in the government of Orel. A ukase was also proclaimed in the streets of Moscow, to the sound of the drum, a ukase which was merely the repetition of an earlier act of Elizabeth's government (June 5, 1757), by which it was forbidden to the inhabitants to occupy themselves with matters which did not concern them. The affairs of state in general were comprised in the enumeration of subjects thus denoted. The interdiction was renewed in 1772.

Almost at the same time, a priest, the Archbishop of Rostof, Arséne Matsieievitch, raised the standard of revolt in a much more audacious manner. The policy of Catherine in regard to the orthodox clergy did not fail to give rise to well-established criticisms. On coming to the throne she had pronounced vigorously against the measures by which Peter III. had brought about the disaffection, if not the active opposition, of the church. She had reopened the private chapels, closed by order of the Czar, forbidden the performance of pagan plays at the theatre, reinforced the censorship of books; finally, she had put an end to the secularisation of ecclesiastical property. Suddenly she changed her mind, and revoked all these measures in protection of interests which she thought it no longer needful to consult. A part of the goods returned to their former possessors was the object of fresh claims. The clergy in general bowed the head, as they had done before. Arsène alone rose in defence of the common rights thus outraged. He went so far as to introduce into the ritual certain new formulas which, under colour of menacing the enemies of the church, were levelled directly against the Empress. Arrested and brought before the sovereign, he broke out into language so violent that her Majesty was obliged to cover her ears. He was condemned to be degraded from his office, and shut up in a cloister, where he was employed, by express order, in the meanest work, in fetching water and chopping wood. Four years later, after a new attempt at revolt, he was removed from the cloister to a better-guarded prison. The fortress of Revel was selected in order that he might not be able to talk in Russian

with his keepers, who only understood Lithuanian.
He changed his name, and called himself the
peasant André *Vral*, that is to say, liar, or *Brodi-
giaguine*, that is to say, brigand. He died in
1772. A year afterwards, a shopkeeper named
Smoline renewed the protest of the unfortunate
bishop against the infringement of the rights of
the clergy. In a letter addressed to the Empress,
and filled with the most virulent invectives, he
openly accused the sovereign of having appropriated the goods of the church in order to
distribute them to Orlof and other favourites.
He ended with this apostrophe: 'Thou hast a
heart of stone like Pharaoh. . . . Of what chastisement art thou not worthy, thou who every day
dost chastise robbers and brigands!' Catherine
proved that the mad creature calumniated her
by showing him mercy. Smoline was only imprisoned for five years, after which, at his own
request, he was made a monk, and nothing more
was heard of him.

Nevertheless, in 1764, the death of Ivan of
Brunswick had already added another stain of
blood to that which the drama of Ropcha left on
the dazzling horizon of the new reign. Ivan, it
may be remembered, was the little Emperor of
two years old, dethroned in 1741 by Elizabeth.
Shut up at first with the rest of his family at
Holmogory, on the White Sea, then, alone, in
the fortress of Schlüsselburg, he had grown up
in the shadow of the dungeon. He was said to
be weak-minded and to stutter; but he had
reigned, and such another act of violence as the
one that had dethroned him might reinstate him
on the throne: he remained a menace. He gave.

some anxiety to Voltaire himself, who foresaw that the philosophers would not find in him a friend. In September 1764 he disappeared. The incident has given rise to contradictory tales and comments, in which history is quite at a loss. To oblige his imperial benefactress, the patriarch of Ferney was good enough to 'arrange' the incident. Others have done the same, Catherine the first of all. Here are the known facts. An officer of the name of Mirovitch, on guard at the fortress of Schlüsselburg, induced a party of men under his command to render him assistance in setting free the 'Czar.' But Ivan had two guardians, to whom the strict command had been given to kill him rather than let him escape. They killed him. Catherine was suspected of complicity in the murder : she was thought to have planned the whole thing with Mirovitch. He, it is true, let himself be judged, condemned, and executed without a word; but had he not been made to believe that he would be reprieved at the last moment? Precedents existed ; under Elizabeth, several high dignitaries, Osterman among others, had profited by the imperial clemency at the very moment when their head rested on the block.

There were certain curious details in the trial : on the express command of the Empress, no attempt was made to find other accomplices, likely as they were to be found, in the crime. The relatives of Mirovitch were not interfered with. It would be unreasonable to try to prove an accusation on such vague grounds. Catherine showed once again, in these circumstances, the force of mind which she possessed. She was travelling in Livonia when the news reached her. She did not hasten her return, or make any change in her itinerary.

But the great crisis in home affairs was that of 1771-1775. At all times, up to the beginning of this century at least, Russia has been the home of pretenders. From the first half of the seventeenth century, after the extinction of the dynasty of Rourik, they followed one another at brief intervals. Under Catherine the series was almost interminable. In 1765 two deserters, Gavrilo Kremnief and Ievdokimof, successively assumed the name of Peter III. In 1769 there was a fresh apparition of the murdered Czar, and it was once more a deserter, Mamykine, who assumed the tragic and ambitious mask. Emelian Pougatchef is thus only the continuation of a series. But this time Catherine has not to do with an obscure plot or a puerile attempt, which a few blows of the knout or the axe will soon set right. A whole tempest is let loose after the wild *Samozvaniets*, a storm which threaten's to shake the throne and the foundations of the empire in a general downfall of the whole political and social structure. It is no more a mere duel between usurpers more or less well-armed for the defence or the conquest of a crown, which has so long been at the disposal of whoever can seize upon it. The contest has another name and another bearing. It is a contest between the modern state, which Catherine is endeavouring to extricate from the unfinished materials left by Peter I. to his heirs, and the primitive state, in which the mass of the people persist in still living; between organisation and the inorganic disorder, which is the natural mode of existence of savage nations; between centralisation and the centrifugal force which is peculiar to that state of nature. It is also the cry of that misery, in which the depths of the populace lie buried, rising against the improvised splendour of a class, how confined! of privileged persons. It is the obscure protestation of the national conscience against the panegyrics of philosophers and poets, of Voltaire and Dierjavine, chanting the splendours of the new reign. For if Catherine, on the heights on which she is surrounded by her crowd of dignitaries and favourites, by all the pomp and majesty of her supreme rank, has done much already to give incomparable lustre to her name, her power, her own greatness, she has done as yet nothing, or almost nothing, for those under her, for the poor, the lowly, who toil and suffer as in the past, who have no share in these triumphs and conquests on high, who know nothing of them, save to be exasperated by the reflection which does but light up the depths of their own misery. Among these, the short reign of Peter III. had awakened hopes and left behind it regrets. The secularisation of the estates of the clergy, begun by the Emperor, had seemed to lead the way towards the enfranchisement of the serfs, and did indeed point in that direction, for the serfs belonging to the secularised domains became free. We have seen that Catherine put an end to this. Peter had also inaugurated a system of absolute tolerance in regard to religious dissent. He had no wish to keep special watch over the welfare of the orthodox church. Legend, as usual, exaggerated his merits. The *skoptsi*, or mutilators, in particular, venerated in him a saint and martyr of their cause. His affiliation to their sect was, they imagined, the real reason of his death; and the accidents of his married life lent some colour to these fables. Catherine, as we have seen, did not follow in this respect either the course of her husband, and what had made her victorious now turned against her. The *raskol* played a considerable part in the movement of insurrection, and with it all the elements of discontent and disorder, even to the turbulent restlessness of the Asiatic races, now in conflict, in the neighbourhood of Kasan and of Moscow, with the Russifying headship of the state: all that entered into conflict with the state and the *régime* which it made and maintained. Emelian Pougatchef was merely the instrument, the nominal leader of this general uprising of the rancours and appetites of an immense *proletariat*. Yet earlier, scattered instances of revolt among the serfs attached to the soil had often been seen. In 1768, in the government of Moscow alone, there were nine cases of proprietors killed by their peasants. The following year there were eight more, and among the victims was one of the heroes of the Seven Years' War, General Leontief, taken prisoner on the battlefield of Zorndorf, and married to a sister of the victorious Roumiantsof.

Emelian Pougatchef was the son of a Cossack of the Don. He too had taken part in the Seven Years' War, where he had distinguished himself, had served also against the Turks, and had then deserted. He was captured, escaped again, and entered upon the career of an outlaw and brigand, by which he came in time to the sanguinary drama which brought his life to an end. The fact of an accidental resemblance with Peter III., which rendered his imposition more practicable, has been denied, and seems to rest on no serious authority. The portraits of the *Samozvaniets* which have reached us show no trace of likeness. Peter III. had the face of a grimacing ape; Pougatchef's was of the common type of the Russian *moujik.* He took the name of the deceased Emperor as others had taken it before him. But he had the fatal luck to appear at the hour marked for the social convulsion, whose causes we have indicated. He did not start the movement, which had long been gathering force; it was rather the movement that bore him with it. He did not even try to direct its course. He put himself at its head and rushed forward blindly, urged on by the tumultuous and threatening flood. It was a terrible course, covering with smoking ruins a half of the empire. After four years, the disciplined force of the organised element got the better of the savage element. Pougatchef, conquered and made prisoner by one of the lieutenants of Panine, was brought to Moscow in a wooden cage, condemned to death, and executed. The headsman cut off his head before quartering him. Catherine declared that it was by her order: she wished to appear more clement than Louis XV. had been with Damiens. She had nevertheless other injuries and other crimes to avenge. The victims made by Pougatchef and his band were beyond all reckoning, and Catherine had been greatly terrified, whatever sallies, more or less witty, she may have sent to Voltaire on the subject of the ' Marquis de Pougatchef.'

An odd characteristic of this incident, but odd in a way which is often seen in similar circumstances, was that, while revolting against the state, as they saw it under Catherine's organisation, Pougatchef and his companions could only copy this organisation, ape it at least, even to the smallest details of its outer forms. After having married a daughter of the people, the false emperor gave her a species of court of honour. Young peasants, beaten into trim, played the *freiline* with immense grotesqueness, attempting ceremonious reverences and a respectful way of kissing the hand. To increase the illusion of his supposed sovereignty, Pougatchef even went the length of naming his principal lieutenants after the principal members of the court of Catherine: the Cossack Tchika took the name of Tchernichef, with the title of field-marshal; others were called Count Vorontsof, Count Panine, Count Orlof, etc.

This comedy cost dear to every one. It took from Catherine the last remains of her former enthusiasm for the redress of social iniquities; Russia, apart from immense material losses, had probably that of a reign which had seemed to be fruitful in great humanitarian reforms. The home policy of Catherine preserved to the last, as we have intimated, the trace of these terrible years, like the scar of blows received and rendered in a fight which was a fight to the death. There were others among the dead than those who perished by fire or steel. Some of the ideas that Catherine had brought with her to the government of the empire remained behind on the field of battle; and perhaps they were among the best that she had brought.

In regard to the department of police, Catherine's *régime*, from 1775 especially, was, in a sense, a *régime* of reaction against that which Peter III. had inaugurated. Peter had suppressed the sinister secret chancellorship, the shameful heirloom of a time which Russia hoped never to see again. Catherine would not re-establish the institution with its hateful obsolete forms, but little by little, without using the name, she restored something very like the thing. She had Stephen Ivanovitch Chechkofski. A legend has been formed about this mysterious functionary, whom Catherine was never without. The reality, without equalling the horror of the memories left by the functionaries of Ivan Vassilevich, was doubtless of a kind to cast some shadow on the reputation that the friend of philosophers desired to preserve in Europe. In her hands it was a cunning and hypocritical machine of state. Chechkofski had neither official titles corresponding with his position nor apparent organisation of his inquisitorial work. But his hand and eye were everywhere. He seemed to possess the gift of ubiquity. He never arrested any one : he sent out an invitation to dinner, which no one dared refuse. After dinner, there was conversation, and the walls of the comfortable and discreet abode betrayed none of the secrets of these conversations. A particular chair was, it seems, set aside for the guest, whom a word, amiable but significant, had induced to cross the formidable threshold. Suddenly the chair, in which he had politely been motioned to be seated, tightened upon him, and descended with him to the floor below, in such a manner, however, that the head and shoulders of the personage remained above. The victim thus preserved his incognito from the assistants of Chechkofski, who subjected the lower part of the body to more or less rigorous treatment. Chechkofski himself turned away at this moment, and appeared to ignore what was passing. The performance finished, and the chair restored to its place, the host turned about, and smilingly took up the conversation at the point where it had been interrupted by this little surprise. It is said that a young man, forewarned of what awaited him, used his presence of mind, and his great muscular strength, to thrust Chechkofski himself into the place reserved for him on the fatal seat. After this he took to flight. The rest can be imagined. Chechkofski died in 1794, leaving a large fortune.

II

The great *ensemble* of laws which Catherine proposed, in 1767, to graft upon Russia, on the model of Montesquieu and Beccaria, was destined never to be achieved, despite certain legislative experiments, done always by fits and starts. The main reason for this, apart from many secondary reasons, is that the work could only be done by beginning at the beginning, and the beginning was the reform, if not the suppression, of serfdom.

This question, be it said to the honour of Catherine, is one of those that occupied her mind the most. When she was yet Grand Duchess, she had, as we have seen, certain projects, quite impracticable indeed, for the enfranchisement of the peasants belonging to the soil. She had found in books, one knows not where, the history of a general and simultaneous emancipation of serfs in Germany, France, Spain, and other countries,—the work of a council! She asked herself if a meeting of archimandrites could not produce the same excellent result in Russia. On reaching the throne she inaugurated the great work by reforming the condition of the serfs in the matter of the ecclesiastical estates confiscated by the Treasury: the peasants, included there, were subjected simply to a light poll-tax; all that they gained in addition was their own property, and they could free themselves altogether for a moderate amount. It was the offer of liberty as a premium on the labour and industry of those concerned; and it was a fruitful idea. Its carrying out was not without inconveniences: the despoiled monks found themselves all at once reduced to beggary. According to the Marquis de Bausset, they had only about eight roubles a year per head to live on; they were forced to beg on the roads; and the degradation of the Russian clergy, one of the most melancholy features of modern Russia, may well be derived, in part at least, from this. But there were about a million peasants enfranchised, or about to be. It was a beginning. For further progress, Catherine counted on her legislative commission. She had to alter her course, as we have seen. Her *Instruction* had in this respect to be retouched as we have indicated. The great mass of peasants belonging with the soil had not even a representative in the assembly, which merely discussed to whom they should belong. Every one sought after this right: the shopkeepers laid claim to it, and also the clergy, and even the Cossacks, jealous of reclaiming their privileges. This reluctance to admit her humanitarian ideas vexed Catherine. Some notes written at this period give us a curious glimpse of her impressions: 'If it is not possible to admit the personality of a serf, he is not a man. Call him an animal, and we shall win the respect of the whole world. . . . The law of serfdom rests on an honest principle established for animals by animals.'

But the deputies of the commission did not read these notes, and probably they would have made no difference to their feelings. On all sides Catherine found an invincible opposition. By 1766 she had already proposed to the Society of Political Economy, founded under her auspices, a question concerning the right of the labourer to the land which he has watered with his sweat. A hundred and twenty replies were sent, in Russian, French, German, and Latin. It was Béardé de l'Abbaye, member of the Academy of Dijon, who won the prize of a thousand ducats. But, by thirteen voices against three, the society opposed the publication of his work.

Catherine finally persuaded herself that the problem was for the present insoluble and dangerous to approach. The revolt of Pougatchef confirmed her in this idea. In the course of a conversation which she had at this time with the head of the excise office, V. Dahl, she expressed the fear that in raising the question there might result a revolution like that in America. She had evidently very vague notions as to what was happening at this moment across the ocean.

'Who knows, however?' she added; 'I have succeeded in so many other things!' In 1775, writing to her Attorney-General, Prince Viazemski, she insisted again on the necessity of doing something for the unhappy serfs, without which 'they will sooner or later take the liberty that we refuse them.' Count Bloudof professes to have seen in the Empress's hands, in 1784, a projected ukase ruling that the serfs born after 1785 should be free. This ukase never saw the light. In the papers of the Empress, found after her death, there is another project concerning the organisation of freedmen, notably the nine hundred thousand serfs who had been emancipated by the secularisation of the ecclesiastical estates. This document has been published in the 20th volume of the *Recueil de la Société d'Histoire* (of Russia). The numerous corrections on the original, written throughout in Catherine's handwriting, prove that she worked over it a long time. She only arrived, however, at the somewhat odd, and probably impracticable, idea of an application of municipal institutions to the very different conditions of rural life. This conception remained equally barren.

There were many reasons why it should be so. In fact, the elevation of Catherine in 1762

had been the work of the nobility, or at least
of the upper classes, and not that of the people.
It was therefore essential that the new Czarina
should stand by this element, and be, in the
first place, sure of it.   Besides, even before her
accession to the throne, the 'philosophical mind'
of Catherine, and her liberalism, did not prevent
her from a certain preference for the old families,
as we see plainly in her memoirs.   In course of
time she substituted little by little for the old
aristocracy of the Narychkines, the Saltykofs,
the Galitzines, an aristocracy of recent creation,
the Orlofs, the Patiomkines.   But this was
merely an exchange.   On the other side, it is
easy to see how a liberal of the stamp of
Diderot could easily, after having examined the
question of Prussian serfdom with the Princess
Dachkof, come to the conclusion that a radical
reform on this point would be premature.   The
observations of the Princess sufficed to shake,
in the mind of the philosopher, convictions
formed and nourished during twenty years.
Probably something of this appeared in the
conversations that Diderot afterwards had with
Catherine herself.   And ten years later, the
Comte de Ségur, having doubtless seen the
peasants through the windows of the imperial
coach, calmly expressed the conviction that their
lot *left nothing to desire.*   Catherine was bound
to end, as indeed she did, by becoming persuaded of it herself.   In her notes on the book
of Radistchef, an avowed and inflexible liberal,
who, in 1790, thought it was still possible to act
on the principles of philosophy, and paid dear
for his error, the Empress goes the length of

declaring, as an incontestable fact, that there is no peasant in the world better treated than the Russian peasant, and no master more kind and humane than a proprietor of serfs in Russia! To know the real truth in the matter, it is needless to go very deeply into the examination of the facts, facts which resemble those of a martyrology. As an example of the humanity shown by the Russian lords to the serfs belonging to them, the Comte de Ségur has pointed in his memoirs to a certain Countess Saltykof. It is an unfortunate instance. The early years of the reign of Catherine were filled with the report of the trial and condemnation of a Countess Daria Saltykof, accused of having put to death, by means of refined tortures, a hundred and thirty-eight of her serfs of both sexes. Seventy-five victims, one of them a girl of fifteen, were proved with certainty by the inquiry. And yet, despite the outcry of popular indignation, which has made the name of the *Saltytchiha* a fearful memory, Catherine dared not do complete justice. The more or less voluntary accomplices of the horrible woman, the pope who presided at the burial of the victims, and the valet who flogged them, received the knout in one of the squares of Moscow; the Countess Saltykof escaped with penal servitude for life. Even this, however, denoted a progress; under the reign of Elizabeth, under that of Peter III., these very facts, universally known, remained unpunished. The knout was brought into play merely upon those who had denounced these abominable crimes!

The case of the *Saltytchiha* was exceptional; the rule, however, was cruel enough. The law appointed no limit to the right of proprietors, in regard to the corporal chastisement of their serfs. It authorised them to send them to Siberia. It was a means of peopling the vast solitudes of the land of exile. Catherine added the power of completing the exile by hard labour. For the rest, the law was dumb, as in the past. And the jurisprudence varied. In 1762 the senate sentenced to transportation a proprietor who had flogged a peasant to death. But in 1761 an identical act was punished merely by religious penance. A curious document has come down to us, a list of punishments inflicted, in the year 1751 and onward, on the estates of Count P. Roumiantsof. It is distressing to read ; a very nightmare. For entering his masters' room while they were asleep, and thus disturbing their sleep, a servant is flogged and *condemned to the loss of his name* : he is to be called only by an insulting nickname, any one infringing this order to suffer *five thousand blows of the stick, without mercy*. Five thousand blows of the stick are, however, far from constituting a maximum. A sort of criminal code, in use on the same estates, includes much severer chastisements. It is further provided that the application of these penalties is not to cause too much inconvenience to the proprietor, by depriving him too long of the labour of the beaten servants. It is ruled that a man who has received seventeen thousand (*sic*) blows of the stick, or a hundred blows of the knout—the two are considered equivalent—*is not to remain in bed more than a week*. If he is longer in rising and returning to work, *he will be deprived of food*.

This code was in force during the reign of Catherine. It corresponds pretty well with the general practice. In fact, after all her contradictory tentatives, Catherine took the initiative in this direction only in two cases, both of them a distinct aggravation of the existing *régime*. In regard to the treatment of the serfs by their masters, by suppressing the right of direct appeal to the sovereign, she suppressed the sole corrective, indeed a very insufficient one, which might, in a certain measure, have attenuated these monstrous abuses. Those who had complaints were sent to their proprietors, that is to say, to the butchers themselves; and there the lash was applied. In 1765 a ukase of the senate substituted for the penalty of the lash that of the knout and hard labour. In 1779 a French painter of the name of Velly, employed to paint the portrait of the Empress, was near making the acquaintance of this new legislation, having taken advantage of a sitting to present a petition to her Majesty. A diplomatic intervention was required to rescue him from the consequences of his false step. In regard to the law of serfdom itself, the great work of Catherine's reign was the introduction of the Russian common law in the ancient Polish provinces of Lesser Russia, that is to say, the transformation of the free peasants into serfs belonging with the soil.

In 1774, in talking with Diderot, who spoke with some disgust of the dirtiness that he had noticed in the peasants round St. Petersburg, the Empress demanded: 'Why should they look after a body which is not their own?' This bitter word, if it was really said, sums up a state of things with which she had finally come to reconcile her humanitarian aspiration.

In 1789, in a series of advertisements in the *Gazette de St.-Pétersbourg* (No. 36), side by side with the offer of a Holstein stallion for sale, we find that of some copies of the *Instruction pour la Commission Législative*, and lower down these lines—

'Any one wishing to buy an entire family, or a young man and a girl separately, may inquire at the silk-washer's, opposite the church of Kasan. The young man, named Ivan, is twenty-one years of age; he is healthy, robust, and can curl a lady's hair. The girl, well-made and healthy, named Marfa, aged fifteen, can do sewing and embroidery. They can be examined, and are to be had at a reasonable price.'

This sums up what Catherine left to her successor by way of result, in regard to her work as legislator.

'As she is ambitious of all sorts of fame,' wrote the Comte de Ségur in 1786, 'she wishes to lay claim, during the peace, to that of legislator; but her subjects have put more obstacles in her way than her enemies, . and she has been forced to acknowledge that it is unfortunately easier to make great conquests than good laws.'

At the same time, sending a memorandum on the general state of the legislation in Russia, the work of his brother, M. d'Aguesseau, he added the following reflections :—

'The result of his work will be one more proof of this truth, that in a land of slaves there can be neither good laws nor good morals, that everything becomes corrupt before being civilised, that there is an inevitable lack of light and help, and that all things betray the irrationality of despotism, even the very measures that are intended to restrain and modify it.'

At the top of his memorandum D'Aguesseau had put this line of Du Bellay: 'Plus je vois l'étranger, plus j'aime ma patrie.'

III

In regard to the administration of justice, Catherine's reign is distinguished by several important reforms, whose merit, however, has been very variously appreciated. Mercier de la Rivière expressed great enthusiasm in regard to an organisation of provincial tribunals put in force after the peace with Turkey in 1774. In the memoirs of a contemporary (Vinski), perhaps a better judge, these tribunals are referred to with not nearly so much praise. The reform has merely put 320 judges where there had formerly been 50, that is to say, in a government divided, according to the new regulations, into four districts with 80 judges each. 'The most obvious result of this benefit to the poor farmer is that instead of three sheep he must now bring fifteen a year to the town,' in order to keep in well with justice. All that, adds Vinski, may be good to dazzle strangers, and make them admire the Semiramis of the North; for us Russians 'it is a mere puppet-play.

Catherine also did her best to quicken the march of justice, always desperately slow. In 1769 a tradesman of Moscow, Popof, having been driven by the exasperating intricacies of procedure into crying aloud in open court that there was no

justice in Russia under the reign of Catherine II.,
the Empress had these audacious words erased
from the minutes of proceedings, but she commanded, at the same time, that the affairs of Popof
should be settled with the greatest despatch,
'so that he might see that there was justice in
Russia.'

The sovereign's zeal was praiseworthy; it produced, as a rule, but little effect. The machine
was too cumbersome for any one hand, even as
energetic as hers, to regulate the heavy wheels.
In 1785 some French shipowners were still
awaiting at St. Petersburg the settlement of
certain indemnities due to them for the losses
they had endured in the first Turkish war. The
Comte de Ségur, who had exerted himself on
their behalf, wrote that he could obtain no more
than a postponement from day to day instead of
from week to week. He added—

'As for the actual debts, I will certainly do
what I can, but I guarantee in advance that it
will be useless. The English minister and I are
convinced by sad experience that it is impossible
here to get the money for letters of credit when
the debtor refuses to pay. The laws are explicit,
but the corruption of the judges, the indolence
of the tribunals, custom and precedent, are always
in his favour. The Empress has at this moment
to decide the case of the Sieur Prory of Lyon,
and the debtor says openly that if it is possible to
make him lose his case, it will be at least quite
impossible to make him pay. This inconceivable
negligence in the execution of the ukases relative
to debts is caused by the general disorder of the
principal people here, who are all in a state of

ruin, and who protect the knavery of the Russian merchants who prop them up.'

The initiative of the Empress, and her supreme right of justice, are frequently put in force, and in the most effectual manner, as we have already intimated, in the mitigation of the excessive severities to which the ordinary jurisdictions still cling. Catherine boasted that she had never signed a death-warrant. She nevertheless allowed both Pougatchef and Mirovitch to be brought to the scaffold. But she employed a subterfuge for these exceptional cases : declaring herself directly implicated in the case of those outrages which were to be punished, she would occasionally renounce her prerogative as high justiciary, in order, as she said, that she might not be at once judge and party. In general, she substituted transportation for capital punishment, and even for the lash. She nevertheless allowed the knout to be sometimes used, even as a means of coercion, in order to obtain the confession of the accused. It must be understood what this kind of torture was. The knout was a whip with a leather thong prepared in such a manner that it possessed at once the elasticity of gutta-percha and the hardness of steel. Wielded by an executioner, who took a spring to strike with greater force, the thong cut into the flesh to the very bone, and left at every blow a deep furrow. A hundred blows were considered the limit, beyond which the resistance, that is to say the life, of the patient, even if exceptionally vigorous, could not go. In general, the 'subjects' lost consciousness at the tenth or fifteenth blow. To continue, was soon to flog a dead body. The skill of the torturer consisted in taking aim, so as to lengthen out the bloody slashes on the patient's back, one by the side of another, without taking away an inch of flesh. At the moment of striking, the *zaplietchnik* (so called because he put the whip-hand behind his shoulder to give more force to the blow) cried to the patient: *Bieriegis!* (Look out! or, literally, get aside) as a last touch of irony. In the torture-chambers the knout was commonly combined with the strappado; the patient was flogged after having been suspended in the air by the arms, which had been pinioned behind the back, so as to put the shoulders out of joint, and cause an intolerable pain.

We know that Catherine was resolutely opposed to the use of torture. Nevertheless, in the course of a trial which lasted from 1765 to 1774, in connection with some fires, the torture was applied three times to the accused.

A legend, of which we cannot verify the source, shows the sovereign, in the part of high justiciary, brought into contact with what is called to-day 'un crime passionnel.' The case is very complicated. A young peasant, the child of rich parents, is in love with a poor young man. Surprised by the father, she hides her lover under the mattress of the common bed; promiscuity in sleeping accommodation being then general in Russia, even among well-to-do people of this class. The father stretches himself on the bed, and the unlucky man is stifled. A neighbour comes in. On hearing what has happened, he takes the corpse and throws it into the sea. But in return he forces the girl to become his mistress. She has a child, whom he also drowns. Then he becomes in want of money, and demands it from the girl, who, in order to satisfy him, steals from her father. Finally, he makes her go with him to the tavern, so that he may parade his conquest. She goes, but, on coming out of the tavern, she sets it on fire. It burns, with all who are in it. She is arrested, and convicted of theft, infanticide, and incendiarism. The tribunals condemn her. Catherine sets her free, restricting her punishment to a religious penance.

IV

It is in the domain of administration, properly so called, that Catherine, from one end to the other of her reign, showed the most sustained, and, to a certain point, the most fruitful activity. She concerned herself with everything. We have a very voluminous personal work of hers on the establishment of manufactures. On the other hand, she takes it into her head, in 1783, to reform the toilette of the lords and ladies of her court, in order to render it less costly : this reform is not at all pleasing to the manufacturers. Elizabeth, we are told by Count Galovkine, in his memoirs, forced the beautiful Narychkine to wear her dresses without a hoop, in order that the charms of her figure did not too much outdo her own beauty. For less personal reasons Catherine had recourse to sumptuary laws, and the Grand Duchess Paul, on returning from Paris, is obliged to send back, without even unpacking them, the marvels that the famous Mademoiselle Bertin had put in her boxes. In general, it must be said, notwithstanding

energy and good intentions, the initiative of
the sovereign is shown in this direction, as
in others, without either consistency or any
particular knowledge of things, fragmentary,
capricious, and at the beck of chance.

'There are too many undertakings in this
empire,' writes the Comte de Ségur, in 1787;
'the disorder that follows on the heels of pre-
cipitation spoils the greater part of the best ideas.
At the same time, there is an attempt to form
a *tiers état*, attract foreign commerce, establish
manufactures of all kinds, extend agriculture,
increase the paper currency, raise the rate of
exchange, build in towns, people deserts, cover
the Black Sea with a new fleet, conquer a neighbouring country, bind down another, and extend
the influence of Russia over all Europe. Certainly
this is undertaking a great deal.'

Catherine, too, had to fight with enormous
difficulties. During the first year of her reign
she discovered that in the Senate, where the
most complex questions regarding the administration of the country were being debated, there was
no map indicating the position of the governmental
centres, whose affairs were settled without the
least notion whether they were on the Black Sea
or the White Sea. She sent a messenger to the
Academy of Sciences with five roubles to bring
one. She worked energetically at the repression
of the many and extravagant abuses which had
crept into the procedure of all the branches of
local government, and Russia is indebted to her
for much serious progress in this respect; yet
there too the task proved to be beyond her
strength. One day she sent an officer of her

guard, Moltchanof, to Moscow, to give a reversion of judgment, and clear up certain official corruptions which had been brought to her notice. Moltchanof required a passport for the journey. Russia has always been the land of passports. He lost three days in going about from office to office in order to obtain one. Meanwhile the delinquents, duly forewarned, had had time to put everything in order. A vast and shameless corruption spreads from top to bottom of the ladder of government. In 1770, during the plague of Moscow, the police officers arranged with the health officers to levy contributions on the rich bourgeois of the city. They were denounced as suspects; the doctor, under pretence of examining them, smeared nitrate of silver over their hands; black spots soon appeared, the supposed plague-stricken people were put in quarantine: if they did not buy themselves out, their houses were pillaged. At St. Petersburg even, a trustworthy witness, the inspector of police, Longpré, sent over from Paris in 1783, on a judicial mission, points out the most shocking disorders: streets unguarded, fires destroying, at every instant, whole quarters of the town, etc. About the same time, the English envoy, Harris, mentions the case of one of his compatriots who, having been robbed of a large sum of money, tries in vain to obtain redress from the under-officers of police, and ends by going to the lieutenant of police in person, whom he finds at ten o'clock in the morning employed in working out combinations with a packet of dirty cards.

One of the most durable, beneficial, and best managed works of Catherine was the

Foundling Asylum, erected in 1763. Privileges
and favours, such as no benevolent institution
ever received before, were granted to this establishment: exemption from taxes and statute-
labour, powers of legal self-government, personal
liberty of inmates, and of those employed in their
care, monopoly of the lottery, share in benefits at
the theatre, etc. A revenue of 50,000 roubles
was assigned by the Empress for the maintenance of the Asylum, while a philanthropist,
Procope Demidof, erected the huge buildings at
his cost. Betzky, appointed director, put into it
his whole fortune (about two millions of francs)
and twenty years of assiduous toil. A work
published by him in 1775, under the title, *Plans
et Statuts des différents Etablissements ordonnés
par l'Impératrice Catherine pour l'Education de
la Jeunesse*, gives a good idea of the greatness of
the scheme. Diderot, who superintended its
translation and publication at the Hague, added
a note in which we find these lines :—

'When time and the steadfastness of this great
sovereign shall have brought (these establishments) to the point of perfection of which they
are all susceptible, and which some have reached,
people will go to Russia for the purpose of seeing
them, as people formerly went to Egypt, Lace-
demon, and Crete, but with a curiosity which
will, I venture to think, be better founded and
better rewarded.'

By this time people are, indeed, beginning to
visit Russia. It is true that it is not precisely
with the object that Diderot prophesied. But,
perhaps we must still wait for the accomplishment
of his prophecy.

V

One side of Catherine's administration presents itself before us under the aspect of a problem defying all solution : this is her financial policy. What the finances of Russia were at her accession she has said in a private journal, of which, unfortunately, a fragment only has been preserved :—

'I found the army stationed in Prussia without pay for the past eight months; in the Treasury 17 millions of roubles of unpaid bonds; a monetary circulation of 100 millions of roubles, of which 40 millions were taken in kind abroad ; almost all the branches of commerce monopolised by private individuals; the excise revenue farmed out for two millions ; a loan of two millions attempted in Holland by the Empress Elizabeth, but without success ; no credit and no confidence abroad ; at home, the peasants in revolt everywhere, and, in certain districts, the proprietors themselves ready to imitate their example.'

This was the result of the *régime* that Peter I. had found in force, and had not attempted to modify, which came from a conglomeration of ideas and traditions, the direct heritage of the Tartar domination, and of the Eastern habit which was summed up, not so much in the squandering, as in the pillage of all the economical resources of the country, and which we have thus characterised, a few years since, in a study of the financial aspect of the great empire—

'Everything that could be taxed was taxed, even to the long beards of the *moujiki*, who found themselves obliged to pay toll at the gates of the towns! To bring in the taxes, those in power resorted to fire and steel, to military warrants, and to ingenuities of torture recom-mended by the experience of centuries. The treasury still remaining empty, the revenues were farmed out, sold, and put up for lottery. Finally, in despair, the whole was taken for the part, the object taxed for the tax, and in 1729 there was established an "office of confiscated goods."'

What does Catherine do with this state of things? She begins by trying to palliate it. She puts the resources of her private purse at the disposition of the state. Then she endeavours to amend the organisation of the public treasury. The capital vice of this organisation is the lack of unity: the finances of the empire are in the hands of different institutions, independent one of another, each acting in a different direction, each seeing which can make the most out of the other. Catherine attempts a unification and a centralisation of these services. Isolated reforms, the suppression of monopolies and indivisible privileges in a certain number of commercial societies, the cancelling of the farming out of the excises, furnish a supplement of receipts. But the sum-total of the revenue remains very low: it is not more than 17 millions of roubles (about 85 millions of francs). Now the question is how to make it even with the new demands of the imperial policy, which would be on a level with that of the great European powers, that of France, which has a budget of five hundred millions of francs, of England, which has one of

twelve million pounds. More than this, Catherine desires to eclipse her rivals in the West.
By her innumerable enterprises at home, by the
pageantry of her court, by her largesses to a
whole crowd of adulators, with which Europe is
soon filled, by the gold which she showers on her
favourites, she desires to efface the memory of
the great king, the *Roi Soleil*, whose dazzling
memory haunts her imagination.

And she well-nigh succeeds! The first Turkish
war costs 47½ millions of roubles. And, after a
few years' respite, she follows up again her great
enterprises abroad with the annexation of the
Crimea, the second Turkish war, the war with
Sweden, the conquest of Poland, the expedition
to Persia, etc. At home the outlay is not less.
Favouritism costs in thirty-four years about 50
millions of roubles. The maintenance of the
court, with its disorder and extravagance, requires enormous sums. From 1762 to 1768 the
keeping up of the palace of Peterhof alone is
debited to the state in 180,000 roubles (900,000
francs), and when the Empress arrives there in
June 1768 she finds everything in absolute dilapidation. The money has all gone elsewhere. In
1796 it is with a budget of about 80 millions of
roubles that Catherine has to meet her liabilities.

And meet them she does. From one end of
her reign to the other she supplies for all. She
pays for everybody and for everything: the
apprenticeship of Alexis Orlof on the fleet in
the Archipelago, the follies of Patiomkine, and
the enthusiasm of Voltaire. She lets the gold
slip through her fingers, and she is never in want,
or never seems to be in want. How? by what

miracle? The explanation is easy to give; but, to understand that explanation, it is needful to penetrate a secret, of which Catherine had (and this was her merit and her great source of strength), if not the profound knowledge, at all events the intuition of genius. In all their struggles with the finances of the empire, it is strange that the governments of the empire never thought, at one time or another, of an expedient which, disastrous as its practice had been in the West, still tempted the fancy. On arriving at power Peter III. did, in fact, decree the foundation of a bank, and the issue of bank-notes for the sum of 5 millions of roubles. The idea of the Emperor did not at first attract the Empress. The paper currency, whose workings she did not exactly understand, did not seem of much use. But, in 1769, the exigencies of the Turkish war overcame her repugnances and scruples, and, from that time, the instrument of her financial power, the magic power which, from 1769 to 1796, sustained the fortune and the fame of the great sovereign, fed the colossal and ever-renewed effort of her reign, and made up for all her prodigalities, was born. In twenty-seven years Catherine issued 137,700,000 roubles'-worth of paper money. Adding 47,739,130 roubles on the one part, and 82,457,426 roubles on the other, for the proceeds of home or foreign loans contracted at the same period, we arrive .at a total of 264,665,556 roubles, or more than a milliard of francs, raised on the public credit. That is how Catherine paid.

VI

There is not much to be said respecting the army in the reign of Catherine. Her reign was warlike; it countenanced neither militarism nor the military spirit. The military spirit lives on discipline, respect for the powers that be, and also ambition. In making Alexis Orlof an admiral and Patiomkine a general in chief, Catherine by no means cultivated these sentiments. In 1772, at the congress of Fokchany, Gregory Orlof, who had never seen a battlefield, assumed the tone of a superior in speaking to Roumiantsof, the con-queror of Kagoul, and was near taking the com-mand in partnership with him. But Roumiantsof only changed rivals. A few years later, he had to retire before a new favourite. When it was no longer commanded by Roumiantsof, and not yet by Souvarof, the army was in general very ill commanded. But the soldier was then as he has since been, as he recently was under the walls of Plewna, and he had before him only the Turks, who were put *hors de combat*, so to speak, before the combat began, by the European tactics; or else the Poles, who, like the Turks, were, in point of view of the art of war, two centuries behind the time. Catherine was careful to avoid fighting with the disciplined troops of the West. When she went against the Swedes, who were never-theless a poor adversary for Russia, she had cause to repent of it. Besides, she conquered cheaply, as Prince Henry of Prussia said. Doubt-less, however, her indomitable energy and her audacity contributed to bring victory to her side.

Competent judges have accused her of having, in all that concerns the military administration, spoilt the work of Peter the Great. In 1763 she sanctioned a reform which put the regiments entirely into the hands of their colonels. Peter had confided the cares of administration to inspectors, employed by a general commissariat, though a commissariat very much centralised. The abandonment of this organisation gave rise to numerous abuses. According to the Comte de Ségur, the Russian army amounted, in 1785, to a fighting force of about five hundred and thirty thousand men, of whom two hundred and thirty thousand were the regular troops. Ségur observed, nevertheless, that the disorder which reigned in the War Office made it impossible to get at the exact figures, and that the official numeration was a little dubious. He added : 'Many colonels have confessed to me that they made from 3000 to 4000 roubles annually out of their infantry regiments, and that those of cavalry brought in 18,000 to their chiefs.' The Comte de Vergennes wrote at the same time · 'The Russian fleets were far from gaining fame by leaving the Baltic. The one which was last seen in the Mediterranean has not left a good reputation. Leghorn complains particularly of the officers, who have bought much and paid for little.'

To sum up, Catherine attempted and began many things ; she achieved hardly any. It was in her nature to go forward without looking at what she left behind her. She left many ruins.

'Before the death of Catherine,' some one has said, 'the greater part of the monuments of her reign were already in *débris.*

There was a demon in her which drove her forward, ever forward, beyond the present hour and the result already attained, without leaving her even the satisfaction of a moment's pause to contemplate the finished work. This demon was perhaps only that of ambition, and of an ambition sometimes poor and trivial. When she had settled the plans and laid the foundations of an edifice, she had a medal struck, and, the medal once struck and put away in her cabinet, she thought no more of what was to be built. The famous marble church, begun in 1780, was still only begun twenty years after.

But perhaps this was the part allotted by Providence to the Czarina, and was it not hers also to carry with her on this headlong course a people whom Peter I. had not succeeded in shaking entirely out of its sleep of ages—a sleeping giant under a shroud of snow—and who needed only to be drawn out of this torpor in order to follow the natural course, a torrent that nothing can intercept, towards a mysterious destiny? And perhaps also Catherine was not entirely at fault when she wrote to Grimm, the day after the day on which was unveiled the monument which she had erected to the great Czar, her predecessor—

'Peter I., seen in the open air, seemed to me to look quite brisk as well as imposing; one would have said he was pleased with the work. For some time I could not look at him fixedly; I felt moved, and when I looked around me I saw that all had tears in their eyes. The face was turned away from the Black Sea, but the pose of his head seemed to say that he could see well enough either way. He was too far away to speak to me, but he seemed to me to have an air of satisfaction, which communicated itself to me, and encouraged me to try to do yet better in the future, if I can.'

CHAPTER III

FOREIGN POLICY

I

THE famous German historian Sybel wrote in 1869 : 'No burning question arises in Germany in our days without our finding some trace of the policy of Catherine II.' This observation might well be generalised and applied to the greater part of Europe. Very ambitious, very feminine, sometimes almost childish, the foreign policy of Catherine was one of universal expansion. The opening of her reign seemed nevertheless to intimate something quite different.

On coming to the throne, the Empress announced herself as a peaceful sovereign, disposed to remain quietly at home if she were not interfered with, desirous, in consequence, of avoiding all conflict with her neighbours, and determined to employ all her activity in the home government of an empire which offered a sufficient field for her spirit of enterprise. This programme corresponded, even from the point of view of international relations, with an ambition which abdicated none of its rights, but which was governed by the most generous inspirations. Writing to Count Kayserling, her ambassador at

Warsaw, Catherine wrote: 'I tell you, in a word, that my aim is to be joined in the bonds of friendship with all the powers, in armed alliance, so that I may always be able to range myself on the side of the oppressed, and in this way become the arbiter of Europe.'

She was not as yet, it is evident, thinking of the spoliation of Poland. She rejected the very idea of conquest. Courland itself did not tempt her. 'I have people enough to render happy,' she said, 'and this little corner of the earth will add nothing to my comfort.' She thought to confirm the treaty of perpetual peace with Turkey. She reduced the fighting force of her army. She was in no haste to fill the vacancies made in her arsenals by the ruinous wars of the preceding reigns. She repeated that it was needful, before all things, to set the country in order and repair the finances.

How did she come to abandon so soon and so entirely this initial point of view? We can cite in this respect a most valuable piece of evidence. The man to whom we owe it is one of those who are the honour of their country, and the frankness of his language is calculated to throw light on this obscure side of Catherine's history; it seems also to indicate that certain sentiments, to-day ignored or discredited in Russia, were not always foreign to noble minds. Some years after the death of Catherine, in a letter addressed to Alexander I., who had just assumed the throne, Count Simon Vorontsof wrote as follows :—

'The late Empress desired peace and desired it to last. . . . Everything was calculated to confirm it. . . . It is Prussia . . . that induced Count

Panine to revoke the ameliorations which had been introduced into the constitution of Poland in order to gain possession of the country with more facility. It is Prussia who persuaded this same minister to insist that all the Polish dissidents should be admitted to all the posts of state, which was impossible without employing violence against the Poles. It was employed, and it was this which formed the confederations, the number of which was carefully concealed from the Empress. Bishops and senators were arrested in full diet and exiled to Russia. Our troops entered Poland, ravaged everything, pursued the confederates into the Turkish provinces, and this violation of territory caused the Turks to declare war against us. It is from the time of this war that we must date the foreign debts, and the creation of paper money at home, two calamities which are the misery of Russia.'

Thus it was Prussia which, in order to gain the assistance of Russia in its Polish policy, drew Catherine into a career of violent and violating enterprises of all kinds in which she found herself caught as in a wheel. This course, nevertheless, was, we incline to believe, inevitable for her in one way or another. Quite apart from Prussia, Catherine had from the first too lofty a notion of her power not to be tempted, one day or another, to make use of it, and too lofty a conception of the part she had to play, not to brush aside any sort of scruples. In October 1762, the court of Denmark having proposed to her to renounce the guardianship of her son, in respect of the Duchy of Holstein, she replied in these characteristic terms—

'The case is perhaps unique that a sovereign empress should be guardian in a fief of empire for her son, but it is stranger still that a woman, who has five hundred thousand men ready to do battle for her ward, should be told that she ought not to be concerned with a *Schvverdt* (*sic*) which can hardly maintain three hundred men.'

It is nevertheless probable, if not certain, that in entering upon the course which was to lead her so far from her first projects of collected and peaceful labour, Catherine did not realise whither she was going, nor that the current was bearing her along, that her first successes had intoxicated her, and that she was thus hurried forward, in her own despite, into a state of war-fever, which rose at times almost to madness, and in which she lost all count of the means at her disposal, and of every consideration of prudence, or, alas! of equity. The Marquis de Virac wrote to the Comte de Vergennes in 1782 : 'Here they snatch at everything, greedily and unthinkingly, which seems likely to add a new glory to the reign of Catherine II. They do not trouble to count the cost; the first thing is to be moving.'

To be moving, no matter how, no matter where, to make a great racket, no matter at what cost, such, in effect, seemed to be the constant concern of Catherine from the time of the first Turkish war onward. Helped by her 'luck,' she reposed on the belief that something for her greater fame and the greater grandeur of her empire would come out of everything. 'The good fortune which crowns all the enterprises of the Russians,' writes the Comte de Vergennes in 1784, 'wraps them, so to speak in a radiant atmosphere, through which they see nothing.' As for political system or general idea at the back of her enterprises, do not ask the Empress for anything of the sort. She will answer 'Cirumstances, conjunctures, and conjectures.' As for conciliating these enterprises with a higher law of morals, of humanity, or of international right, she has no thought of such a thing. 'It is as useless to speak to her of Puffendorf or of Grotius,' writes the English envoy Macartney from St. Petersburg in 1770, 'as if one spoke of Clarke or Tillotson at Constantinople.'

Catherine, moreover, inaugurates, in the conduct of foreign affairs, a rule of personal initiative, which itself cannot but give to them an adventurous turn, for she flings herself into it with her nervous and excitable woman's temperament. She expends, especially at the outset, an extraordinary activity. She dictates herself all the diplomatic correspondence. She soon finds out, it is true, that she cannot manage it all, and that the service suffers by it. She then reserves to herself the most important matters, leaving to the minister, that is to say, to Count Panine, the bulk of the work. She writes on April 1, 1763, to Count Kayserling: 'In future I hope secrecy will be better kept, for I do not choose to take any one into my confidence in regard to what is in the air.' Her predecessors had only short extracts communicated to them from the despatches of her foreign ambassadors. She insists on seeing the originals; she reads and annotates them. These annotations are curious. On the margin of a despatch from Prince Galitzine, her ambassador at Vienna, informing her that the courts of Vienna and of Versailles are inciting the Porte to meddle in the affairs of Poland, she writes : ' He does not keep his eyes open, for he does not know even what the street children know, or else he says less than he knows.' Prince Repnine, writing from Warsaw, that in the course of a conversation with the Prussian ambassador, Baron Goltz, the latter has recognised that the orders of the King, his master, do not seem to him in the interests of his subjects, though they are perhaps in those of the sovereign, she annotates : ' Is there then auy other glory than the good of the subject. These are oddities beyond my pale.' In 1780, on the first visit that he makes to the sovereign, Joseph II. is informed of this method of work, and is amazed at it. Up to the time of this meeting, however, which played a decisive part in the history of Catherine, the influence of Panine, as head of the department of foreign affairs, had been very great. It is this influence which, in spite of wind and tide, in spite even of the personal repugnance of the Empress, had kept her policy in touch with the Prussian alliance. The visit of Joseph brings about a sudden change. Catherine promptly brushes her minister aside in order to form, on her own account, the new alliance which opens new horizons before her on the side of the North Sea. And soon Panine is quite out of the reckoning. A mere clerk, obedient in carrying out the inspirations of the imperial mind, will suffice. One is soon found, excellent for the purpose, Bezborodko. ' Properly speaking, the Empress has no longer a minister,' writes the Marquis de Verac in September 1781.

This personal policy, superior as are the qualities of mind and temper of which Catherine gives proof, is not slow to subject her to numerous failures. There are infatuations, followed by disenchantments equally arbitrary. Fancy has full play, and the woman is too often seen in the place of the sovereign. It is a woman, and an angry woman, who from the 4th to the 9th of July 1796 draws up for Count Budberg, Russian minister at Stockholm, a communication intended to take the King of Sweden to task for thinking of coming to St. Petersburg without entering into an engagement beforehand to marry the grand-daughter of the Empress. Let him stay at home, then, this ill-bred prince! She is tired of all the crotchets that cloud his brain. When one means to do anything, one does not make difficulties at every step. The document, an official document which has to pass through the chancellor's office, is all in this tone. But can it be called a diplomatic communication? One would say rather, a confidential letter to an intimate friend, on whom one pours out all one's wrath and impatience, simply and solely to ease one's nerves. And to make the resemblance complete, there is a postscript. There are even four, each of which says something different, and indeed precisely opposite, to what has just been said by the last; the whole summed up by agreeing, unconditionally and without reserve, to the visit which had been so vigorously objected to at the outset.

At times Catherine realises the action of her temperament on her state policy, and the unbalanced elements that this influence brings into it. *A propos* of her declaration of armed neutrality, issued April 28, 1780, she writes to Grimm : 'You will say that it is *volcanic*, but there was no means of doing otherwise.' She adds a reflection which we have already found her making, and which seems to intimate that she has not forgotten her German origin, but still desires to make what capital out of it she can : '*Denn die Teutschen*,' she says, '*hassen nicht so als wenn die Leute ihnen auf die Nase spielen wollen; das liebte der Herr Wagner auch nicht.*'

But this is only a way of putting things, or, at the most, a proof that she sometimes misjudges the transformation which has taken place in her, and which links her to her adopted country by the deepest fibres of her being; for her foreign and home policy alike are essentially Russian, as is her mode of thinking and feeling, indeed her whole nature. Russian, and not German, are the personal elements of success that she puts at the disposal of her ambition, as are also the defects which hinder their free course. For there is nothing German in this way of rushing forward with one's eyes shut, or dreaming with one's eyes open, which is peculiar to her, this way of leaving reflection and calculation out of the question. It may be said that her success is due to qualities the most precisely opposed to the German temperament. A cold and calculating German would never have undertaken the first Turkish war. 'The army,' writes Count Simon Vorontsof, 'was reduced, imperfect, and scattered all over the empire. It had to march in the depth of winter against the Turkish frontier, and the cannons, mortars, bombs, and explosives had to be sent with the greatest possible speed from the arsenal at St. Petersburg to Kief.' When the second Turkish war and the Swedish war broke out, it was worse still. In 1783 the rupture with the Porte being imminent, a regiment of dragoons, which should have consisted of 1200 to 1500 men, was summoned from Esthonia. Only 700 men were to be found, with 300 horses, and not a single saddle. Catherine was by no means daunted. She had the faith which scorns obstacles, and will not admit impossibilities. This faith, which removes mountains, and sets cannons travelling from one end to the other of an empire some thousand miles in length, is not a German quality.

Meanwhile, in the domain of foreign politics, Catherine accomplished great things with means which the constant illusion in which she lived doubled or tripled in her eyes, but which were really most moderate. She supplied their lack by her moral force, which was immense.

From the point of view of the administration of the department of foreign affairs, she brought a distinct progress to Russia. Nothing daunted by the labour of which Frederick alone among contemporary sovereigns showed himself careful and capable, and adding to it the authority that she always carried with her, she gave to the administration of this department a unity of direction that it had never yet had. At the same time she insisted on habits of probity and professional dignity quite alien to the modes of a not very distant past. In June 1793 the

English ambassador Buckingham, urging upon the chancellor Vorontsof the conclusion of a treaty of commerce, thought it quite natural to supplement his demand by the offer of a personal gratuity of £2000. But Vorontsof at once replied : ' I leave it to those who are well versed in these shameful traffickings to decide whether 2000 or 200,000 pieces would balance the sale of my sovereign's interests.' Bestoujef, the chancellor of Elizabeth, did not speak this language.

BOOK III

THE FRIEND OF THE PHILOSOPHERS

CHAPTER I

LITERARY AND ARTISTIC TASTES

I

Count Hordt, a Swede, serving in the Prussian army, has left some interesting notes on his visit to St. Petersburg. The first five months of it were spent in prison. This was under the reign of Elizabeth. Peter, on coming to the throne, liberated the prisoner and invited him to dinner.

'Were you well treated in your captivity?' asked the Emperor. 'Don't be afraid to tell me.'

'Very ill-treated,' replied the Swede. 'I had not even any books.'

At that a voice was heard, saying loudly · 'That was barbarous indeed.' It was the voice of Catherine.

We shall endeavour to show what were the relations, so often commented upon, but still so little really known, between the Empress and those who were the main instruments of her European fame. Voltaire and his rivals in the honour and adulation of the 'Semiramis of the

330

North' demand a separate study. We shall here concern ourselves with Catherine alone.

She loved books, as she has abundantly proved. Her purchase of Diderot's library is well known Dorat has celebrated this acquisition in an epistle in verse which figures in the edition of his *Œuvres Choisis*, embellished with a vignette in which are seen little Loves dressed in furs and travelling in sledges. Diderot asked 15,000 francs for his treasure. The Empress offered him 16,000, on condition that the great writer should remain in possession to the time of his death. Diderot thus became, without leaving Paris, librarian of Catherine the Great in his own library. For this he had a pension of 1000 francs a year. It was to commence in 1765. The following year the pension was not paid. This was then the common lot of pensions and pensioners, not only in Russia. On hearing of it from Betzky, Catherine wrote through him to her librarian that she did not wish 'the negligence of an official to cause any disturbance to *her library*, and, for this reason, she would send to M. Diderot for fifty years in advance the amount destined to the maintenance and increase of *her books*, and at the expiration of that period, she would take further measures.' A bill of exchange for 25,000 francs accompanied the letter.

One can imagine the transports of enthusiasm in the philosophic camp. Later on, the library of Voltaire joined that of Diderot in the Hermitage collection. It was Grimm who, after the death of the patriarch of Ferney, arranged with Madame Denis for this new acquisition. The

conditions were, 'a certain sum' at the discretion
of the Empress, and a statue of Voltaire which she
would place in one of the rooms of her palace.
Madame Denis relied on the generosity of
Catherine, so much belauded by the illustrious
dead and by his friends, and Catherine was resolved, as Grimm expresses it, 'to avenge the
ashes of the greatest of philosophers from the
insults that he had received in his own country.'
The great man's relatives, his grand-nephews
particularly, MM. Mignot and d'Hornoy, protested against the transaction, which, they considered, infringed upon their rights and upon
those of France. M. d'Hornoy even attempted
to procure an official intervention. But the
Empress held to her bargain. Voltaire's books
now form part of the Imperial Library, to which
they have been removed from the palace of the
Hermitage. A special room is assigned to them.
In the middle is the statue of Houdon, a replica,
from the hand of the master, of the one in the
foyer of the Comédie Française at Paris. There
are about 7000 volumes, the greater part half-
bound in red morocco. Every volume contains
annotations in Voltaire's handwriting.

One need not be a Frenchman to feel, on
entering this room, the indefinable sensation
caused by the sight of things which are not in
their proper place. These relics, the monument
of one of the greatest glories of France, should
assuredly not be here.

These were not, however, the largest part of
the additions to the imposing collection of printed
books and manuscripts with which Catherine
endowed Russia. The king Stanislas Ponia-

towski was, we know, a cultivated man. On arriving at the throne, he endeavoured to satisfy his tastes and to share them with his fellow-citizens. The capital of Poland profited by this. It had already a considerable library, founded in 1745 by two brothers, who were distinguished savans and good citizens, the Zaluskis. Ponia-towski enlarged it. On taking possession of Warsaw, Catherine transported the king to St. Petersburg, and the library along with him. Having no longer any political independence, the Poles were supposed to have no longer any need of books.

Thus Catherine loved books : did she equally love literature ? The question may seem strange. It demands an answer, nevertheless. The reign of Catherine corresponds, in the history of literary development in Russia, to a well-marked epoch. The preceding epoch, dominated by the great figure of Lomonossof, stands out clearly. It was, during the lifetime of Elizabeth and for some years after her death, a period of absorption and assimilation of foreign elements *en masse*. Euro-pean culture entered into the national life by the door, one might say rather by the breach that Peter the Great had hewed open. A period of reaction and of struggle followed. The national genius, submerged, trampled upon, oppressed, revolted and demanded back its rights. It came finally to treat foreign litera-ture and science as enemies. The poet Dier-javine, and the satirical journalist and thinker Novikof, were the heroes of this campaign of liberation. What part was played in this crisis by Catherine ? We know what she did with

Novikof: she broke his pen and his life; fifteen years of imprisonment were the last reward that she gave to his labours. She treated Dierjavine worse still: she made him a *tchinovnik* and an abject courtier.

For all this there is a reason. Catherine's was an intelligence specially, and, so to speak, solely organised for politics and the government of men. She is a little German princess, who, at the age of fourteen, comes to Russia with the idea that she will be one day the absolute mistress of this immense empire, and who has conscientiously applied herself to prepare for the part she will have to play, a part, judging by the examples before her, which has nothing in common with that of a literary Mecaenas. Consequently, all her ideas, all her tastes, are subordinated to this definite conception of her destiny, and of the rights and duties resulting from it. What she appreciates in Voltaire, when the fame and the books of Voltaire reach her, is not the charm of style—does she even know what style is?—but the support that the prose, good or bad, of the author, his poetry, melodious and full of sentiment, or dry and hard to the ear, might afford to the development of the programme of government that she has vaguely mapped out in her mind. She has no sense of harmony, and, beyond her family relations and her love-episodes, she pays little heed to sentiment. At one moment, at the beginning of her reign, influenced a little by her reading and a great deal by her friend of some years' standing, Princess Dachkof, she is wishful to take part in the artistic, scientific, and literary movement which she perceives about her. She flings herself into the *mêlée* with the ardour she puts into everything. She becomes a writer. She becomes a journalist. But we know already the lamentable shipwreck of her liberal ideas. And what happens to her ideas happens also to her tastes. All the love she may have ever had for letters founders in this disaster, which even the glory of Voltaire does not survive.

But let us first look at her tastes. Voltaire apart, French literature, the only literature with which she is familiar up to a late period of her life, is far from attracting her as a whole. She makes her selection, and what she selects are the works of Le Sage, and those of Molière and Corneille. After studying Voltaire, she has en- joyed Rabelais, and even Scarron. But she has gone back upon her tastes in this direction, only remembering them with a sort of shame that she has ever had them. As for Racine, she simply does not understand him. He is too literary for her. Literature with him is art for art's sake, and art for art's sake, to Catherine, is nonsense. When she applies herself to the task of writing comedies and tragedies, she does not for an instant dream of making a work of art : what she does is criticism, satire, and, above all, politics. She attacks the prejudices and vices that she perceives in the morals of the country, the ideas, and even the men, that offend her. She makes war upon the *Martinists*, and occa- sionally upon the King of Sweden. Literature, to her, is merely a branch of her military and repressive powers. Rhetoric, for her, does not exist : she replaces it by logic and her authority as *samodierjitsa*, ruler of forty millions of men.

She, nevertheless, makes a solitary choice in the work of Racine: she likes *Mithridate*. One sees why.

Still her disputatious instincts and her moralising intentions come in collision with continual obstacles in the surroundings in which she lives. The incident in connection with Sedaine is characteristic in this respect. She had liked Sedaine for his simple gaiety, and the easy flow of his couplets, so pleasantly brought out by the music of Philidor. This pupil of Montesquieu and of Voltaire had a taste for comic opera. In 1779 it occurred to her to utilise, after her own fashion, the talent of the witty and prolific writer. Why should he not compose, on her lines, and for her theatre at the Hermitage, a comedy which might follow up her own satirical pieces? Urged on by Grimm, encouraged by Diderot, Sedaine composes a piece, *L'Épreuve Inutile*. 'Tell him,' writes Catherine immediately to Grimm, 'that if instead of one, two, or three pieces, he were to do a hundred, I would read them all with the greatest eagerness. You know that, after the Patriarch, there is no one whose writing I like so much as Sedaine's.' But Betzky, who has read the piece aloud to his august benefactress, is much less enthusiastic. He points out 'that the piece, if it were played before the court, would give umbrage to the spectators, and that the master plays a very small part in it.' Catherine at first rebukes these timid objections; she intends to have the piece acted, 'if it were only to show that she has more credit herself than Raymond.' Betzky insists; he considers such a tentative not merely useless, but dangerous; and the Empress finally comes round to his point of view. She tells Sedaine that she thinks his play 'good, very good'; she sends him 12,000 francs for his trouble, but she informs him that his masterpiece will not be acted, 'from precaution.' *L'Epreuve Inutile* does not even receive the honours of print. We are unaware if it was preserved in manuscript.

Some years later a polemical writer of quite other range appeared on the scene, before a public at first surprised and terrified, but soon in great part won over, and doing all that could be done to atone for its first scandal by the vehemence of its present applause. Catherine ranges herself on the side of those whom the new work still continues to shock or frighten.

'If I ever write a comedy,' she says, 'I shall certainly not take the *Mariage de Figaro* as a model, for, after *Jonathan Wild*, I have never found myself in such bad company as at this celebrated marriage. It is apparently with an idea of imitating the ancients that the theatre has recurred to this taste, from which it had seemed to be purified. The expressions of Moliére were free, and bubbled up like effervescence from a natural gaiety, but his thought is never vicious, while in this popular play the undertone is constantly unworthy, and it goes on for three hours and a half. Besides that, it is a mere web of intrigues, in which there is a continual effort, and not a scrap of what is natural. I never laughed once all the time I was reading it.'

But Catherine's business is not to play the part of a critic, it is to govern Russia, and what Russia needed at this period was assuredly not

to be set in the van of European progress, intellectual and artistic; it was to follow, at a great
distance, those who were ahead, to try to come
up with them, not by a servile imitation, but
doubtless by finding inspiration in them for the
development of the original resources of the
national genius. What did Catherine do to help
on this event, as was her duty and even her
ambition in the radiant days when she accepted
the title of 'the Semiramis of the North,' and
Voltaire declared that the sun seemed to have
taken to shining on the world from another
quarter? We hold with those who think that
the best way of protecting literature that can be
found by a ruler, is to leave it alone without
interfering in its concerns. Such was not the
opinion of Catherine. She wished to assert, in
this as in all other domains, her personal initiative and her supreme command. She professed
in vain to have 'a republican soul'; the republic
of letters was transformed in her eyes into a
monarchy governed by her despotic will. Did
she, however, bring to light a force, a glory, or
did she even aid the outcome of a new period in
letters, which could balance the merit and the
reputation of the writers of whom the reign of
Elizabeth could legitimately boast? We cannot
see that she did. No name of the importance
of Lomonossof and Soumarokof, whose fame
belongs to the former reign, can be found in hers.
Catherine confined herself to making the most of
this heritage, always for her own personal interests,
which were far from being those of art and
literature. Lomonossof, now grown old, served
as a sort of figure-head; Soumarokof, with his

imitations of the French dramatists, was sufficiently good as a set-off. There was perhaps in
Dierjavine the making of a great poet ; she sees
nothing of it in him, and in time he ceases to see
it in himself. *Felitsa*, the poem on which his
literary reputation rests, is merely a pamphlet
done to order, half panegyric, half satire. The
panegyric, we need not say, is for the Empress ;
the satire for the court nobles, to whom Catherine
desires to read a lesson, and to whom she sends
copies of the work, with the passages concerning
them carefully underlined. At the end of the
reign the author of *Felitsa* is a mere buffoon,
wallowing in the antechambers of the favourite,
Plato Zoubof. The serious rivals of Lomonossof,
—those who try to react against the current
of foreign importation, by which Soumarokof is
carried along, Kherasskof too, in his *Rossiade*,
and Bogdanovitch, in his *Douchenka*, made up
from the insipidities of the centuries on the
subject of the loves of Psyche—Kniajnine, Von-
Visine, Loukine, add some interesting plays to
the national drama. Kniajnine writes the *Fan-
faron*, a comedy which remains one of the classics
of Russian literature, and, in *Vadime à Novgorod*, attempts the historical drama, drawn from
the fresh sources of national tradition. Von-
Visine, the Russian Moliére, ridicules in his
Brigadier the acquirements of Muscovite Tris-
sotins, founded on the reading of French novels ;
and, in his *Dadais*, takes off the educators of
aristocratic youth, brought at great expense from
abroad. But. this national drama is not that of
Catherine. She never visits it, until in her later
years, when the whim takes her, or rather she finds

it good policy, to be interested in the dramatisa-
tion of scenes taken from the history of the
country

Meanwhile, literature, national or otherwise,
feels itself so little under her protection, that the
contributors to the *Sobiessiednik*, founded by the
Princess Dachkof, dare not sign their articles,
even though they are aware that the Empress
herself is one of their number. They are not
unwise, if one may recall the fate of Prince
Bielossielski, who wrote so charming an 'Epistle
to France,' won so flattering a reply from Voltaire
on 'the laurels thrown to his compatriots and
falling back upon himself,' and who, then being
Minister at Turin, was recalled in disgrace, for no
reason but that he was a man of wit, that he
showed it in his despatches, and that he turned
agreeable verse. Kniajnine, too, knew what it
cost to cultivate the national drama. His *Vadime
à Novgorod* was torn up by order of the
Empress, and came near being burnt by the
public executioner.

An Academy, founded in 1783 on the model of
the French Academy, under the inspiration of
the Princess Dachkof, is the sole monument that
Russian literature owes to a sovereign to whom
Russia owes so much in other respects. To this
Academy was confided the mission of fixing the
rules of orthography, the grammar and prosody,
of the Russian language, and of encouraging the
study of history. It began, one need hardly say,
by undertaking a dictionary, to which Catherine
herself contributed.

II

'Tragedy offends her, comedy bores her, she does not care for music, her *cuisine* is quite unstudied; in gardens she cares only for roses; she has, in short, no taste for anything but for building and for domineering over her court—for what she has for reigning, and figuring in the world, is a passion.'

It is thus that Durand, the French *chargé-d'affaires*, summed up, in 1773, the intellectual position of Catherine the Great. His observation was correct, especially from the artistic point of view. Was it lack of knowledge in her, or lack of natural disposition? It was as much the one as the other. She herself was well aware of it. In 1767, when Falconet submitted to her judgment the design for the statue of Peter the Great, she excused herself from passing an opinion; she understood nothing about it, and she recommended the artist to the judgment of his own conscience and of posterity. Falconet was foolish enough to insist—

'My posterity is your Majesty. The other may come when it will.'

'Not at all,' replied Catherine. 'How can you submit yourself to my opinion? I do not even know how to draw. This is perhaps the first good statue I have ever seen in my life. The merest school-boy knows more about your art than I do.'

We often find in her mouth, and in her writing, this *parti pris* of incompetence and self-abnegation, so alien from the general tendency of her mind and temperament.

She has an opera for which the best singers are sought all over Europe. She pays heavy incomes to the 'stars,' whose demands at that time were without limit. But she acknowledges that all this expense is not in the least for her own pleasure. 'In music,' she writes, 'I am no more advanced than formerly. I can recognise no tones but those of my nine dogs, who in turn share the honour of being in my room, and whose individual voices I can recognise from a distance; the music of Galuppi and Paisiello I hear, and I am astonished at the tones that it combines, but I cannot recognise them at all.'

Nevertheless, certain comic operas of Paisiello succeed in charming her. She has a sense and taste for the grotesque. She is enchanted by the *Pulmonia*, and even remembers some of the airs, which she hums over when she happens to meet the *maestro*.

Sometimes, too, even in the domain of art, where she feels so out of place, her despotic instincts claim their rights; and, as if by miracle, she has certain inspirations which are not without a certain savour. Here is a letter, written at the time of her first triumphs over Turkey—

'Since you speak to me of festivities in honour of the peace, listen to what I am going to say, and do not believe a word of the absurdities of the gazettes. The original project was like that of all festivities: temple of Janus, temple of Bacchus, temple of the Devil and his grandmother, stupid and intolerable allegories, because they were gigantic, and because not to have common sense was supposed to be an effort of genius. Disgusted with all these fine and mighty

plans, which I positively would not have, one fine
day I summon M. Bajenof, my architect, and .I
say to him : My friend, three versts from the city
there is a meadow ; imagine that this meadow is
the Black Sea ; that there are two roads leading
to it from the city ; well, one of these roads shall
be the Tanaïs, the other the Borysthène : at the
mouth of the first you will build a banqueting-
hall, that you will name Azof; at the mouth of
the other you will build a theatre, that you will.
name Kinburn ; you will trace out with sand the
peninsula of the Crimea ; you will there enclose
Kertch and Iénicalé, as ball-rooms ; on the left of
the Tanaïs you will place buffets of wine and
eatables for the people ; opposite to the Crimea
you will have illuminations which will represent
the joy of the two empires over the re-establishment of peace ; on the other side of the Danube
you will have the fireworks, and on the land
which is supposed to be the Black Sea' you
will place illuminated ships and boats ; you will
garnish the banks of the rivers which serve as
roads with landscapes, mills, trees, houses, all lit
up ; and there you will have a *fête* without anything imaginary in it, but perhaps as good as
many others, and much more natural.'

There is something, indeed, very natural and
charming in this plan of a *fête*, but there is also
a stroke of policy. There is always this in everything that Catherine thinks and does. All her
prepossessions, artistic and literary included, tend
in this direction. She accumulates in her Hermitage considerable artistic collections, but she
confesses that it is not for love of the things of
beauty that are heaped up in the galleries and

cabinets that she prepares expressly for them. One cannot delight in what one does not understand, and she does not understand in what consists the merit of a fine picture or of a fine statue. She admits that it is part of the glory of a great sovereign to have these things in his palace. All her famous predecessors, all the monarchs in history whose renown she envies or seeks, Louis XIV. at their head, have had them. But she hits on a word which, coming from any one but herself, would have the air of a cruel epigram, but which characterises the purchases, very extensive during the first part of her reign in particular, to which she submits in order to carry out this part of her programme of imperial magnificence. 'It is not love of art,' she says, 'it is voracity. I am not an amateur, I am a glutton.' In 1768 she buys for 180,000 roubles the famous Dresden gallery of Count Brühl, ex-Minister of the King of Poland. In 1772 she purchases, at Paris, the Crozat collection. In reference to this Diderot writes to Falconet: 'Ah, my friend Falconet, how things have changed! We sell our pictures and our statues in time of peace; Catherine buys them in time of war. The sciences, the arts, taste, and wisdom, all make for the North, and barbarism with its attendant train comes down upon the South. I have just carried through an important affair: the acquisition of the collection of Crozat, increased by his descendants, and known to-day under the name of the gallery of the Baron de Thiers. There are Raphaels, Guidos, Poussins, Van Dycks, Schidones, Carlo Lottis, Rembrandts, Wouvermans, Teniers, etc., to the number of about eleven hundred. It has cost her Imperial Majesty 460,000 francs. That is not half its value.'

Her usual good luck accompanied Catherine in these proceedings. Three months later, fifty pictures of not greater worth were sold for 440,000 francs at the sale of the Duc de Choiseul's collection. She herself paid 30,000 francs to Mme. Geoffrin for two pictures of Van Loo, *La Conversation Espagnole* and *La Lecture Espagnole*. It is true that this is, perhaps, on her part, a way of establishing friendly relations with the influential matron, who gains on the bargain two-thirds of the amount. She has one misfortune, in 1771, with the Braancamp collection, bought in Holland for 60,000 écus, which goes down on the coast of Finland with the vessel that brings it. But, says Catherine, there is only 60,000 écus lost. She can easily make up for the rest. She buys *en bloc* the engraved gems of the Duc d'Orléans. Through Grimm and Diderot she sends order after order to French artists : from Chardin and Vernet she demands landscapes; from Houdon a Diana (which has been refused admittance at the Louvre, on the ground that it is too little clothed); from Vien, a ceiling for the grand staircase at Tzarskoïe-Sielo; from the painter on enamel, De Mailly, an artistic inkstand for the room of the Order of St. George, for which he charges 36,000 francs, and which he executes very unwillingly, and only on being forced to do so by an intervention of Government. In 1778 she has copies made at Rome, by Gunterberger and Reiffenstein, of the frescoes of Raphael in the Vatican; and she has a gallery erected at the Hermitage with panels of the same dimension to receive these copies, which, being done on canvas, have been since utilised in the reconstruction of the palace. They can still be seen there. In 1790, in sending to Grimm her portrait, 'in a fur cap,' she writes : ' Here is something for your museum ; mine, at the Hermitage, consists of pictures, the panels of Raphael, 38,000 books, four rooms filled with books and prints, 10,000 engraved gems, nearly 10,000 drawings, and a cabinet of natural history contained in two large rooms. All that is accompanied by a charming theatre, admirably adapted for seeing and hearing, and also as to seating accommodation, and with no draughts. My little retreat is so situated that to go there and back from my room is just 3000 paces. There I walk about in the midst of a quantity of things that I love and delight in, and these winter walks are what keep me in health and on foot.'

All that is her own doing. In accomplishing it she has had to fight with serious difficulties, for, though she may make gold at will, her power in this respect is unlimited only within the limits of her empire—outside, the paper money loses too much in change. Thus, from the year 1781 she feels obliged to use moderation. She writes to Grimm : ' I renew my resolution to buy nothing more, not a picture, nothing ; I want nothing more, and consequently I give up the Correggio of "the divine."' That is indeed a 'glutton's' vow, as valid as a drunkard's! A veritable conflict commences, from this moment, in the mind of Catherine, between her desires as a collector, now á passion with her, and her forced instincts of economy. It is not the latter that most generally win the day. The letter to Grimm that we have just cited is dated March 29; on the 14th of April we find in the correspondence of the Empress with her art-purveyor this passage: 'If "the divine" [Reiffenstein] would send her, direct to St. Petersburg, some very very fine old cameos, in one, two, or three colours, in perfect state and keeping, we should be infinitely obliged to those who would procure them for us. That is not to be called a purchase, but what is one to do?' And on the 23rd she writes: 'Now, you may say what you like, you may rail at me as you please, but I must have two copies of coloured prints, according to the list I am going to give you . . . for we are gluttons, and so gluttonous for everything of that kind, that there is no longer a house in St. Petersburg where one can decently live if it does not contain something faintly resembling the panels, the Eternal Father, or the whole string that I have enumerated.'

'Lord, one would say that the good resolutions of Thine anointed are wavering!' observes Grimm maliciously in his reply. He has his doubts, too, as to what has provoked this return of 'gluttony.' In using the collective pronoun 'us,' Catherine does not use the plural instead of the singular by a mere trick of speech. The 'gluttons' of whom she speaks are indeed two at present. After the favourite Korssakof, who was a mere boor, has come, since the end of 1780, the handsome Lanskoï, who is a man of education and refined tastes. And the handsome Lanskoï has a real passion for prints and cameos. In July 1781, sending Grimm new orders for purchases, Catherine explains that these are not for her, 'but for gluttons who have become gluttons through knowing me.' The money is certainly hers, that is to say, Russia's. In 1784 she renews her resolution of buying nothing more, 'being poor as church mice.' But Lanskoï sends 50,000 francs to Grimm 'for the purchase of a cabinet of pictures,' and promises a further amount shortly. This new course of things goes on for some time. In 1784, it is true, there is a momentary pause : Catherine will have no more cameos, nor anything of the kind. Lanskoï is dead, and with him is dead also the taste for things which, as she frankly confesses, she does not understand a bit. But in April 1785 it begins again. What has happened ? Mamonof has taken the place of Lanskoï, and with the place he seems to have inherited the artistic tastes of the deceased. It is not till 1794 that this intermittent fever comes finally to an end. 'I shall not buy anything more,' says Catherine, on January 13. 'I must pay my debts and save up money ; so refuse all the bargains that are offered you.' It is Plato Zoubof who reigns now, and Zoubof cares for nothing engraved save the gold circles bearing the effigy of his imperial mistress.

Up to now the Empress has not merely been increasing her collections ; she has also been building. We should say, she has especially been building. And this time the pleasure has all been her own, as Durand intimated in 1773. We have seen what the Prince de Ligne thought of the sovereign's taste and knowledge in regard to architecture. But in default of judgment and

sense of proportion she has at least plenty of
spirit. She replaces artistic sense by enthusiasm,
and quality by quantity. 'You know,' she
writes in 1779, 'that the mania of building is
stronger with us than ever, and no earthquake
ever demolished so many buildings as we have
set up.' She adds in German these sad reflections : 'The mania of building is an infernal
thing; it runs away with money, and the more
one builds, the more one wants to build; it is a
disease, like drunkenness.'

At this moment she sends to Rome for two
architects—Giacomo Trombara and Geronino
Quarenghi. She thus explains her choice: 'I
want Italians because our Frenchmen know too
much, and make horrid houses, inside and out,
because they know too much.' Always the same
contempt for care, the same *penchant* for impro-
visation! She nevertheless frequently consults
the learned Clérisseau, who sends her plans of
palaces in the Roman style. Perronnet furnishes
her with the scheme of a bridge over the Neva;
Bourgeois de Chateaublanc, another of a light-
house for the shores of the Baltic. In 1765 she
demands of Vassé a design for an audience-
chamber 120 feet long and 62 high.

With all that, does she give good cause to
artists, whether architects, painters, or sculptors,
to praise her treatment of them? Let us not ask
Falconet, on his return from St. Petersburg; his
reply would be too bitter. We shall have to speak
elsewhere of the visit to the capital of the North of
the man to whom the city of Peter the Great and
of Catherine owes to this very moment its finest
ornament. We shall try also to show what were

his relations with the sovereign, beginning, on her part, with more than courtesy, and ending with more than indifference. Let us say here that, not having the least comprehension of artistic things, Catherine could not in any way be likely to understand the soul of an artist. Falconet pleased her at first by his original and somewhat paradoxical turn of mind, still more perhaps by the oddities of his disposition; she soon grew tired, and finally impatient of him. He was too much of an artist for her liking. She had always her own way of interpreting the part to be played in the world by the men of talent whom she wished to employ in improving her capital. She frankly confesses it in one of her letters to Grimm: '*Si il signor marchese del Grimmo volio mi fare* [*sic*] a pleasure, he will have the goodness to write to the divine Reiffenstein to look me out two good architects, Italians by birth and skilled in their profession, whom he will engage in the service of her Imperial Majesty of Russia for so many years, and whom he will send from Rome to St. Petersburg *like a bundle of tools*.' Tools—it is just that; tools that one uses, and then throws away when they are done with, or one finds better and handier ones at hand. It was thus that she did with Falconet. She gives this further piece of advice to Grimm: 'He will choose honest and reasonable people, not dreamers like Falconet; people who walk on the earth, not in the air.' She will have nothing aspiring. 'A Michael Angelo,' it has been justly said, 'would never have remained three weeks at the court of Catherine.' To remain there nearly twelve years, required in Falconet an extraordinary power of resistance, and a veritable passion for the work he had begun, into which he had put all his soul. But when at last he went, he was broken down. Apart from him, Catherine did not keep by her any foreign artists who were not mediocrities : Brompton, an English painter, a pupil of Mengs, and Koenig, a German sculptor. Brompton paints allegories which delight the sovereign, for they are political allegories. 'He has painted my two grandsons, and it is a charming picture : the elder amuses himself by cutting the Gordian knot, and the other has proudly put the flag of Constantine about his shoulders.' Koenig does a bust of Patiomkine. Mme. Vigée-Lebrun, arriving at St. Petersburg in 1795 with an achieved reputation, meets with a flattering reception everywhere but at the court —Catherine finds little pleasure in her society, and considers her pictures so bad 'that one must have a very distorted sense of things to paint like that.'

And the Russian artists—what does she do in this respect? Does she try to discover native talent, to encourage it, and bring it to the front? The list of national glories, contemporaneous with her reign, is easy to establish in this sphere. There is Scorodoumof, an engraver, who had studied art in France, and whom she sent for at Paris in 1782, in order to take him into her service ; and whom a traveller, Fortia de Piles, found, a few years later, in an empty studio, engaged in polishing a copper plate for a wretched design done to order : he explained that there was not a workman in St. Petersburg capable of doing this kind of work ; was astonished that a stranger took any interest in what he was doing; was quite resigned to the low uses of his profession. There is Choubine, a sculptor, discovered by the same visitor in a narrow room, without models, without pupils, with only one order, a bust, for which an admiral has offered him 100 roubles, the marble itself costing 80 roubles, which he has to take out of the price. There is, lastly, the painter Lossienko. Here is what Falconet says of him: 'The poor fellow, starving and in the depths of misery, wishing to live anywhere but at St. Petersburg, came and told me all his troubles; then, sinking into drunkenness in his despair, he little knew what he would gain by dying: we read on his tombstone *that he was a great man!*'

The glory of Catherine wanted one great man the more, and she had him cheaply. The artist once dead, she willingly added his apotheosis to all her grandeurs. She had not taken any pains to keep him alive. All her artistic ideas reduce themselves, in the last resort, to a question of show. And, for this object, the 'divine' Reiffenstein, whose name is known all over Europe, is obviously worth more than the poor Lossienko, though he was no more than a good copyist. National art, in short, owes to Catherine some models furnished by her to the study and emulation of Russian artists. Beyond that, she did not give it so much as a morsel of bread.

CHAPTER II

CATHERINE AS A WRITER

I

DURAND certainly made a mistake in his reckoning when giving his list of the things in which Catherine took pleasure. He forgot one at least of her favourite pastimes: she liked to write. We do not believe there was anything she liked so much. It was not only a taste in her—it was in some sort a necessity, almost a physical necessity. It seems that the mere fact of holding a pen in her hand, and having before her a white sheet of paper, on which she can set her fancy roving, gives her a pleasant sensation, not only mental, but like a thrill of physical delight. She says herself, in one of her letters to Grimm, that the sight of a new pen makes her fingers itch. She never dictates. 'I do not know how to dictate,' she says. All that she writes is written with her own hand, and what does she not write? Besides her political correspondence, which is very active, and her private correspondence, which, with the enormous budgets sent regularly to Grimm, attains huge proportions; besides her work in regard to signatures, to reports sent in to her, which she covers with marginal notes, to her dramatic and other compositions, she writes much and often for herself, for her own satisfaction, sometimes for no apparent reason, unless for that of calming that itching of the fingers. She makes extracts from old chronicles relating to the life and glorious actions of St. Sergius, in which we cannot imagine that she has any particular interest. She works at copying the old church Sclavonic, an acquaintance with which would not seem to be indispensable to her duties as Orthodox sovereign. She cannot read a book without covering the margins with her great scrawling writing. She draws up plans for *fêtes* and programmes for concerts. Contrary to that statesman of our days who could only think when he was talking, one might say of her that she could only think when writing. So, like the other with his words, she was carried away by what she wrote. Her pen ran away with her thought, and sent it astray. She was well aware of it herself. She wrote to Grimm—

'I was going to say that I would write for you, so much in the scribbling mood am I; but I recollect that I am here and you in Paris. I advise you to dictate, for I have been advised a hundred times to do so myself: happy is the man who can do so; for my part, it would be impossible to talk nonsense with the pen of another. . . . If I said to this other what flows from my pen, he would often not write what I said.'

How does she find the time to write all that she writes? She rises at six o'clock in the morning to chat at her ease with her confidant, pen in hand. Despite these laborious habits, the question remains for us an enigma. On May 7, 1767, the Empress, on a voyage of inspection, finds herself on the Volga in 'frightful' weather. She takes the opportunity to write a long letter to Marmontel, who has just sent her his *Bélisaire*. It is miraculous. Note that, thinking and writing being the same thing to her, and her inaptitude to precede the manual labour of putting things down by the intellectual labour of putting them together being complete, she goes over and over again anything to which she attaches much importance. We have thus two rough drafts of a letter addressed by her in 1768 to the Academy of Berlin, which had offered her the title of honorary member. She sometimes makes more, for she does not like erasures. If the expression or the phrase which comes up does not suit her, she throws aside the sheet— generally a large-sized sheet, gilt-edged—and begins over again.

Her phraseology is at times very happy, translating her thought with a single vigorous or picturesque expression. In refusing to evacuate the Crimea, as the cowardice of Patiomkine advises her in 1788, and looking for arguments to justify her decision, she writes : 'Does a man who is in the saddle get down in order to hold on to the horse's tail?' Her letters, especially her letters to Grimm, are full, at the same time, of words and turns of phrase in which the *bonhomie* and carelessness of thought and language alike are unbounded, and sometimes become positively gross. Not content with interlarding her incorrect French with German or Italian words and phrases, she often writes in slang. She puts 'sti-là' for 'celui-là,' 'ma' for 'mais.' Probably she speaks in the same way. She is not averse from a certain triviality. We shall not venture to reproduce here the *gaul-*

oiseries—are they indeed *'gauloiseries* ?—which
sometimes crop up when she is in the jocose and
familiar vein, and we should certainly tire or
even disgust our readers with the quips and
quibbles which she is for ever sprinkling over
her epistolary conversation.

It is true that this is her 'undress' style, her
language of asides. Let us see now what is her
style as a writer, her way of writing for the
public.

II

It is in her works written for the stage that
the pen of Catherine is most prolific. She does
something of everything in literature, but especially dramatic writing.

'You ask me,' she writes to Grimm, 'why I
write so many comedies. I will reply, like
M. Pincé, with three reasons: *primo*, because it
amuses me ; *secundo*, because I should like to
restore the national theatre, which, owing to its
lack of new plays, is somewhat gone out of
fashion ; and *tertio*, because it was time to put
down the visionaries who were beginning to hold
up their heads. *Le Trompeur* and *Le Trompé*
have had a prodigious success. . . . The most
amusing part of it is that at the first performance
there were cries of "Author!" who, however,
kept completely incognito, despite his huge
success. Each of these pieces has brought in,
at Moscow, 10,000 roubles to the management.'

It is not needful, we see, to be an author
played at Paris to secure the welcome that a
happy idea always receives from the public, and

the imperial diadem does not preclude happy ideas.

In *Le Trompeur* and *Le Trompé* Catherine has brought Cagliostro and his dupes on the stage. The greater part of her plays are thus polemical or satirical, philosophical, social, or religious. She bravely attacks the ideas or tendencies, or even persons, that she disapproves of or dislikes. One may say that she has put into them her best work as a writer. She has, nevertheless, not the least sense of the dramatic. The dramatic element, properly speaking, is absent from her comedies as from her serious dramas. There is no art of composition, no knowledge of effect, no creative faculty, not a type among all these characters; but here and there certain traits caught *sur le vif* in the manners of the country, a certain wit, good-humour, and a real gift of observation. The general tendency is that of Voltaire, toned down by the respect of certain sentiments, the religious sentiment among others, which she is obliged to treat so carefully in the surroundings in which she is placed. The principal aim is to oppose the current of mysticism which begins to penetrate the upper strata of society, finding in the natural leanings of the Russian mind an element highly favourable to its propagation. It is with Freemasonry and *Martinism* that she has most often a bone to pick. One day she assimilates the Freemasons to the Siberian sect of *Chamanes*, whom she tries to turn into ridicule by accusing them of extorting money from the weak-witted folk on whose credulity they trade. This is the theme of *Chamane Sibirski* (Chamane of Siberia), a piece for which an article in the *Encyclopédie* (Theosophy) has furnished her with the canvas; it is also that of *Obmanchtchik* (The Deceiver), and *Obolchtchenie* (The Deceit). But she also attacks occasionally other errors and absurdities. One of the characters of *O Vremia !* (translated into French under the title, *O temps ! O mœurs !*), Madame Hanjahina, in the fervour of her religious devotion, is in the act of performing fifty genuflections before a holy image. A peasant enters, and, after kissing his mistress's feet, puts a paper into her hand. How dare he trouble her at such a moment. 'Leave me, demon, imp of hell!' she cries. 'Fear the wrath of God, and mine.' She nevertheless glances at the paper: it is a petition, on the part of a lover who wishes to marry, and who, in his capacity of serf, requires the authorisation of his mistress 'The idea of coming and disturbing with such requests a proprietress of serfs, who is at her devotions!' Mme. Hanjahina turns the luckless importunate out of doors, and returns to her genuflections. But she has lost the reckoning. Must she do them all over again? She begins the task, but before beginning she summons her people, and orders them to give fifty times fifty blows to the peasant, who must have been sent by Satan himself, and who shall never marry, let him be assured of that, as long as she lives and continues to reverence the holy images.

Catherine also, it appears, wrote fiction. In the third volume of his *History of German Literature*, Kurtz includes the Empress among the number of German writers of the eighteenth century, as author of an Eastern romance,

Obidach, written in 1786. He attributes to her several other works in her mother tongue, of which he does not mention the titles.

We have also some fragments of the Empress's work as a fabulist. In writing for her grand-children one of the tales that Grimm published for the first time in 1790, in his *Correspondence*, Catherine was a little out of her reckoning. The *Tsarevitch Chlore*, as well as the *Tsarevitch Febei*, are philosophical tales in the style of Voltaire, with allegorical turns, moralising intentions, and scientific pretensions, quite out of the range of childish minds. Catherine had, nevertheless, what we now call ' a knowledge of children,' the art of putting herself on the level of young, fresh, naïve imaginations ; she had also a love of children. But, pen in hand, she sometimes forgot what she knew the best. Nor has she given evidence, in these compositions, of much fertility of invention, or of a particularly in-genious turn of mind, or an original inspiration. She has once again stolen some one's ideas— those of Jean-Jacques and of Locke this time.

Finally, Catherine has had her poetical moments. The taste came to her late in life. 'Imagine,' she writes in 1787, to Grimm, 'that on my galley, going down the Borysthène, he [the Comte de Ségur] wanted to teach me to write verse ! I have been rhyming for the last four days, but it takes too much time, and I have begun too late.' Nevertheless, the year before, she had already asked Chrapowicki to send her a dictionary of Russian rhymes, if there was one in existence.

We do not know what success attended her

secretary's researches in this direction, but after 1788 we often enough find the Empress rhyming, both in Russian and in French. In August 1788 she writes burlesque verses on the King of Sweden, while composing a French comedy, *Les Voyages de Madame Bontemps*, which she intends to have acted, by way of surprise, in the apartments of the favourite Mamonof on his birthday. In January 1789 she sends to Chrapowicki two Russian quatrains on the taking of Otchakof. One of them is somewhat remarkable for its vigour of thought and the energy of some expressions. As for the poetic form, it escapes our estimation. Here is a French quatrain, without date, which will permit the reader to see for himself the skill of Catherine in this branch of literature. It is an epitaph composed by her on the occasion of the death of the Count I. I. Chouvalof, who, since 1777, had been the Empress's high chamberlain—

'Ci gît
Monseigneur le grand chambellan
À cent ans blanc comme Milan ;
Le voilà qui fait la moue ;
Vivant il grattait la joue.'

We shall doubtless be excused from giving more.

Catherine also undertook to translate the *Iliad*. Three sheets of attempts in her handwriting are preserved in the archives of the empire. Certainly, she attempted many things.

CHAPTER III

CATHERINE AND EDUCATION

I

THE institutions founded by Catherine for the furtherance of national education, her educational ideas and writings, hold too large a place in the history of her reign, and in that of the intellectual development of her people, for us to omit some consideration of them in this study, brief as must be the space that we can give them. On arriving at power, Catherine was quick to see what advantage she had derived, in the struggle from which she had come out victorious, from the superiority of her intellectual culture, the relative extent and variety of her knowledge. At the same time, she was able to judge how much it cost in Russia, even on the throne, to arrive at the little knowledge that she possessed. Finally, the handling of power must soon have shown her the enormous difficulties that the best-intentioned rulers have always had to meet with from the ignorance of their subjects. The reform, or rather the establishment, of national education is, from the first, one of the principal ideas brought by the Empress to the government of her empire. In this regard she had everything, or almost everything, to do. The lower classes did not count, the middle class hardly existed ; there was therefore nothing to do but to raise the level of studies at the summit of the social ladder.

But this level was terribly low. The children
of the nobility were brought up by serfs or by
foreign tutors. We can guess what they had to
learn from the former; as for the latter, we can
guess also what sort of people they were—French
for the most part—who at that time entered upon
the career of private tutor in the far-distant
Russia. Méhée de la Touche tells the story
of the governess who, being asked by the
parents of her future charge if she spoke French,
replied : ' *Sacrédié!* I should think so ; it is my
own language.' She was engaged without further
question; only, the name of Mlle. Sacrédié always
stuck to her.

As ever, Catherine would do everything, and
everything at once. In the second year of her reign,
Betzky, the collaborator whom she picked out for
this purpose, received the order to set to work
on a project, which included a whole new system
of education, able to serve as basis for a number
of scholastic institutions, to be set on foot sub-
sequently. The result was the publication, in
1764, of *General Regulations for the Education
of Children of both Sexes.* Betzky has admitted
that the ideas developed in this document were
those of the Empress herself. They must be
considered bold, if not original : they are more
or less those of Locke and of Jean-Jacques
Rousseau ; those of Jean-Jacques especially, little
as Catherine generally professed to think of his
genius. It was a project for fabricating men and
women not in the least like any that had ever
been seen in Russia, taken radically away from
the soil which had given them birth, transplanted
from their natural surroundings, and developed

in an atmosphere artificially prepared for the culture to which they were destined. They were to be taken at the age of five or six, kept strictly shut up, and removed from all outside influence, to the age of twenty or more.

Catherine seriously thought of carrying out this programme. If this was not done, at least within the desired limits and proportions—that is to say, throughout the whole length and breadth of public education—it is because she encountered great difficulties on the way, and that here, too, patience, firmness of resolution, and continuity of effort were once again lacking to her will. Difficulties arose at the outset from the opposition that she met with, not only in her immediate surroundings —but little enlightened itself, as a rule, and consequently indifferent, if not hostile, to the development of any programme whatever, relating to this order of ideas—but also among even the most open-minded and cultivated of those to whom she could appeal, outside the official sphere, for some amount of help in her enterprise. The ideas of Jean-Jacques were by no means those of Novikof, for example, nor those of the circle in which the influence of the publicist was exercised. Now, this was perhaps the most intelligent circle in the Russia of that time. Novikof had pedagogic views of his own, entirely different, giving a large place, in national education, to local feeling, to custom, tradition, to the ways of the country, averse from the introduction of foreign elements. As for the officials at Catherine's disposal, they were inclined to ask whether public education, and schools in general, were of any real value. In 1785, at one of the Empress's evening recep-

tions, as Patiomkine was discussing the necessity
of starting a large number of universities throughout Russia, Zavadofski, the director of the
recently established normal schools, observed that
the University of Moscow had not produced a
single distinguished man in science during the
whole of its existence. 'That,' replied Patiomkine, 'is because you hindered me from continuing
my studies by turning me out.' This was a fact;
the favourite had been sent down, and obliged to
enter a regiment, which was the beginning of his
fortune. He forgot to say that his idleness and
misconduct had quite justified the punishment.
Catherine thereupon declared that she herself
owed much to the university education : since she
had had in her service some men who had carried
out their studies at Moscow, she had been able to
make out something in the memoranda and other
official documents presented for her signature.
It was after this conversation that she decided
upon founding the Universities of Nijni-Nov-
gorod, and Iekatierinoslaf. But the latter town
had itself yet to be founded.

Another difficulty presented itself in the selection of a staff of teachers. In organising the
establishment of the corps of cadets, Betzky
took for director a former prompter from the
French theatre, and for inspector of classes a
former *valet de chambre* of Catherine's mother.
One of the professors, Faber, had been a lackey
in the service of two other French professors,
Pictet and Mallet, whose colleague he now
became   Pictet and Mallet having ventured to
protest, Betzky contented himself with giving
Faber the rank of lieutenant in the Russian army,

which, it appeared, put things straight. The master of police in the establishment was a certain Lascaris, a mere adventurer, who afterwards became director, with the title of lieutenant-colonel.

The greatest liberty reigned in this school, if we may believe the testimony of Bobrinski, the natural son of Catherine, who was brought up there: the ideas of Jean-Jacques were liberally applied.

Catherine was thus forced to complicate her programme of scholastic organisation; she had first to think of *training the masters* for the future pupils that she meant to intrust to them. She sent to Oxford, to the Academy of Turin, to the schools in Germany, young men who were to be prepared for the delicate duties of professorship. But many other things were yet wanting for the founding of national schools, and first, to know how to set about it. She confessed it naïvely to Grimm—

'Listen a moment, my philosophical friends · you would be charming, adorable, if you would have the charity to map out a plan of study for young people, from A B C to the University. I am told that there should be three kinds of schools, and I who have not studied and have not been at Paris, I have neither knowledge nor insight in the matter, and consequently I know not what should be learnt, nor even what can be learnt, nor where one is to find out unless from you. I am very much concerned about an idea for a university and its management, a gymnasium and its management, a school and its management.'

She intimates, however, the means by which she intends to get over the difficulty for the present—

'Until you accede or do not accede to my request, I know what I shall do: I shall hunt through the *Encyclopédie.* Oh, I shall be certain to haul out what I want and what I don't want.'

The philosophers remaining silent, it is the *Encyclopédie* that has to afford matter for the conceptions to which the universal genius of Catherine betakes itself, in this new order of things.

II

These conceptions were destined to remain sterile, with one exception. Some scholastic establishments date, it is true, from her reign, But these are special schools, that, for instance, of artillery and engineering, founded in 1762, the school of commerce founded in 1772, the academy of mines in 1773, the academy of Beaux Arts in 1774. In 1781 there was even an attempt at popular schools, and in 1783 Jankovitz was summoned for the foundation of normal schools, after the order of those in Austria. Ten were at once founded at St. Petersburg, and the following year they had 1000 pupils. Catherine was full of enthusiasm on the subject, and wrote to Grimm: 'Do you know that we are really doing fine things, and getting along famously, not in the air (for, from dread of fire, I have expressly forbidden aerostatic globes) but *ventre à terre,* for the enlightening of the people.'

In reply Grimm conferred upon the sovereign the title of *Universal-normalschulmeisterin.*

But all that was not the national education according to Locke and Jean-Jacques, of which the Empress dreamed, and which ought, she thought, to regenerate Russia. The dream was unrealised save in the establishment founded in 1764 for the education of girls, in the famous *Smolnyi Monastyr*, which was one of the favourite achievements of Catherine, the one among all others to which she was most constant; the majestic edifice on the banks of the Neva is even now the admiration of travellers from the West. *Demoiselles nobles* are still educated there in the most careful manner, and but lately the two daughters of the Prince of Montenegro grew up within these walls, where so often the Empress was to be seen surrounded by her pupils, following their studies with solicitude, and interesting herself in their recreations. Rigorous seclusion, during twelve years, the removal of all outside influences, even family influences, even religious influences : all the details of the plan sketched out in 1764 were to be found in the scheme of this institution. No one was allowed to go out, except to go to the court, whither the Empress frequently summoned the scholars whom she had particularly noticed. There were hardly any holidays. Every six weeks the parents were admitted to see their children, and to witness a public examination which showed what progress they were making. That was all. The lay schoolmistresses never spoke to their pupils of God or the Devil save in general terms, without any attempt at proselytism ; the clergy

were admitted to this singular monastery, and
to some part in the instruction given there, but
within prescribed limits. It was a convent having
as abbess a philosophising Empress ; monastic
life with a door of communication opening on the
splendours and seductions of the imperial palace ;
St. Cyr, *minus* Christianity, and not merely the
severe and gloomy Christianity of Madame de
Maintenon, but Christianity in general. A long-
bearded pope was sometimes seen there ; the
Christian teaching was absent. The very plan
of the establishment was alien to it, for could
anything be more absolutely contrary to its spirit
than the separation into two divisions of the
inmates, kept absolutely apart and distinct, by
the very first principles of the undertaking ? In
this establishment, in which there is room for 500
pupils, there are daughters of the nobility and of
the middle classes. They have nothing in common one with another, either in mode of living,
of education, or even of costume. The former
are indulged with fine clothes, the refinements of
the toilette, of the table, and of accommodation, a
course of study in which the arts of pleasing hold
a large place ; the latter have to put up with a
coarse kind of clothing, with simple dishes, with
lessons in sewing, washing, and cooking. The
colour of the clothes is the same, but the 'corset'
takes the place of the elegant 'fourreau,' and is completed by a pinafore, which denotes the humility
of their condition. All that is Pagan, utterly
Pagan, as is the plan of the teaching itself, into
which Diderot would have wished to introduce
thorough instruction in anatomy ; as are the sallies
into the frivolous and corrupt world of the court.

As it has been noted, Catherine is the first Russian sovereign to give attention to the education of women. She gave to her undertaking all the breadth and magnificence that we find in all her creations, and that would seem to be in some sort the natural emanation of herself. But she also put to proof principles which she had not sufficiently gauged. The germs that she thus introduced into the intellectual and moral development of her sex still bear fruit in Russia, not perhaps always for the best.

We have had means of judging, in the Empress's confidences to Grimm, what point she had reached, after fifteen years of sway, in her own studies and notions in regard to this delicate and difficult matter : she obviously went right ahead, picking up principles and ideas for her plans of education as she picked up soldiers for her plans of conquest. In the very numerous writings on educational subjects that she has handed down to posterity, some ideas and ingenious intuitions alternate with the most paradoxical assertions, as, for example, that 'the study of languages and sciences ought to hold the last place in education,' or that 'the health of the body and the inclination of the mind towards what is good make up the whole of education.' The idea of enlightened despotism, coming out in the blind subjection of pupil to master, accords as best it can with that of the progressive development of the spirit of independence, in which one is to endeavour to fortify the child's mind. As a whole it is almost incoherent. Catherine saw clearly that the way in which the youth of Russia in her time was educated was useless alike to them and to Russia, and she admitted the necessity of a change of system, as an absolute necessity of national progress. It was only on this one point that she had quite made up her mind. At her time, and in the place that she occupied, coming after Ann, Elizabeth, and Peter III., it was something already to have made this discovery and cherished this conviction. But the glory of having been the founder of the national education was not to be hers. The judgment of posterity has given this title to a name more humble than hers, that of a man whom she treated as a foe, to whom she gave a dungeon and a chain as the reward of the labours of which Russia reaps the benefit to-day. It was in the educational establishments founded at St. Petersburg by Novikof that the programme of studies and the plan of scholastic organisation now in force throughout the empire were really mapped out.

BOOK IV

INNER ASPECTS

CHAPTER I

HOME LIFE

WE shall try to give an account of a single day in the life of the Empress, an ordinary day, one of those which show the habitual course of her existence. We are in winter, let us suppose, and about the middle of the reign, in 1785 for example, a year of peace. The Empress occupies the *Zimnyi Dvariets*, the Winter Palace. The private suite of rooms, on the first story, is not very large. On mounting the little staircase, we come to a room in which a table, covered with writing materials, awaits the secretaries and others employed in her Majesty's immediate service. We pass through this first room, and enter the dressing-room, whose windows look out on the square of the palace. It is there that the Empress's hair is dressed before a small circle of intimate friends and high functionaries, admitted to the early morning audiences. It is the *petit lever* of her Majesty. There is no *grand lever*. Two doors open before us: one leads to the Diamond Room, the other to the bedroom. The bedroom communicates at the back with a private dressing-room, and at the left with a work-room opening on the Mirror Room, and the other reception-rooms.

It is six o'clock in the morning, the hour at which the Empress rises. By the side of her bed is a basket, where, on a couch of pink satin ornamented with lace, sleeps a whole family of little dogs, Catherine's inseparable companions. They are English greyhounds. In 1770 Dr. Dimsdale, whom the Empress, as we know, summoned from London to inoculate her, brought over for her a couple of these creatures. They have increased and multiplied, so that one sees a greyhound in all the aristocratic houses in St. Petersburg. The Empress always has half a dozen about her, sometimes more. The bell-ringer of the palace having rung the hour of six, Maria Savichna Pierekousihina, the head *femme de chambre* of her Majesty, enters the bedroom. Formerly Catherine had no one about her at this time; she rose by herself, and in winter even lit her own fire. Time has changed this habit. But to-day her Majesty is late in waking. The night before she was not so early as usual in going to bed; an interesting conversation detained her at the Hermitage after ten. Maria Savichna coolly finds a divan, opposite to the sovereign's bed, lies down on it, and seizes the happy chance of a little additional nap. But now the Empress awakens. She gets up, and in her turn awakens the slumbering Maria Savichna. She goes into her dressing-room. A little warm water to rinse out her mouth, and a little ice to rub over her face, are all that her Majesty is in need of for the moment. But where is Catherine Ivanovna, the young Calmuck, whose business it is to have these things ready? She is always behind her time, this Catherine Ivanovna! What, already a quarter past six! The Empress has a movement of impatience; she taps her foot nervously on the ground. Here she is at last: beware of her Majesty's wrath! Catherine snatches from her hands the silver-gilt ewer, and, hastily making use of it, she apostrophises the lazy girl—

'What are you thinking about, Catherine Ivanovna? Do you think you will always be able to go on like this? One day you will get married, you will leave my service, and your husband, be sure, will not be like me. He will be much more particular. Think of your future, Catherine Ivanovna!'

That is all, and that is repeated day after day. Meanwhile the Empress goes briskly into her work-room, followed by her dogs, who have waited till now to leave their luxurious bed. It is time for *déjeuner*. The coffee is waiting: good. Is it strong enough? It needs a pound of coffee for the five cups that the Empress is accustomed to take. One day one of her secretaries, a certain Kozmine, coming to make his report, is benumbed with the cold. The Empress rings. 'A cup of coffee for the poor shivering wretch!' She insists on his swallowing the steaming cup at a draught. But what is the matter? He is unwell; he has palpitations of the heart. He has had the coffee that is prepared for her Majesty, and which she alone can drink. It never occurred to any one that the cup was for the secretary; who could imagine that her Majesty would share her *déjeuner* with a mere *tchinovnik* like him? Generally Catherine only shares her *déjeuner* with her dogs. The imperial coffee is not in their line; but there is thick cream, biscuits, sugar. The whole contents of the sugar-basin go to them, and the biscuits too.

Her Majesty has now no further need of any one. If her dogs want to go out, she opens the door for them herself. She wishes to be alone, and to give herself entirely to her work or correspondence, till nine o'clock. But where is her favourite snuff-box, which should always be on her work-table? A portrait of Peter the Great, which is on the cover, is there, she says, to remind her that she has to continue the work of the Great Czar. Catherine takes a great deal of snuff. But she never carries a snuff-box. There must be one at hand in every corner of her palace. She uses only a particular kind of tobacco that is specially grown for her in her garden of Tzarskoie-Sielo. When writing, she needs to take snuff almost all the time. She rings. 'Will you kindly,' she says to a *valet de chambre* who enters, 'look for my snuff-box.' 'Veuillez,' 'Prenez la peine de,' are formulas that she invariably uses in speaking to the people about her, however humble.

At nine precisely Catherine returns to her bedroom. It is there that she receives the officials who come to give in their report. The prefect of police enters first. Her Majesty is

dressed, at this moment, in a white dressing-
gown of *gros de Tours*, with large folds. She
wears a cap of white crape, which the vigour of
her work or the excitement of her conversation
with Grimm has accidentally pushed aside, to
right or left. Her complexion is fresh, her eyes
bright; nevertheless, in reading the papers presented for her signature, she puts on glasses.

'You don't need this, do you?' she says to her
secretary Gribofski. 'How old are you?'

'Twenty-six.'

'You have not had time, as I have, to lose
your sight in the service of the empire.'

On entering, Gribofski has bowed very low.
The Empress has replied with a slight inclination
of the head, after which, with an amiable smile,
she ends her hand to the secretary. At this
moment Gribofski can notice that a front tooth
is missing from the otherwise well-furnished
mouth of the sovereign. On stooping to kiss
the imperial hand, a white, plump hand, he has
felt a pressure of this august hand, and he has
heard the words 'sit down,' which summon him
to his task. It is a task often interrupted.
Ministers, generals, high officials, who have been
granted audiences, are announced, and the Empress is often considerate enough not to make
them wait. Now General Souvarof is ushered
in. Without looking at the Empress, he marches
with his automatic soldier's step straight to the
right, where, in a corner, a lamp is always kept
burning before the image of Our Lady of Kasan.
He stops short before the *icone*, and bends three
times, striking the ground with his forehead.
Having accomplished this rite, he turns sharply,

as if he were at drill, takes a few steps forward, and a fourth genuflection brings him to the sovereign's feet.

'Pray, are you not ashamed?' she murmurs. She makes him sit down, addresses two or three questions to him, one after another, to which he replies in the tone of a trooper catechised by a corporal, and she dismisses him after two minutes. Other personages arrive. But, all at once, some one whispers a word in the Empress's ear, she gives a sign of the head, and all retire: it is the favourite, Patiomkine, Lanskoï, or Mamonof, who wishes to come in. For him her Majesty is always visible, and, when he comes, every one else goes.

This goes on till mid-day, afterwards till one o'clock when the dinner-hour has been changed from one to two. After dismissing her secretary, the Empress retires to her private dressing-room, where she makes a complete toilette, dresses, and has her hair dressed by her old *coiffeur* Kozlof. Her costume, except on great occasions, is extremely simple: a loose and open gown, *à la Moldave*, with double sleeves; the under ones of a light material, plaited to the wrist, the over ones very long, of similar material to the skirt, and caught up at the back. The gown is of violet or grey silk; there are no jewels, no indication of supreme rank; comfortable shoes with very low heels. Catherine puts no coquetry in anything but the arrangement of her hair: she wears her hair drawn back, showing the whole of the forehead, the development of which she perhaps likes to emphasise. Her hair is long and heavy; when she sits before her toilet-table,

it touches the ground. On state occasions a
diadem crowns the cunning edifice raised by the
skilful hands of Kozlof; but then the silk dress
is replaced by red velvet, and the costume thus
transformed, though it keeps much the same easy
character, takes the name of 'the Russian dress.'
It is obligatory at court, despite the heavy
sacrifices it imposes on the young women, who
are distressed at not being got up in the Paris
fashion.

Her private toilette over, Catherine goes into
the official toilette-chamber, where she finishes
dressing. It is the *petit lever*. The number of
those who have the privilege of being present is
limited; but in spite of this, the room is full.
There are, first, the Empress's grandchildren, who
are invariably brought in; then the favourite; with
a few friends, such as Léon Narychkine. There
is also the court fool, who is a person of much
wisdom : Matrena Danilevna holds this office, to
which she adds that of tale-bearer. She diverts
the sovereign by her jokes, and Catherine is
kept *au courant* of all that is going on at court
and in the city, the scandals in the air since the
night before, and even the best kept family-
secrets. Matrena Danilevna has an eye and ear
everywhere, and admirable police instincts. One
day she is very severe upon Ryleïef, the chief
of imperial police. Catherine summons him to
her, and advises him in a friendly manner to send
some fat fowls and geese to Matrena Danilevna,
who seems to be in want of them in order to duly
celebrate the *Prasdnik* (Easter). A week passes.
'And Ryleïef?' asks the Empress of the worthy
gossip, who is dishing up to her the string of

daily tattle. Matrena Danilevna has nothing but praise for the official, for whom, a week before, she had nothing but abuse. 'Ah! ah!' interrupts Catherine. 'I see what it is: he has sent you some fowls and geese.'

But now the Empress is seated before her toilet-table, a superb table in massive gold. Her four *femmes de chambre* approach her. They are four old maids, whom she has had in her service since her accession to the throne, and who have passed their heyday in her service. They were all of them very plain. One of them, Maria Stiepanovna Aleksieïevna, paints her face in the most preposterous way. They are all Russian. To give her subjects an example that they have never, up to the present time, followed, Catherine has absolutely none but Russian servants. Now Maria Stiepanovna presents to the sovereign a piece of ice, which she rubs over her cheeks in public, to prove that she herself has no recourse to the coquettish tricks employed by her *femme de chambre*; the old Palakoutchi places on her head a little crape cap, this time carefully adjusted; the two Zvieref sisters add some pins, and her Majesty's toilette is over The whole ceremony has lasted about ten minutes, during which Catherine has spoken to several of those present.

And now to table. Up to the time of the Swedish war, dinner was at one o'clock. At that time the pressing occupations with which Catherine was burdened made her put off the hour of dinner, which remained afterwards at two o'clock. On ordinary days there are generally about a dozen guests at her Majesty's table: the favourite first of all, as a matter of course, a few friends,

Count Razoumofski, Field-Marshal Prince Galitzine, Prince Patiomkine, the Count of Anhalt,
the two Narychkine brothers, the General
Aide-de-Camp, Count Tchernichef, Count Strogonof, Prince Bariatinski, Countess Bruce, Countess Branicka, Princess Dachkof, and, later on,
during the last years of the reign, the General
Aide-de-Camp Passek, Count Strogonof, the
Maid of Honour Protassof, Vice-Admiral Ribas,
the General Governor of the Polish provinces,
Toutolmine, and two of the French émigrés,
Comte Esterhazy and the Marquis de Lambert.
Dinner lasts about an hour. The dishes
are very simple. Catherine cares nothing
about elaborate cookery. Her favourite dish is
boiled beef with salted cucumber; her drink,
water with gooseberry sirup. Later, on the
advice of physicians, she takes a glass of Madeira
or Rhine wine. For desert, some fruit, apples or
cherries by preference. Among her cooks there
is one who cooks abominably. For years she
has never noticed it. When it has been pointed
out to her, she has refused to dismiss the
man, saying that he has been in her service
too long. She merely inquires when his turn
comes, and then says on sitting down to
table : 'Ladies and gentlemen, we must exercise our patience; we have a week's fast before
us.'

Twice a week her Majesty keeps *jour maigre*,
and on these occasions she has only two or three
people to dinner.

It should be added that her guests are not
obliged to go beyond the palace to find better
cheer. Her Majesty's table is poorly served,

and Catherine sees that the expenses are kept
down ; but the table of the favourite, Zoubof,
that of his protector, the Count N. J. Saltykof,
and that of the Countess Branicka, Patiomkine's
niece, which are all three paid for out of the
imperial treasury, come to 400 roubles (2000
francs) a day in 1792, without counting the
drink, which, with tea, coffee, and chocolate,
comes to 200 roubles a day extra.

After dinner there are a few minutes' conversation ; then every one retires. Catherine
takes up her embroidery, at which she is very
skilful, and Betzky reads aloud to her. When
Betzky, now growing old, begins to lose his
sight, she does not have him replaced; she reads
herself, with the aid of her glasses. An hour
passes in this way, and now her secretary is
announced : twice a week he comes with the
courier, who is immediately despoiled. The
other days, it is the officials who come, one
after another, handing in reports, demanding
instructions. All the while the Empress generally has with her her grandchildren, with whom
she plays in the intervals of her business. By
four o'clock she has well earned the rest and
recreation which she now allows herself. She
betakes herself to her favourite Hermitage,
through the long gallery which connects it with
the Winter Palace. Lanskoï or Mamonof or
Zoubof accompanies her. She examines her new
collections, sees to their arrangement, has a game
of billiards, and sometimes amuses herself with
turning ivory. At six o'clock she returns to the
reception-rooms. Slowly she makes the round of
her *salons*, giving an amiable word here and

there, and then sits down to her whist-table.
She plays whist at ten roubles the rubber,
rocambole, piquet, and Boston; always very
cheaply. Her usual partners are Count Razoumofski, Field-Marshal Count Tchernichef, Field-
Marshal Prince Galitzine, Count Bruce, Count
Strogonof, Prince Orlof, Prince Viazemski, and
the foreign ministers. Catherine gives the preference to the two first, because they play well,
and do not try to make her gain. She herself
plays her very best. The chamberlain Tchertkof, whom she sometimes admits to make up
a party, generally gets in a rage, reproaches her
with not playing fair, and, sometimes, in his
vexation, throws the cards in her Majesty's face.
She never loses her temper, defends her way
of playing as best she can, appealing to the
bystanders. One day she calls on the two
French exiles, who are of the party, to give
their opinion.

'Fine arbiters!' cries Tchertkof 'They betrayed their own king!'

This time Catherine has to impose silence on
the too reckless player. One sees that she has
no easy task to maintain at her court the tone
that should reign there. Another time, as she
is playing at whist with Count Strogonof, General
Arharof, and Count Stackelberg, Strogonof constantly loses. At last, unable to contain himself
any longer, and forgetting all the *convenances*, he
rises in a heat, leaves the party without finishing
it, and, with purple cheeks, begins to stride to
and fro in the Diamond Room, giving free course
to his irritation—

'I shall lose all my money! As for you, it

makes no difference for you if you lose. But as for me, I shall soon be in destitution.'

Thinking that this is going too far, Arharof would interfere, but Catherine stops him : 'Let him be! He has been just like that for fifty years. You will never change him, no more shall I.'

The play invariably stops at ten o'clock. Her Majesty then retires. Except on reception-days, there is no supper, and even on these days Catherine only sits down to table as a matter of form. Returning to her private suite of rooms, she goes immediately to her bedroom, drinks a large glass of boiled water, and goes to bed. Her day is ended.

II

This is a quiet enough course of existence, and the picture that we have just presented will not, perhaps, be much in agreement with the very different pictures presented to us by the usual legend. We have, however, drawn from the best sources ; but we find a very natural explanation of the contrast between legend and history. The former draws its inspiration, for one thing, from what was really reprehensible, and might well have justified the most ill-natured suppositions in regard to one side of the Empress's private life, on which we shall enlarge later. Legend and ill-feeling have also made capital out of certain periods of dissipation which were nevertheless only accidental and occasional in the history of the great Empress, such as that which followed the great crisis of despair after the death of

Lanskoï. The general course of life of Catherine appears under quite a different light, and, if we can make up our minds to throw a veil over certain pleasures, which, for the rest, never disturbed, in a permanent fashion, the harmonious balance of her faculties, nor the wisely planned programme of her occupations, the other distractions, associated with them, were quite mild and innocent. Those who, on the strength of certain reports, have looked upon her existence as one continual orgy, would find it hard indeed to justify such a conception by the testimony of fact. History gives no support to it. But is this history well informed? Did not the more or less edifying outside of the Empress's private life hide something far more scandalous underneath? Were there not, in the palaces of St. Petersburg and Tzarskoïe-Sielo, in the rooms of the Hermitage, certain hidden corners, concealing more unmentionable pleasures? We do not think so, for reasons founded as much on the character of Catherine as on the very organisation of her private life, itself, in one way, so much a scandal, but a scandal which was official, cynically but frankly avowed. The Empress has given the lie, for the rest, not in words but in actions, to the greater part of the infamous accusations that were brought against her during her lifetime. The Englishman Harris wrote in January 1779: 'The Empress becomes from day to day more disordered and dissipated, and her society is composed of the lowest set among the courtiers; the health of her Majesty is certainly tried by the life she leads.' And the Foreign Office concluding that the sovereign, 'worn out

by debauch,' had only a short while to live, all
Europe soon found out, rather at its expense,
that Catherine was quite alive, healthy in body
and mind.   Never was she in better health,
physically and mentally, than at this time.

Catherine was certainly sensual, licentious if
you will, but she was nothing of a Bacchante.
Insatiably amorous, as she was infinitely ambitious, she accommodated her love affairs, as she
accommodated her ambition, to certain rules of
conduct, from which she never varied.   Favourites had always a large place in her palace and
in all the material, moral, and even political
organisation of her life ; but the sovereign always
held her own, and, strange as it may sound, the
quiet housewife as well.

Catherine was passionately fond of children ;
it was one of her favourite pastimes to play with
them.   In a letter addressed to Ivan Tchernichef
in 1769 she brings herself before us, with the
usual company of her leisure hours, and we see
her, Gregory Orlof, Count Razoumofski, and
Zahar Tchernichef, Ivan's brother, playing with
the little Markof, whom the sovereign has just
adopted, gambolling, rolling on the ground, com-
mitting a thousand absurdities, and all the time
in fits of laughter.   The little Markof, then six
years old, is afterwards replaced by the son of
Admiral Ribeaupierre.   The child is hard to
tame, having got into his little brain the idea
that he has been brought to the palace that he
may have his head cut off.   But Catherine
gradually wins him over, cutting out paper
figures, making toys for him.   One day she tears
a ribbon out of her collerette to make the reins

of a horse and pair that she has cut out of cardboard. She has him with her for hours together,
sends him away when any one comes to her on
business, then sends for him again ; at the age of
five she makes him an officer of the Guards.
He is not the only one to be thus favoured : two
little Galitzines, four grand-nephews of Patiomkine, the son of the Field-Marshal Count Saltykof, the son of the hetman Branicki, the young
Count Chouvalof, who afterwards accompanied
Napoleon to Elba, and young Valentine Esterhazy, all have their share. Little Ribeaupierre
lives under her Majesty's roof till the age of
twelve. On sending him away, Catherine wishes
him to write to her, and she replies to his letter
in her own handwriting. But her letter is so full
of erasures—she has not, this time, taken the
trouble to begin over again—that she has it
copied out by her secretary, Popof, who afterwards sends on the original.

After children, we dare not say before, but it
would perhaps be more correct, dogs, and animals in general, play a large part in Catherine's
private life. The family of Sir Tom Anderson
is certainly, of all the families of the empire, the
one whose position at court is most solidly
established. Here is the list, in one of the
Empress's letters—

'First comes the head of the race, Sir Tom
Anderson, his spouse, Duchess Anderson, their
children, the young Duchess Anderson, Mr.
Anderson, and Tom Thomson : the last is
established at Moscow under the guardianship of
Prince Volkonski, Governor-General of the city.
There are also, besides these, whose reputation

is made, four or five young people of infinite promise, who are being brought up in the best houses in Moscow and St. Petersburg, as for example that of Prince Orlof, MM. Narychkine, and Prince Toupiakine. Sir Tom Anderson has taken as second wife Mlle. Mimi, who has since taken the name of Mimi Anderson. But up to now there is no family. Besides these legitimate marriages (since the faults as well as the virtues of people must be told in their history) M. Tom has had several illegitimate attachments: the Grand Duchess has several pretty bitches who have greatly taken him, but up to the present no bastards have been seen, and it would seem that there are none; anything to the contrary is a mere calumny.'

But Catherine was not content with dogs alone. In 1785 she takes a fancy to a white squirrel, which she brings up herself, and feeds out of her hand with nuts. And about the same time she gets a monkey, of whose cleverness and pretty ways she often boasts. 'You should have seen,' she writes to Grimm, 'the amazement of Prince Henry' (brother of the King of Prussia) 'one day when Prince Potemkin let loose a monkey in the room, with which I began to play, instead of going on with the conversation we were engaged in. He opened his eyes, but in spite of all, he could not resist the tricks of the monkey.' At that time she had also a cat, the present of Prince Patiomkine: 'the most tom-cat of all tom-cats, gay, witty, not obstinate.' The present is in return for a service in Sévres porcelain, which she has had made for the favourite, saying that it was for her, 'so that it should be finer.' The Anderson family, however, loses none of its rights. 'You will excuse me,' says the Empress in one of her letters, 'if all the preceding page is very badly written. I am extremely hampered at the moment by a certain young and fair Zemire, who of all the Thomassins is the one who will come closest to me, and who pushes her pretensions to the point of having her paws on my paper.'

Let us quote also this fragment of the *Souvenirs* of Madame Vigée-Lebrun: 'When the Empress had returned to town, I used to see her every morning open the shutters and throw out crumbs to hundreds of rooks who came every day at the same hour to seek their pittance. In the evening, about ten, when the rooms were lit up, I used also to see her send for her grand-children and some persons of the court, to play at hot cockles and hide-and-seek.'

Madame Vigée-Lebrun lodged in a house opposite to the imperial palace. Regardless of local colour, legend has since transformed the rooks into pigeons; but, legend or history, does not all that the one and the other tell us of the tastes and habits of Catherine stand out in anything but the colours of a Messalina? Doubtless the objection that we have ourselves raised retains its force. Is what we know of the interior of a palace in which Catherine dwelt in company with an Orlof or a Patiomkine the whole truth, the true truth, as the Italians say? Doubt is the first virtue of the historian, and we would not forget it. Nevertheless, as we have already said, Catherine was no hypocrite; she lived openly before the world, and she had the pride, or the shamelessness, to seek no disguise, and to defy rebuke, at the point where our respect and admiration must needs forsake her.

III

From the outside, the Empress's life offers little material for the chronicler, favourably inclined or the reverse.

Apart from the great tours which stand out in the history of her reign, that in the Crimea for instance, she preferred generally to keep within the bounds of her vast and luxurious palaces. Sometimes, during the carnival, on a fine sunny day, she would make a longer expedition. Three great sledges, drawn by ten or twelve horses, carried her and her ordinary retinue. To each of these sledges a dozen smaller ones were fastened on behind with ropes, and into these the lords and ladies of the court crowded pell-mell, and the strange cavalcade set out at a gallop. They have dinner in the suburbs of the capital, in the Tchesmé Palace, and afterwards cross the Neva and go on as far as Gorbilevo, an imperial villa where there are *montagnes russes*; returning to the Taurida Palace for supper. On one of these excursions, after having dined and returned to her place in one of the large sledges, which she has all to herself, Catherine inquires of her squire if the drivers and lackeys have had their dinner. On his replying in the negative, she gets down from the sledge. 'They want dinner as much as we do,' she says. And, as there is no meal ready for them, she waits patiently until the hunger of the poor servants is appeased.

But these escapades are rare. The sovereign does not care to be seen too often, except in her palace, in the midst of the decorative *mise-en-scène* that surrounds her; she fears to lessen her prestige. One day when she has a headache, and a walk in the open air has done her good, she is recommended to try it again next day, the headache having returned. 'What would the people say,' she replies, 'if they saw me in the street two days following?' Twice in the course of the winter she goes to the masked ball. Those whom she invites to accompany her find masks and costumes at the court. Generally, on these occasions, in order the better to preserve her incognito, Catherine goes in some one else's coach. She likes to put on a man's costume, and to puzzle the women, to whom she pays court, and whose curiosity she puts off the track. Her voice, rather deep, lends itself to this disguise. One of those whose fancy she takes, carrying her imaginary conquest to some lengths, is so curious that she ends by violently tearing off the mask of the mysterious cavalier. Catherine is very angry, but she merely reproaches the too susceptible fair one of having broken the etiquette in usage at *fêtes* of this kind.

She accepts no invitations. The opulent Prince of Taurida, Count Razoumofski, Prince Field-Marshal Galitzine, the two Narychkines, the Countess Bruce, and Madame Batiouchkine are almost the only persons who have sometimes the honour of having her as guest. But as a rule she will not have herself announced, delighting in the confusion caused by her unexpected apparition.

In spring she leaves the Winter Palace for the Taurida Palace, when that magnificent abode, built by Patiomkine, has been bought by her from the wealthy favourite.   She generally goes there on Palm Sunday, and pays her Easter devotions.   She remains there till the month of May, when she returns to the shades of Tzar-skoïe-Sielo.   This abode that she has built, in place of the residences of Peterhof and Oranien-baum, about which there cling too mournful souvenirs, is the spot where she is most happy. There, no more reception, no more court cere-mony, no more tiresome audiences.   Affairs even are in some sort suspended, or at least reduced to what is strictly necessary.   The Empress rises at six or seven, and begins her day with a walk. Lightly dressed, a cane in her hand, she strolls through her gardens.   The faithful Pierekousihina, a *valet de chambre*, and a huntsman, are the only ones who accompany her.   But the Anderson family, one may be sure, is of the party, and the sovereign's presence is known from afar by the joyous barking of the band that gambols before her on the grass.   Catherine is passionately fond of gardening, and *plantomania*, as she calls that taste, rivals with her the taste for building.   She follows, in this respect, the fashion of the age.

'I am madly enamoured at present,' she writes in 1772, 'of gardens in the English manner, curved lines, gentle slopes, pools in the form of lakes, archipelagos in *terra firma*, and I have a profound scorn for straight lines.   I hate foun-tains that torture the water to make it take a course contrary to nature : in a word anglomania dominates my plantomania.'   And five years

later: 'I often enrage my gardeners, and more
than one German gardener has said to me : *Aber,
mein Gott, was wird das werden!* I found that
the greater part were mere pedantic followers of
routine : the departures from routine that I often
propose to them horrify them, and, when I see
that routine is too strong for me, I employ the
first docile young gardener that comes to hand.
There is no one who laughs at my plantomania so
much as Count Orlof. He spies on me, mimics
me, makes fun of me, criticises me, but, on going
away, he asked me to look after his garden
during the summer, and this year I am going to
play pranks there after my own fashion. His
land is close to mine ; I am very proud that he
has recognised my merits as a gardener.'

The gardens of Tzarskoie are public. One
day, sitting on a bench with la Pierekousihina,
Catherine sees a man pass, a citizen of St. Petersburg, who, seeing the two old women, and not
recognising the sovereign, casts a scornful look
upon them, and goes on his way. La Pierekousihina is indignant, but Catherine replies : 'What
would you have, Maria Savichna? Twenty
years ago that would not have happened to us ;
we have aged : it is our fault.'

After her walk, at nine, Catherine begins
work, and till six o'clock the rest of the day goes
on much as it does in town, except that there are
fewer officials and tedious clerkly people, and
that the private retinue is lessened. One or two
invited guests from the capital sometimes appear
at dinner. At six o'clock, another walk, this
time in larger numbers, but in the most complete
liberty. The Empress's grandchildren play at

base-ball, with Count Razoumofski as umpire. If it rains, Catherine gathers together her people in the famous gallery of colonnades covered with glass, in which one sees the busts of the great men, ancient and modern, for whom she has a particular admiration.

The foreign ministers are sometimes admitted to share the pleasures of the imperial *villegiatura*. The Comte de Ségur, who had this honour, thus recounts his recollections of it :—

'Catherine II. had the extreme kindness to show me herself all the beauties of this magnificent pleasure-house, whose limpid waters, fresh groves, elegant pavilions, noble architecture, priceless furniture, cabinets panelled in porphyry, in lapis-lazuli, in malachite, had a fairy-like air, and recalled to those who admired them the palace and gardens of Armida. . . . The entire liberty, the gaiety of conversation, the absence of all ennui and constraint, might have made me believe, had I turned away my eyes from the imposing majesty of the Palace of Tzarskoïe-Sielo, that I was in the country among the pleasantest of private people. . . . M. de Cobenzel manifested his unquenchable gaiety ; M. Fitz-Herbert, a fine and finished wit ; General Potemkin, an originality that made him always new, even during his frequent moments of moroseness or dreaminess. The Empress chatted familiarly on all subjects, politics excepted ; she liked to hear amusing stories, and to tell them, and if by chance the conversation flagged, the chief equerry, Narychkine, recalled the laughter and gaiety by his mad humour. Catherine worked almost all the morning, and we were all free to write, read, walk, or do whatever we felt inclined. The dinner, very limited as to dishes and guests, was good, simple, without display; the time after dinner was devoted to play and conversation. In the evening the Empress retired early, and after that we met together, Cobenzel, Fitz-Herbert, and I, either in the room of one of our number, or in Prince Potemkin's.'

Catherine rested in this pleasant retreat from the fatigues of her position, from those especially which came from the necessity of her presence in the court festivities and ceremonies. We owe our readers a few words on the celebrated soirées of the Hermitage.

In the amplitude of its proportions, the magnificence of its interior decoration, the palace thus called did not by any means answer to its name. A series of rooms and galleries led to a circular *salle de spectacle*, a reduced copy of the ancient theatre at Vicenza. The receptions were of three different kinds, the great receptions, the medium, and the small. To the first were admitted generally all the persons of distinction and the foreign ministers. Balls alternated with performances, in which all the famous artists took part: Sarti, Cimarosa, Paisiello conducted the orchestra; Biotti, Puniani, Dietz, Lulli, Michel, displayed their talents on different instruments; la Gabrielli, la Todi, the baritone Marchesi, the tenor Majorletti, sang; in pantomime there were Pic, Rossi, Santini, Canucciani. After the concerts and Italian operas came the performances of Russian comedies and plays, with Volkof, Dmitrefski, Choumski, Kroutitski, Tchernikof, Sandounoff, la Trepolskaïa. The French drama and opera also had their place, with Sedaine, Philidor, Grétry, whose works found elegant interpreters, such as the famous Aufresne. At the ball, each lady had two cavaliers, who supped with her. After supper one more polonaise was danced, and the ball was over before ten.

The *medium* receptions differed from the grand receptions merely by the smaller number of guests.

Quite different was the character of the *small* receptions. As a rule no one was present except the members of the imperial family and some special friends carefully selected—a score of people in all. An invitation to a stranger was a mark of exceptional favour, to which the greatest value was attached. In the orchestra, when there was a play, as was often the case, there were sometimes only three or four picked musicians, Dietz with his violin, Delfini with his violoncello, Cardon with his harp. After the play, every one did as he liked. In the rooms thrown open to the guests there was really no longer *un soupçon d'impératrice*, as she is made to say to the Baron Grimm in a passage of his memoirs. On the walls is a notice: it is forbidden, among other things, to rise before the sovereign, even if one is sitting down, and the Empress comes over, and chooses to enter into conversation while standing. It is forbidden to have an ill-tempered air, to exchange unkind words, to speak ill of any one whatever. It is forbidden to remember the quarrels or the friendships that one may have out of doors: they must be left at the door, with sword and hat. It is forbidden also to lie and to talk idly. A fine of ten kopecks, which is received in a poor-box, is inflicted on those who break these rules. Bezborodko is appointed cashier. Among the *habitués* there is one who, by his constant blunders, continually has the cashier after him with his moneybox. One day when the bore has gone before the other guests, Bezborodko says to the Empress that she ought to refuse him admission to the Hermitage, otherwise he will ruin himself in fines. 'Let him be,' replies Catherine, 'after having passed the day in hearing your reports and those of your colleagues, I need some rest, and such idle talk is quite pleasant.' 'Then, Matouchka,' says Bezborodko, 'come and pay us a visit in the senate: you will get as much of it as ever you want.'

Games are all the rage in these gatherings, and Catherine herself is the life and soul of the company, stirring up the gaiety of her guests, and authorising every liberty. The forfeits are, to drink a glass of water at one draught, to recite a passage of the *Télémachide* of Trediakofski without yawning, etc. The evening ends with a game of cards. Often, in the middle of a rubber, the sovereign is interrupted to execute some forfeit. 'What must I do?' she asks meekly. 'Sit on the ground, Matouchka.' She obeys at once.

All that is far enough from the imaginary orgies which haunted the minds of her contemporaries. In a way, it is true, Catherine afforded some excuse for suppositions of this kind, which have done some harm to her reputation. She had from the first, and she kept to the last, ways and manners which are unusual enough in sovereigns.   In 1763 the Baron de Breteuil, just as he was leaving his post, received from her the following letter, the style of which might have surprised a diplomatist accustomed to the ceremonious forms in use in courts :—

'Monsieur le Baron de Breteuil will have the kindness to be at the cottage, on whose beauty he has promised to keep eternal secrecy, on Sunday at eleven o'clock in the morning, and if he will be so good, he will remain till after supper on the pretext of paying a visit to Count Orlof.'

The note, without date or signature, was in the Empress's handwriting.   The cottage referred to was a villa newly built in the neighbourhood of Moscow.   Breteuil answered as follows :—

'The Baron de Breteuil renews his vows of secrecy in regard to the cottage, where he looks forward to the pleasure of being publicly admitted on Sunday at eleven o'clock.   He will be there, in all respect and gratitude, and he will take advantage of the kind permission to remain all day, but M. le Comte d'Orlof will excuse him from making the pretext of paying him a visit.'

One would say that this was written at the dictation of the Baroness.   But if she really saw anything dubious in the sovereign's invitation, she was well deceived, and her husband well taken aback, when he found out the real cause of it.

CHAPTER II

FAMILY LIFE—THE GRAND DUKE PAUL

I

CATHERINE did not show a very profound affection for her parents; she seemed to forget that she had a brother; she was on bad terms with her husband, if she had not even some share, direct or indirect, in his tragic end; finally, her son, the only one of her legitimate children who survived her, had not much cause for gratitude to her, if even, as it has been supposed, she did not think of disinheriting him. These are facts. It has been inferred from this that she had no sort of family feeling, and that even the maternal feeling, found in the lowest of the low, and even among the animals, was alien to her cold and corrupt heart, depraved by ambition and by vice. These are questions to be considered.

What were the relations of Catherine with her husband, we have already said. Her relations with the heir to the throne have been variously interpreted. Some have imagined them to have been excellent up to the time of Paul's first marriage. From this moment the presence of a stranger may have exercised, in their regard, a jarring influence, such as one finds in the history of many families. Besides this, in the first year of this union, in 1774, a conspiracy is said to have been discovered, the aim of which was to raise the Grand Duke to the throne in place of his mother, and at the head of this plot

was the new daughter-in-law of Catherine, the
Grand Duchess Nathalie Aleksieïevna, *née* Princess of Darmstadt.   A secretary of Count Panine,
Bakounine, betrayed the secret to the Empress,
who threw the list of conspirators in the fire:
among the names she had found that of her
Prime Minister, side by side with her former
friend, Princess Dachkof.

This story, which is founded merely on a family
tradition, has been doubted by many.   It raises,
in fact, many objections.   Plots, real or imaginary, having for object the support of the incontestable rights of the son of Peter III., were
frequent throughout the whole reign of Catherine.
In his despatch of June 26, 1772, Count Solms
notifies to Frederick the discovery of an intrigue
of this kind set on foot by some officers of the
Preobrajenski regiment.   But he speaks also of
blows of the knout distributed, of noses and ears
cut off.   Such was the natural order of things.
The fact admitted of an almost hostile tension
between mother and son, in place of the former
harmonious, if never very intimate and affectionate, relations, another explanation has been
given and another date attributed to this change
of things.   The tour that Paul wished to make in
Europe, in company with his second wife, the
Grand Duchess Maria of Würtemberg, brought
about the crisis.   Having authorised this excursion only against her will, Catherine wished her
son, at all events, not to stop at Berlin.   She was
on the point of breaking with the court there.
Paul took no heed of all that.   He let himself
be fêted, flattered, and cajoled by Frederick, and
when he made his appearance at Vienna, people

were astonished to find that he knew nothing, or professed to know nothing, of the alliance which had already linked that court with his. He put himself forward everywhere as a severe critic of his mother's policy. At Florence, talking with Leopold, the brother of Joseph, he expressed himself in the most unguarded manner in reference to the principal assistants of Catherine, Prince Patiomkine, Bezborodko, Panine himself, declaring that they were all without exception in the pay of the Emperor. 'I will stamp them all out,' he repeated wrathfully.

This second version seems to us as arbitrary as the first, and neither appears to have any foundation ; it remains to be proved that at any period whatever Catherine treated her son better than she did after his marriage, or after the 'grand tour' which separated them for a time. Doubtless, in her letters to Madame Bielke, which date from 1772, it pleases the sovereign to paint in the most agreeable colours the life that she leads at Tzarskoïe, in company with Paul; but we know already what Catherine's epistolary sincerity is worth. Doubtless also, in the course of the September of that year, the Prussian ambassador, Count Solms, mentions several times a revival of tender demonstrations of the Empress to the Grand Duke. 'She cannot make a step without having him with her,' he writes. But this is at the very height of the crisis which, in separating the sovereign from her first favourite, and thus putting her at variance with the powerful tribe of the Orlofs, causes her serious misgivings as to the security of her throne. 'I know on sure authority,' adds Solms, 'that the Grand Duke is not too sure himself of the meaning of this excess of friendliness on the part of his mother.' And not without reason. About the same time, writing to her son, and beginning her letter twice over, Catherine first wrote these words :—

'It seems to me that you were either afflicted or sulky during the day; both would distress me as a mother; but as for the sulkiness, I confess I am not much concerned about that, either as mother or as Empress.'

She tore up the page, and began again thus:—

'It seems to me that you were either afflicted or sulky during the day; if you were in affliction, I should be distressed by it; if it was sullenness, I leave you to imagine what attention I should pay to that.'

But the first draft probably rendered her thought more exactly, and it does not indicate, to our view, very cordial relations. Catherine supposed that the affliction or sulkiness of the Grand Duke came from her refusal to admit him to her council, and this refusal was assuredly not in itself a proof of confidence or affection. As early as 1764 Bérenger wrote from St. Petersburg to the Duke of Praslin—

'This young Prince gives evidence of dark and dangerous dispositions. It is known that his mother does not love him, and that, since her accession, she shows him none of the marks of tenderness that she showered upon him before. . . He asked, a few days ago [Bérenger had this detail from one of the Grand Duke's *valets de chambre*], why his father had died, and

why the throne which belonged to him had been
given to his mother.   He added that when he
was grown up, he would get at the bottom of
all that.   They say that the child makes too
many such remarks for them not to reach the
ears of the Empress.   Now, no one doubts that
this Princess takes all possible precautions against
such an event.'

It is possible, however, that the tour undertaken by Paul against the wish of his mother,
and the attitude that he often assumed on that
occasion, may have helped to bring about some
ill-feeling on the part of the Empress, and to
urge her forward on a path on which her accession to the throne, that is to say, properly
speaking, her usurpation of the rights of her
son, had made her enter.

But the intimacy and affection had ceased
before this.   They were incompatible with the
respective position of these two beings, one of
whom had violently taken the place of the other.
Had these affectionate feelings and relations
ever existed?   Could Catherine ever have had
a mother's heart for the child who had been
torn from her arms as soon as he was born,
whom she had never nursed, whom she had
never brought up, whom she had never even seen
except at rare intervals?   Did she ever really
shower upon him those caresses of which Bérenger speaks?   Perhaps, before she had become
Empress, when the child, her son, might one day
become her Emperor and her master.   If there
was a change in her demeanour, the event must
have been simultaneous with that of July 5, 1762,
as indeed the report of the French *chargé-*

d'affaires clearly indicates, and the reason is sufficiently apparent.

II

We have already spoken several times of the tour of the Count and Countess du Nord. The departure, which took place on October 5, 1781, produced a great sensation at St. Petersburg. The people surrounded the carriage which bore the heir to the throne, with tears and sobs and every sign of the warmest affection. Some enthusiasts threw themselves under the wheels of the carriage to hinder it from advancing. This alone might well have alarmed Catherine She was, however, at first well pleased, rather than otherwise, by the homage with which Paul was greeted at Berlin. A conversation that she had with her son, after his return, changed her feelings on the subject. Then only she bethought herself that he had been made too much of by Frederick. As Paul made no disguise of his opinions and sympathies, she grew angry, declaring in her wrath that after she was dead 'Russia would become a Prussian province.'

The Grand Duke's travels were in the strictest incognito. Their Highnesses refused even the apartments that had been prepared for them, putting up in furnished lodgings with all their suite, which must have been considerable, since it required sixty horses at every posting station. Paul and his wife consented, however, to be guests at Versailles for a few days, and their visit seems to have left a favourable impression. 'The Grand Duke,' wrote Marie Antoinette, the day after their departure, 'has the air of an ardent and impetuous man who holds himself in. . The King has not noticed that he professed extravagant opinions.' There was a mythological and allegorical *fête* at Trianon, where a young *Hebe* particularly charmed the august spectators. It was—how can one record it without a pang? —*Madame Elizabeth!* The royal family wished also to make good the reputation of French hospitality. At *Mouceaux* (*sic*), in the gardens of the Duc de Chartres, 'after having traversed a thousand winding byways, arched over with sycamores, lilac-trees, Italian poplars, and a thousand shrubs of the Indies; after having breathed the fresh air, and rested on plots of grass and wild thyme, visited rustic huts and crumbling Gothic manor-houses, the Comte and Comtesse du Nord partook of the simple repast of the labouring shepherds.'

At Paris the passage of their Highnesses, coinciding with the effervescence of Russian sympathies that we have noted above, had almost the air of a triumphal progress. Everywhere agreeable surprises were in store for the visitors. At the Royal Library, a number of Russian books were taken down for the Grand Duke's benefit from the shelves, where no doubt they found few readers, and the librarian, Desolnais, called his attention to a volume that had served, said he, in the education of a prince whom Paris had long learned to admire, and was now learning to love. It was a manual composed for the use of Paul himself by the Archbishop Plato. Their Highnesses did their utmost to repay all this courtesy. After having reviewed Marshal Biron's

regiment of Gardes-françaises, the Grand Duchess
sent to the marshal a gracious letter, enclosing
ten bank-notes of 1200 francs, for the soldiers to
drink the health of their chief. The parsimony,
a forced parsimony indeed, of Paul in 1776 was
still remembered at Berlin, where the Grand Duke
had come to marry his second wife. Imperious
orders from St. Petersburg had cut short his
generous intentions. The proceeding was much
criticised, even at Paris, and the present difference was all the more appreciated. There was,
however, the painful incident of Clérisseau.
Paul, naturally, was surrounded in the capital
of arts and letters by the literary clique with
which his mother was connected. He did not
always give it satisfaction, or consider all its
susceptibilities. But for the distance which separated Paris from St. Petersburg, Catherine herself
might not have succeeded. Madame d'Ober-
kirch relates this scene in her memoirs, much as
follows. The scene took place at the house of
M. de la Reynière, now occupied by the Cercle
de l'Union Artistique. M. de la Reynière was
a wealthy *fermier-général*, and his house, which
was decorated by the best artists in Paris,
Clérisseau at their head, was famed as one of
the wonders of the city. Paul wished to see it.
He had already been introduced to the irascible
architect, and he had not been too attentive to
him : so at least Clérisseau thought, and he had
written a letter to Prince Bariatinski, the Grand
Duke's aide-de-camp—a very dignified letter,
according to Grimm—in which he had stated
that he would acquaint the Empress with the
reception that persons honoured by her esteem

met with from her son. A few days after, the
artist and the prince met in the dining-room
of de la Reynière's house, one of Clérisseau's
masterpieces. On entering, the Comte du Nord
perceived a man who bowed without speaking.
Paul returned the bow, but the man barred the
way.

'What do you want, Monsieur?'

'You do not recognise me, Monseigneur?'

'I recognise you perfectly; you are the Sieur
Clérisseau.'

'Why then do you not speak to me?'

'Because I have nothing to say.'

'Then you are going to be here as you were
at home, Monseigneur, slight me, treat me as a
stranger; I, the architect of the Empress, and
in correspondence with her! And I have written
to her, to complain of your unworthy treatment
of me.'

'Write her also, then, that you are hindering
me from passing, Monsieur. She will certainly
thank you for it.'

The version that Grimm gives of the incident,
in his correspondence with Catherine, is quite
different, and it seems to us more probable. It
was Paul who first made overtures to Clérisseau,
wishing to repair the wrongs he might have done
him, showing himself most amiable, and recalling
the flattering words that he had used on their
first meeting. But Clérisseau cut short these
tardy demonstrations—

'Monsieur le Comte, you may have intended
to say all that to me, but I heard nothing of it.'

'You must have neither ears nor memory,
then,' said Paul, with some heat.

With this, some people coming up just then, the conversation ended. 'Never was I so uncivilly used,' said the Grand Duke, laughing, to those about him; 'it gave me quite a shock.' The Grand Duchess tried to smooth over matters; but Clérisseau was unmanageable, and ended by becoming rude. The Princess having asked him to send her the plan and sketches of a *salon* that she had admired, he replied dryly—

'I will send them to my august benefactress, where Madame la Comtesse can have them.'

Catherine did not, in this circumstance, attempt to justify her architect against the heir to her throne; she knew too well the interests of her rank and dignity; but the incident doubtless left an unpleasant impression on her mind · she was only too much disposed to think her son and heir a clumsy creature. The letters that she sent to the travellers, during their absence, were, however, always affectionately maternal. It would seem even as if this separation exercised a calming influence over her mind. When he was present, and by her side, Paul became a menace and a source of perpetual uneasiness. Had it not been publicly stated that she was only awaiting his coming of age to restore to him his own, that is to say, the place that she herself occupied ?

III

After his return these disagreements grew worse. Paul and his wife complained that the Empress took out of their hands the education of their children. At the time of the Crimean tour,

Catherine had wished to take with her the little Grand Dukes Alexander and Constantine. This time the parents' objections were so strong that she hesitated to go against them. But questions of policy played a considerable part in the quarrel, which grew worse from day to day. In July 1783 the Marquis de Vérac, then French minister at St. Petersburg, wishing to prevent a conflict between Russia and Turkey, renewed the representations that the Court of Versailles never ceased to urge, and complained of the unfavourable, almost scornful, reception that was given them on the part of the Empress and her ministers; he insisted in these terms on an antagonism in which he saw some hope for the future : 'The Grand Duke is entirely opposed to all this system of ideas; this Prince, brought up in the wise principles of the late Count Panine, regards with mortal dissatisfaction the deplorable state to which the empire has come through the boundless prodigality of the Empress. He considers the plan of campaign against the Turks a project likely to lead Russia to utter ruin, and he is personally much incensed against the Emperor, whom he regards as the prime mover in the matter.'

When the war had broken out, Catherine objected to the Grand Duke's taking part in it. 'It would be a fresh inconvenience,' she wrote to Patiomkine. She allowed him to go to Finland, during the Swedish war; but Knorring, who commanded the army in the field, declared afterwards that he had been commanded not to communicate to his Highness any plan of operations. In 1789, when there was question of a rupture with Prussia, the situation of Paul assumed a certain likeness, irritating for Catherine, but still more threatening for him, with that occupied by Peter during the last years of Elizabeth's reign. Dark rumours were in the air. The famous Greek project of the Empress was yet another source of continual conflict: on the part of the Grand Duke it met with open opposition. Finally, in the course of the changes which came about from year to year in those who were about the Empress, Paul sometimes went so far as to forget his duty as a son, and, in return, the favourites, whether Patiomkine or Zoubof, did not feel obliged to be very respectful to his Highness. One day, at table, the Grand Duke having approved of an idea put forward by Zoubof, 'Have I said anything stupid?' said he.

The young count was frequently in difficulties about money. In 1793, when Catherine was engaged in looking through the accounts of the court banker, Sutherland, who had made some bad speculations, and was on the point of suspending payment, her secretary, Dierjavine, comes, in his enumeration of the assets, to a sum due to the banker 'from a person in high position, but who has the misfortune not to be loved by the Empress' Catherine was not long in discovering who was meant. 'How absurd!' she cries; 'what does he want with such sums?' Dierjavine ventures to observe that the late Prince Patiomkine had been accustomed to borrow much larger sums; he points out some in Sutherland's assets. The Empress pays no heed, and the examination of the accounts goes on. They

come to another item of the 'person in high
position.' 'Another!' cries Catherine, furiously.
'No wonder, after that, Sutherland became
bankrupt!' Dierjavine thinks the occasion
favourable to pay a bad turn to the new favourite,
Plato Zoubof, by whom he does not consider
himself sufficiently well paid. He turns to a
long sum recently put to his account. The
Empress, without replying, rings a bell. 'Is
there any one in the secretary's room?' she asks.
There is Vassili Stiepanovitch Popof. 'Send
him in.' Popof enters. 'Sit down there, and do
not leave me till the end of this report. This
gentleman' (pointing to Dierjavine) 'wishes to
come to blows with me, I think.'

At this period the Grand Duke lives with his
wife at Gatchina or Pavlovsk, entirely apart from
his mother and also from his children, who are
with her, and whom he sometimes does not see
for months together. To see them he requires
the permission of Count Saltykof, their governor.
We have already spoken of the opinion, general
enough during the last years of Catherine's reign,
according to which she intended to disinherit her
son. This measure was hoped for by a large
number of persons. A manifesto deciding this
important point was anxiously expected. It was
thought that it would appear on January 1, 1797.
According to one version, the manifesto was
already drawn up, and was intended to inaugurate
constitutional government·in Russia under the
sceptre of Alexander, the character of Paul being
utterly opposed to the adoption of this form of
government. In the memoirs of Engelhardt, in
a fragment of the memoirs of Dierjavine, which

has been preserved, there is, on the other hand, some reference to a testament of the Empress, having the same object, except for the enigmatic and doubtful introduction of constitutionalism, so little in accord with the ideas then prevailing in the mind of Catherine.   The Ode written by Dierjavine for the coronation of Alexander seems to allude to it, as well as a curious document which circulated after the death of the Empress under the title, *Catherine II. in the Elysian Fields.*   The sovereign reproaches Bezborodko, to whom the testament in question was supposed to have been confided, with having inflicted the reign of Paul on her country.

It is certain that in alluding, frequently enough, in her correspondence, to the future of Russia after her death, Catherine never speaks of the reign of her son.   It is always Alexander whom she speaks of as her heir.   According to certain authorities, she finally took stringent measures against the difficulties that she anticipated on the part of the natural heir.

Mother and son now met only in official ceremonies.   They exchanged ceremonious letters.   During the very short visit of the Grand Duke to the army in Finland, where he soon discovered that he had nothing to do, the correspondence is almost daily.   It recalls a little that of the King of Spain with Maria of Neubourg, in the version that Victor Hugo has given of it.   Here is a specimen :—

'My dear Mother,—The letter of your Imperial Majesty has caused me the greatest pleasure, and I am deeply touched by what is said in it. I beg her to accept the expression of my gratitude, and at the same time that of the respect and affection with which I am . . .'

Here is Catherine's reply :—

'I have received, my dear son, your letter of the 5th, with the expression of your sentiments, to which mine respond. Good-bye. I hope you are well.'

The letters are all after this fashion, almost without variation.

IV

What bears witness against Catherine in these unhappy events—the seamy side of the splendours of the great reign—is the way in which she acted in regard to another son, in whom there was nothing to alarm her ambition or her responsibility as a sovereign. She had, as we know, a second son, a love-child, who was known as Bobrinski. Did she love him? It does not seem so. Did she look after his welfare? She gave him enough to live comfortably, to travel abroad, and even to commit some extravagances. He carried them to excess : she hears of it, and betrays an astonishing indifference on the subject.

'What,' she writes to Grimm, 'is this affair of Bobrinski? The young man is singularly unconcerned. If you could manage to find out the state of his affairs at Paris, you would oblige me. . However, he ought to be well able to pay his way ; he has 30,000 roubles a year.'

Two years afterwards she writes—

'It is tiresome that M. Bobrinski will get into

debt; he knows the amount of his income, and is quite honest. Beyond that, he has nothing.'

It is thus that she announces her resolution not to meet the debts of this son; beyond the modest quota that she allows him, he and his creditors must not count upon her. And she keeps her word. At the end of 1787 young Bobrinski is in Paris, in the greatest distress, several million francs in arrears, besides the amount that he owes in London, whence he has just fled his creditors. For one thing, he has given the Marquis de Ferriéres a bill of credit for 1,400,000 francs. Catherine up to now has made no attempt to arrest this disordered career. She now makes up her mind to act; she recalls the young man to Russia, and confines him to Revel, where she has all his movements carefully watched, without, however, caring to see him or to know what becomes of him. As long as he leaves her in peace, and does not ask her for money, and she does not hear him referred to, she is quite satisfied.

Nothing could be more definite than that. But is there no touch of nature in the heart of this insensible mother? How can we maintain the contrary? But how also can we affirm it? We have seen her relations with her son. But now let us see her relations with her grand-children. From 1779 onwards, every day at half-past ten, the little Alexander is brought to her. 'I have said it to you before and I say it to you again,' she writes to Grimm, 'I dote on the little monkey. . . . Every day we make new acquaint-ances, that is to say that of every toy we make

ten or twelve, and we try which of the two can
best develop his talents. It is extraordinary how
industrious we have become. . . . After dinner
my little monkey comes back as often as he likes,
and he spends three or four hours a day in my
room.' The same year she begins to teach his
A B C to 'Mr. Alexander, who cannot yet talk,
and who is only a year and a half old.' As we
have seen, she makes his clothes for him. 'This
is how he has been dressed ever since he was six
months old,' she says, when sending to Grimm
the facsimile of a costume of her invention. 'All
that is sewn together, and goes on at once, and
fastens behind with four or five little hooks. . . .
There is no ligature anywhere, and the child
scarcely knows that he is being dressed : his
arms and legs are put into the dress at once, and
it is all done; it is a stroke of genius on my part,
this dress. The King of Sweden and the Prince
of .Prussia have demanded and received a pattern
of the dress of Mr. Alexander.' Then come the
inevitable anecdotes that we find in the letters of
all mothers, in which are narrated day by day
the great deeds of the infant prodigy, the clever
sayings, the indications of intelligence, 'wonderful for his age.' One day when the precious
'little monkey' is ill and shivering with fever,
Catherine finds him at the door of her room,
wrapped up in a great cloak. She asks what that
is for, and the child replies, 'It is a sentinel dying
of cold.' One day he asks one of the Empress's
femmes de chambre whom he is like. 'Your
mother,' she replies; 'you have all her features,
her nose, her mouth.' 'No, not that; but my
temper, my ways, what are they like?' 'Oh, in

that you are more like grandmamma than any-body.' Thereupon the little Grand Duke throws his arms round the old woman's neck, and kisses her effusively. 'That is what I wanted you to say!'

This story is very significant in regard to the place that Paul and Catherine occupied respec-tively in this family, in which the widow of Peter III. usurps all the supremacy. Read one more passage from a letter to Grimm, referring to the adored little being : ' He will, to my thinking, become a most wonderful personage indeed, provided the *secondaterie* does not hinder his progress.'

Secondat, secondaterie, are words after the manner of Catherine, used by her to describe her son and her daughter-in-law, as well as the educational, political, and all kinds of ideas that prevail at Pavlovsk, and are in general entirely opposed to her own.

The little Constantine does not at first get into the good graces of his grandmother to the same extent as his brother. Catherine finds him too frail, too delicate, for an Empress's grandson. 'As for the other,' she says, after having spoken enthusiastically of Alexander, 'I would not give ten *sous* for him ; I am very much mistaken if he is likely to live very long.' But by and by the younger wins his way. With time the child grows and becomes stronger, and, dreams of Byzantine sovereignty showing themselves on the horizon, the affection of Catherine awakens little by little for the nursling of the Greek Helen.

Alas! it must needs be said that her state

policy plays its part, and even a main part, in this chapter of the great sovereign's history. Policy! we are sure to find that wherever we follow Catherine: in her feelings as in her thoughts, in her likes as in her dislikes, and her family feelings themselves make no exception to the rule. It is there, to our mind, that we must seek the starting-point and the solution of all the doubts, all the enigmas, to which the study that this book is devoted to may give rise. Naturally, as we think, in this woman, who, in certain sides of her character and certain details of her conduct, deserves all reprobation, as on other sides she merits all the praise, the moral sensibility, without being of a high order, was neither absent, as some have fancied, nor yet deadened, nor vitiated and reduced to the level of the lowest instincts. Her heart was on a level with her mind, which, as we have intimated, never reached a very great elevation. She could love, but she subordinated love, as she subordinated everything else, to the motive force of her life, which was of exceptional force and vigour : she lived, above all things, by and for politics. At one time she loved the handsome Orlof because he was handsome, but also because he declared that he would risk his life to give her a crown, and she believed him capable of carrying out his word. She was cold and even harsh towards Paul, a little because she had not had the leisure to develop the maternal sentiments, thwarted from the cradle, but very much because she saw in him a dangerous rival in the present, and a pitiful successor in the future. She manifested a passionate affection for the little Alexander under the influence of just opposite causes, in the same category of ideas and feelings.

The letters that she wrote to her grandchildren when she was away from them, in 1783, during her stay in Finland, in 1785, when she spent some time in Moscow, and in 1787, during her Crimean tour, are full of freshness, of communicative warmth, of loving abandonment. It was a great trial to her not to have them with her on the fairyland roads of Taurida. It was a reason of economy that decided her to cut short the endless negotiations, on this subject, between St. Petersburg and Pavlovsk : every day's delay cost her 12,000 roubles. One may judge from that what must have been the total expense of the tour, which all Europe looked on in wonderment.

Catherine had the opportunity, in directing the education of Alexander and Constantine, of applying her own theories in the matter. Her success seems to have been doubtful. The sovereign was almost alone, it would seem, in being satisfied with the progress of her scholars. La Harpe, among others, did not share her opinion. He had often to complain of the bad instincts and defects that he found in the elder. He gives several unpleasant enough traits. In 1796 the visit of the young King of Sweden caused comparisons to be made, not to the advantage of the two boys. Catherine, however, did her best, not allowing her affection to hinder her from a sometimes necessary severity. One day she noticed that in changing the squad on guard under the windows of the palace the men were kept under arms longer than was needful : it was a sight intended for the little Grand Dukes. She immediately sent for their tutor, and reprimanded him severely. The service of the state, the military service in particular, was not made for the amusement of children. If the Grand Dukes complained, they were to be informed that grand-mamma had forbidden it. This was an accidental instance of a very wise principle. But perhaps the system as a whole was less wise.

Catherine was much concerned, and she was the only one to concern herself, as to the marriage of her grandchildren. The parents were not even consulted. Paul was scarcely consulted, indeed, in regard to his own marriage. Eleven German princesses were successively brought to Russia by the sovereign, solicitous as to the well-being of her son and her grandchildren : three Princesses of Darmstadt, three Princesses of Würtemberg, two Princesses of Baden, and three Princesses of Coburg. Choice was to be made from the lot. The Princesses of Würtemberg only went as far as Berlin, Frederick having insisted on Paul being sufficiently gallant to come half way to meet his *fiancée*. It was Prince Henry of Prussia, who was at St. Petersburg in 1776, who arranged the marriage. The eldest of the Princesses was already promised to the Prince of Darmstadt, but it was understood that he would give her up if, as Prince Henry wrote to his brother, 'he had the least good feeling,' and did not desire to trouble the happiness of two states.' The Prince of Darmstadt did indeed prove his 'good feeling.' Being deprived of the eldest, he turned his attention to the younger, 'because, at bottom, that came to the same thing.' Besides, as

Frederick gave him to understand, the father of the Princess had not waited to consult him before 'playing for the biggest stake that presented itself to his daughter.' He had had no difficulty beyond that of finding a Lutheran minister sufficiently 'enlightened' to make the future Grand Duchess understand that she would please God by changing her religion. But, as the court of St. Petersburg had sent 40,000 roubles for the cost of the Princess's journey, 'a real help,' as their mother said, to the rickety finances of the family, that difficulty was soon overcome.

Two years later, the Princesses of Darmstadt went all the way to St. Petersburg. Then came the turn of the two Princesses of Baden-Durlach. As they were orphans, the Countess Chouvalof, widow of the author of the *Epître à Ninon*, was sent to bring them over; and she was accompanied by a certain Strekalof, who appears to have conducted himself like a Cossack who had been ordered to carry off girls into Georgia. But the German courts were not susceptible at this time. On the arrival of the Princesses, the Empress asked to see their *trousseau*. Having examined it, she said, ' My friends, I was not so rich as you when I arrived in Russia.'

The elder remained in Russia, and married Alexander; the younger returned to her own country : Constantine would not have her. She was only fourteen, and not yet developed. Later on she married the King of Sweden. The *fêtes* which were given on the occasion of the marriage of Alexander mark the last brilliant and happy moment of the reign of Catherine. The following epithalamium was composed :—

'Ni la reine de Thèbes au milieu de ses filles,
Ni Louis et ses fils assemblant les familles,
Ne formèrent jamais un cercle si pompeux.
Trois générations vont fleurir devant elle,
Et c'est Elle toujours qui charmera nos yeux.
Fière d'être leur mère et non d'être immortelle :
Telle est Junon parmi les dieux ! '

The year after, the arrival of the Princess of
Saxe-Coburg with her three daughters produced
less effect.   This time Catherine considered that
the belongings of their Highnesses were quite
too mean.   Her own penury at the time of her
arrival in Russia was exceeded   The wardrobe
of the family had to be renewed before it was
presentable to the court, and Constantine, in
spite of all, was still unsatisfied.   He ended,
however, by deciding on the youngest.

Catherine, then, resolutely disregarded certain
family affections and responsibilities imposed on
her both by nature and the proprieties; she
entered into others with at least equal intensity.
We have pointed out the most admissible solution, in our eyes, of this moral problem ; we do
not profess that it answers every objection.
But, with regard to the great figures of history,
there are many of these insoluble enigmas, in
which no one can say the last word.

CHAPTER III

PRIVATE LIFE—FAVOURITISM

I

THERE is a whole legend in regard to the love
affairs of Catherine.   We shall try to replace it

by a few pages of history.   It is certainly not in
the character of historian that Laveaux has recorded Catherine's first taste of intrigue, at a
time when she had not yet arrived in Russia.
Even at Stettin she would have had as lover a
Count B., who imagined that he was marrying
her, when leading one of her friends to the altar.
It is an absurd fabrication.   The small courts of
Germany were certainly not temples of virtue ;
nevertheless, at the age of fourteen, princesses
were not exactly on the streets.   Afterwards, at
Moscow and at St. Petersburg, Laveaux shows us
Catherine abandoning herself to the first comer,
in the house of a Countess J., where she had innumerable lovers, who had no idea who she was.
Saltykof gives place to a Venetian actor named
Dalolio, who, in turn, arranges new rendezvous for
his mistress of a day in the house of Ielaguine.
In all this Laveaux echoes mere *on dits* without the
slightest shadow of proof.   Sabatier de Cabre is a
witness really well informed and really serious, and
one, too, who cannot be suspected of partiality.
Now, in a memorandum drawn up by him in 1772,
we read : ' Though not free from reproach, she is
far from the excess of which she has been accused;
nothing has been proved beyond the three known
connections—with M. Saltykof, the King of
Poland, and Count Orlof.'

On arriving in Russia, Catherine finds a court
and society, we dare not say more debauched than
those of the other great European centres, but at
least equally so, and, to crown it all, a form of
regal debauchery, similar also, though with an
inversion of *rôles*, to the examples afforded
elsewhere by the morals of the time, by French

royalty among others. This is *favouritism.*
Since the death of Peter I. the throne of Russia
has been constantly occupied by women ; they
have lovers, as Louis XV. has mistresses, and,
when the imperial lover is called Biron, he is as
powerful in Russia as a royal mistress, when she
is called Pompadour, can be in France. As
Louis XIV. married Madame de Maintenon, so
Elizabeth marries Razoumofski. He is only the
son of a little Russian peasant, once choir-boy in
the imperial chapel; but Scarron's widow is of
no very illustrious line. Choubine, who had
preceded Razoumofski, was a mere soldier in
the Guards : he was at all events the equivalent
of the du Barry. And, going back a little further,
when, by the cradle of Louis XIV., royalty had
provisionally fallen to the female line, the presence
of Signor Mazarini on the steps of the throne
must have seemed not less extraordinary to the
people who are easily astonished than, a hundred
and fifty years later, that of Patiomkine. Need
one even, to parallel the favourites of Catherine,
go back so far ? Struensee, Godoy, Lord Acton,
are contemporaries.

Favouritism in Russia is what it is or has been
elsewhere, allowing for the difference of scale. It
is just this which gives it, under the reign of
Catherine, a place apart. This time it is a
woman who has the gift of going to extremes
in everything. She has favourites, as Elizabeth
and Anne have had ; but urged by her temperament, her character, her inclination to do things
grandly, she gives unparalleled proportions to
this usual, traditional order or disorder of things.
Anne merely made Bühren the groom a Duke of

Courland; Catherine makes Poniatowski King of
Poland. Elizabeth was content with two admitted favourites, Razoumofski and Chouvalof;
Catherine has them by dozens. Nor is this all.
Her mind is not only of vast reach, scorning the
ordinary limits, passionately desirous of what lies
beyond; it is also, and especially, imperious,
absolute, disregardful of established rules, but
readily turning into rule or law the inspiration of
the moment, will or caprice. With Anne and
Elizabeth, favouritism is a mere caprice; with
Catherine it becomes almost an institution of state.

It is only gradually, however, that things reach
this height. Up to 1772 Catherine is merely a
sovereign who takes her pleasures as all those
who preceded her on the same throne have done.
Her caprices are talked of just as were those of
Elizabeth, in the most unconcerned way. Writing to Frederick, the Comte de Solms does, it
is true, *à propos* of Gregory Orlof, make this
observation, that 'one might find to-day artisans
and lackeys who have been seated with him at
the same table'; but he adds, 'One is so accustomed to favouritism in Russia, so little surprised at any rapid ascent, that one can but
applaud the choice of a young man who is mild
and polished in his manners, who betrays neither
pride nor vanity, who lives with his old acquaint-
ances on the same terms of familiarity, and never
loses sight of them in the crowd, avoiding mixing
himself up in affairs, except sometimes to recom-
mend a friend.' Gregory Orlof, it is true, does
not long content himself, or rather Catherine is
not contented on his behalf, with this modest and
retiring part, and the Comte de Solms writes

later on: 'Her Majesty's passion having increased, she has wished to bring Orlof into
affairs. She has put him into the commissions
established for the reform of government.' And
it is then, if we may believe the Prussian ambassador, that discontent breaks out. The
hetman Razoumofski, Count Boutourline, both
generals aides-de-camp, do not willingly suffer
that a man who has been so far below them,
just before, should now become their equal.
Other lords, princes, and generals are scandalised at being obliged to wait in the Sieur Orlof's
antechamber, to be admitted to his *lever*. Count
Cheremetief, the high chamberlain, one of the
first and wealthiest lords of the land, as well as
all whom their offices oblige to accompany the
Empress's carriage on horseback, see with dissatisfaction the favourite seated in the coach
beside their sovereign, while they trot by at
the side.

But that is an old tale, and those of the great
Russian lords who remember the favouritism of
Biron under the reign of the Empress Anne, the
Bironovchtchina, as the detested period has been
called, must find the present state of things very
acceptable in comparison, especially as Gregory
Orlof rarely shows much inclination to avail himself of the somewhat forced part that the loving
attentions of Catherine impose upon him in the
government of the country. His ambitious fits
are few and far between. Generally, as we have
pointed out, he merely obeys the exigencies of
the sovereign in this respect, and with a constrained and unwilling air. He is backward and
retiring, a lover of voluptuous ease, careless and

inoffensive. On the giddy heights, in the intoxi-
cating atmosphere, where the stroke of fortune
has suddenly raised him, he lives in a half dream,
and a day comes when his reason gives way
altogether, sinking into the black abyss of
madness.

With him the weakness of Catherine has an
excuse, a defence; the man has risked his life
for her, the man has given her a crown, and she
loves him, or imagines she loves him, with a love
not only of the senses. Separated from him, she
will suffer in all his sufferings, and at his death
she will shed real tears, tears coming from the
heart.

The scandal really commences only after the
disgrace of this first favourite. With Vassiltch-
kof, in 1772, it is the mere lust of the flesh, gross
and shameless. With Patiomkine, in 1774, it
is the division of power with mere chance lovers
that enters into the history of the reign. Then
comes the long procession of passing favours: in
June 1778 the Englishman Harris announces the
elevation of Korssakof; in August, he speaks of
competitors who are already canvassing his succession, some supported by Patiomkine, others
by Panine and Orlof acting in concert; in September, it is a certain Strahof, 'a low buffoon,'
who seems to win the day; four months after,
it is a major of the Siemionofski Guards, a
certain Levachof, a young man protected by the
Countess Bruce, Svieikofski, stabs himself in
despair at seeing a rival preferred to himself.
Then Korssakof seems once more to gain the
upper hand. He struggles with a new com-
petitor, Stianof, then is blotted out entirely by

Lanskoï, who is replaced by Mamonof, who struggles in turn with Miloradovitch and Miklachefski ; and so on, and so on. It is the rising of a tide that is to go on for ever ; in 1792, at sixty-three years of age, Catherine begins again with Plato Zoubof, and probably also with his brother, the same old story that has been gone over with twenty predecessors.

Is it, nevertheless, even in this last descent into nameless depths, sheer shameless sensuality on her part? and is her reason, the reason of a woman of genius, carried away, along with her modesty and her dignity, by the impetuous current which bears her forward? In our belief, no. A phenomenon of another order is to be met with, raising the old and ever new problem which, now once more, is being passionately discussed. The question in regard to Catherine and her favourites is the broad question of 'sexuality,' from the material and moral point of view, and this question resolves itself, we can almost say, in the clear light of historical experiences. Here is an exceptional woman, exceptionally endowed with aptitudes and energies, both intellectual and moral, even physical, exceptionally exempt also from the bondage common to her sex. She has all liberty, all independence, and all power, an absolute power. How does she make use of it? No, it is not alone the imperious and unwearying appeal of the senses that throws her, now into the arms of a Zoubof, now into the arms of a Patiomkine. Another need, another imperative demand, comes into play, by its side, in the amorous Odyssey whose changing fortunes we are about to sketch. And ir the first place, whatever may be the energy of her character, the firmness of her mind, and the good opinion that she has of her own abilities, Catherine does not profess that they can suffice to themselves and to her for the accomplishment of her task ; she feels the need of support from a virile mind and re-solution, however inferior these may be to hers in actual value.   And she proves this necessity! When she writes to Patiomkine that without him 'she is without arms,' it is not a mere phrase. In 1788, when the favourite is in the Crimea, the letters that her confidential agent, Garnofski, sends to him from St. Petersburg are full of pressing objurgations, showing the urgent need of his return, as much on account of the disorder into which his absence has thrown affairs, as of the state in which the Empress herself is, 'de-jected, subject to constant terrors, and vacillating from lack of support.'   And it is here, too, that the part played in history by the conqueror of the Crimea and his fellows differs from the ex-amples given at the same time, at the other end of Europe, by feminine favouritism : Louis XV simply endures the influence of his mistresses and their intervention in affairs of government : Catherine encourages and demands it.

Nor is this all.   Lanskoï, Zoubof, are twenty-two when they succeed to the place of Patiom-kine.   Now Nicholas Saltykof, who retains his freedom of speech with the Empress, expressing his astonishment at a choice so utterly out of keeping with the age of the sovereign, she makes this reply, which may perhaps cause a smile, but which contains a characteristic trait of the 'eternal feminine' : 'Well! I am serving the empire in the education of such capable young men.' And she believes it! In her anxiety to initiate these young 'scholars' of a particular kind into the handling of the great interests of the state, there is really a sort of maternity. And it is thus that in her the irremediable weaknesses of a woman's nature join with her highest vocation in necessitating the presence and assistance of the male, near this proud and headstrong female autocrat.

Naturally,—for without this Catherine would not be herself,—political calculation has its share in this particular complication of her existence, strange as it may seem to say so. The statement is verified by the facts, and, so fantastic as a whole is the fortune of this great handler of men, the facts decide in her favour even on this point. Her intentions, extravagant as they may seem, are not entirely unjustified; 'educated' by her, trained, rough-hewn, raised from step to step, rapidly it is true, in the hierarchy of high civil and military functions, Patiomkine finally cuts a certain figure as all-powerful minister. When a whim of the sovereign installs him for a few months in the special suite of rooms communicating with the Empress's by an inner staircase, Zovitch is merely a major in the Hussars. He comes afterwards to fill an important place in the history of national education. We are not inventing : this favourite was the first to conceive of a military school modelled on the foreign establishments of the kind. At Chklof, a magnificent estate near Mohilef, which was given him as a residence after his disgrace, a school founded by him for the children of poor gentle-folk served as nucleus for the establishment of the *Corps de*

Cadets of Moscow, now the principal military gymnasium of the city.

Doubtless, such miracles came about through a peculiar concourse of circumstances presiding over the material and moral development of the great empire, become so entirely her own. But the complete history of her life is unintelligible; indeed, none such is possible, when it is not seen in this light. With Zovitch, Patiomkine, Mamonof, and ten others, the court of Catherine is quite that of Gerolstein, but a Gerolstein in which the comic, the grotesque, and the extravagant combine with serious elements, which make of this amalgam one of the most singular pages in the annals of the world. The Russia of to-day is still a unique country, existing, so to speak, on the verge of the European community; and Catherine was also a most extraordinary woman. These two conditions were required in order that it might be possible for operatic heroes to thus enact by her side, on one of the great stages of the universe, the great parts of the human drama. But these conditions being realised, and the history of the Russia of that day being thus played out amid pantomime scenery, it would be idle to try to explain it on the ordinary lines of analysis, which belong to the ordinary run of things.

Lastly, from a final point of view, favouritism such as Catherine practised was by no means the reign of sensuality pure and simple, blindly reaching after ever new pleasures. There was method in the madness of Hamlet; and in the veins of Catherine there was a little Danish blood. As we have said, she made of favouritism an institution.

II

We read, under date September 17, 1778, the following lines in the despatch of the day sent from St. Petersburg to the Comte de Vergennes by M. de Corberon :—

'We may observe in Russia a sort of interregnum in affairs, caused by the displacement of one favourite and the installation of his successor. This event eclipses everything else. On it hang all the interests of a certain side of things, and even the cabinet ministers, succumbing to the general influence, suspend their operations until the choice has been made, and things fall back into the accustomed groove, and the machine is once more in proper order.'

All this is an essential part of the machinery of government, and, this once lacking, everything comes to a dead stop. The interregnums are, however, as a rule of very short duration. Only one lasts for several months, between the death of Lanskoï (1784) and the succession of Iermolof. Generally it is a matter of twenty-four hours, and the slightest ministerial crisis is a much more serious inconvenience to-day. There is no lack of candidates. The place is good, and those whose ambition it tempts are legion. In the regiments of the Guards, the traditional home of *vremienchtchiks* (favourites), there are always two or three handsome officers who turn their eyes in the direction of the imperial palace with a hope and longing more or less concealed. From time to time one of them makes his appearance at court, introduced by some great personage, who tries his chance of making a 'creature' for him-

self, and in a post which is the source of all riches
and honours.   In 1774 a nephew of Count Zahar
Tchernichef, a Prince Kantemir, young, dissolute,
deep in debt, *beau garçon*, prowls for some weeks
around the Empress.   Twice, pretending to have
lost his way, he reaches the private apartments of
the Empress.   The third time, he finds her, falls
on his knees, and begs her to use him as she will.
She rings, he is seized, put in a *kibitka*, and sent
back to his uncle, who is advised to teach his
nephew a little wisdom.   Catherine is indulgent
for this kind of folly.   Patiomkine, more for-
tunate, makes his way by a bold stroke almost
exactly similar.   In general, however, this post, so
much sought after, is the price of some intriguing.
After 1776 it is Patiomkine, now honorary favourite,
who brings forward deputies discovered, trained,
and managed by him, and offers them to the
choice of the sovereign.   But both they and
he have no easy task to keep the position, once
attained : an absence, an illness, a momentary
default, are enough to ruin all their chances.
The very name, so expressive in Russian (*vremia*
means time, moment ; *vremienchtchik*, the man of
the moment) tells the chosen ones that the favour
is fleeting.   In 1772 it is at Fokchany, where he
has gone to negotiate peace with Turkey, that
Gregory Orlof learns of the installation of Vassiltchikof in the place that he has imprudently
quitted.   He sets out at full speed, covers 2000
miles without stopping, travelling post, without
sleep, almost without food, in order to reach the
capital as quickly as he can.   In spite of all, he
arrives too late.   In 1704, Lanskoï, fallen ill, has
recourse to artificial stimulants, which irreparably

ruin his health. Sometimes, too, on the height by the throne, reached at a bound, these spoilt children of fate grow giddy : Zovitch thinks he may even defy her who has raised him from nothingness. Mamonof even imagines that he can share her favour with a court lady, for whom he sighs. It is over in an instant : at an evening reception, it is noticed that the Empress has gazed attentively at some obscure lieutenant, presented but just before, or lost sight of till then among the crowd of courtiers; next day, it is reported that he has been appointed aide-de-camp to her Majesty. What that means is well known. Next day he finds himself in the special suite of rooms, in which the abode of the favourite is as brief as, in our days, are those of the heads of departments in the ministerial quarters. The rooms are already vacated, and everything is prepared for the new-comer. All imaginable comfort and luxury, a splendidly appointed house, await him ; and, on opening a drawer, he finds a hundred thousand roubles (about 500,000 francs), the usual first gift, a foretaste of Pactolus. That evening, before the assembled court, the Empress appears, leaning familiarly on his arm, and on the stroke of ten, as she retires, the new favourite follows her.

He will never leave the palace except at the side of his august mistress. From this moment he is a bird in a cage. The cage is fine, but it is carefully guarded : the Empress is on her guard against accidents, such as the generally far from reassuring antecedents of the chosen ones might reasonably lead her to fear. And it is for this reason, among others, that we can

give no credit to the stories that represent the
favours of Catherine as shared by casual comers
and goers. No doubt the place to which Patiomkine, Lanskoï, and so many others have found
their way is not an inviolate sanctuary; still, it
is by no means accessible to the first comer.
At the outset of her reign, Catherine certainly
committed some imprudences, which caused her
no little inconvenience. In 1762 an officer of
the name of Hrastof, charged with the inventory
of the wardrobe of the late Empress Elizabeth,
was accused of making away with 200,000
roubles'-worth. A woman had been seen wearing jewels that had belonged to the deceased
sovereign. She was recognised as one of the
innumerable mistresses of the favourite, Gregory
Orlof, who probably shared the fair lady's favours
with Hrastof. Now, the latter, according to the
report of the French *chargé-d'affaires* Bérenger,
had been living for some time in considerable
intimacy with the new Czarina.

Since then, Catherine has put all that in order :
the favourite is a person whose slightest movements are subjected to an invariable routine and
a minute scrutiny. He pays no visits, accepts no
invitations. Once only was Mamonof authorised
to accept a dinner, to which he had been invited
by the Comte de Ségur. Even then Catherine
became uneasy, and the French minister and his
guests, on rising from table, see the Empress's
coach under the windows : it goes slowly backward and forward, with a persistence which
betrays all the distress of the momentarily abandoned lover. A year later, the *vremienchtchik*
nearly loses his place through a very natural

and a very innocent infraction of the severe discipline to which he is subjected. On his birthday the Czarina has authorised him to present her with a pair of earrings, which she herself has purchased for the sum of 30,000 roubles. The Grand Duchess sees the earrings and admires them greatly: upon which Catherine makes her a present of them. She puts them on, and next day she summons Mamonof to her, to thank him for having, however indirectly, contributed to this unexpected liberality. He is on the point of going, considering himself bound to obey a command from one so high in position; but the Empress, on finding it out, falls into a violent rage; she apostrophises him in violent terms, and sends to the Grand Duchess the most severe of reprimands: let her take care never to do it again! Paul thinks to make himself agreeable by sending to the favourite a snuff-box set with diamonds; Catherine allows Mamonof to go and thank the Grand Duke, but not by himself: she designates the particular person who is to accompany him. Paul refuses the visit.

We must add that, on their side, the favourites do their best to guard against the danger of an unfaithfulness, even accidental, which would put them into competition with a rival perhaps capable of supplanting them. Their power, and it is great, is employed in a vigilance not less active than that of Catherine herself. So long as Patiomkine is in favour, and he is in favour, 'honorary' after a certain time, for fifteen years, from 1774 to 1789, his imperious will raises an insurmountable barrier against every caprice that he does not choose to sanction. He can even, at need, use violence to her who, in giving herself to him, has found a master indeed.

Catherine's choice, it should be noted, falls, without exception, on men in the prime of life, and, for the most part, of Herculean build. As she grows older, she chooses them younger and younger. Of the two brothers Zoubof, one was twenty-two and the other eighteen at the time when she was first attracted by them. We know the age of Lanskoï, and the circumstances of his premature end.

What was the actual number of favourites, from the day of Catherine's accession to the day of her death ? It is not easy to say with absolute precision. Only ten officially occupied the post, with all the privileges and responsibilities of the post : Gregory Orlof, from 1762 to 1772 ; Vassiltchikof, from 1772 to 1774 ; Patiomkine, from 1774 to 1776 ; Zavadofski, from 1776 to 1777 ; Zovitch, from 1777 to 1778 ; Korssakof, from 1778 to 1780 ; Lanskoï, from 1780 to 1784 ; Iermolof, from 1784 to 1785 ; Mamonof, from 1785 to 1789 ; Zoubof, from 1789 to 1796. But at the time when Korssakof was in favour, a crisis came about which called forth several aspirants, and brought at least one of them, Strahof, very much into the good graces of the sovereign. Strahof never occupied the special apartments of the favourite ; it is almost certain, however, that he took the place, for a short time, of the official favourite. Very likely something similar happened on various occasions. On visiting the Winter Palace, shortly before the death of Catherine, a traveller was particularly struck

by the decoration of two little rooms close to
the Empress's bedroom : the walls of one of
these rooms were completely covered with miniatures of great price, set in gold, and representing
different lascivious scenes ; the other room was
similarly decorated, but the miniatures were portraits, portraits of men whom Catherine had
known or loved.

Among these men, some showed themselves
singularly ungrateful for the excess of favours
which Catherine heaped indiscriminately upon
them all. She herself behaved well to every one
of them, and not one, even of those who were
unfaithful to her, had to suffer the weight of her
wrath and vengeance For she was betrayed
and abandoned like the most vulgar of mistresses :
all her power, all her fascination, and the immensity of the price set on her favour, could not
shield her from the mishaps that have tortured the
hearts of empresses and of grisettes alike since
the beginning of the world. In 1780 she surprises Korssakof in the arms of the Countess
Bruce. In 1789 it is Mamonof who gives her up
to marry a *freiline.* Taking everything into consideration, it is she who was the least changeable.
Referring to the departure of Mamonof, simply
sent to Moscow with his lady, with whom he is
soon in disagreement, the Comte de Ségur wrote
in a despatch to the Comte de Montmorin—

'One can shut one's eyes indulgently on the
errors of a woman who is a great man, when she
shows, even in her weaknesses, such mastery
over herself, such mercy, and such magnanimity.
It is rarely that one finds in union absolute
power, jealousy, and moderation, and such a

character could only be condemned by a man without a heart, or a prince without a weakness.'

Perhaps the Comte de Ségur was too indulgent. Perhaps, too, Saint-Beuve was not sufficiently so, when he observed that Catherine's way of treating her lovers, when she got tired of them, so different from that of Elizabeth of England and Christina of Sweden, really told against her. That she should load them with gifts, instead of having them assassinated, 'is too much, betrays too openly the scorn that she has of men and of nations.' There is, at all events, an error of fact in this severe judgment : Catherine was not tired of either Korssakof or Mamonof when she learned how they had deceived her. She clung to them still, to the latter especially, and her pride was not alone in suffering from the disgrace that they inflicted upon her. Her weaknesses were often, too often, those of a woman who takes her pleasure where she finds it ; but the English statesman who wrote ' she was a stranger to love,' understood very little, to our mind, of the psychology of a woman.

III

Before making up her mind to abandon Gregory Orlof, Catherine endured from him what few women would have endured. In 1765, seven years before the rupture, Bérenger writes from St. Petersburg to the Duc de Praslin :—

'This Russian openly violates the laws of love in regard to the Empress. He has mistresses in town, who, far from calling down the indignation of the sovereign through their complaisance to Orlof, seem, on the contrary, to gain her favour by it. The senator, Mouravief, who had found his wife with him, attempted to make a sensation by demanding a separation : the Empress appeased him by giving him some land in Livonia.'

But at last things get to such a pitch that Catherine can endure it no longer, and she profits by the absence of the favourite to break her chain. At the moment when Orlof, travelling post, is coming to reclaim his rights, he is stopped by command a few versts from St. Petersburg, and banished to his estates. But he will not admit that he is beaten; now suppliant, now menacing, he begs to be allowed to see the sovereign again, if only for a moment. She has only to say the word to be rid for ever of his importunities : Patiomkine is already at hand, and he would willingly make away with all the Orlofs at once. But this word is never said. She parleys, comes to an agreement, and finally sends to the lover,—how lightly punished for a part that might justify quite other measures!—a plan of agreement which is a very poem of supreme tenderness of heart ; the past forgotten, an appeal to the reason of the guilty one that painful mutual explanations may be spared, the necessity of separation for a time, indicated how mildly, almost imploringly—nothing is wanting. He is to take leave of absence, to settle at Moscow, or on his estates, or elsewhere, if he will. His allowance of 150,000 roubles a year will be continued, and he will receive 100,000 roubles in addition, to furnish a house. Meanwhile he may make use of any of the Empress's houses near Moscow, use the court equipages as before, and keep the servants in the imperial livery. Catherine remembers that she has promised him 4000 peasants for the victory of Tchesmé, in which it happens he took no part; she adds 6000 more, whom he can pick out as he likes, in any of the domains of the crown. And as if she were afraid of not doing enough for him, she multiplies the proofs of her munificence: now a silver service, and then another 'for ordinary use,' and then a house at the *Troïtskaia Pristagne,* furniture, and everything that is found in the apartments that had belonged to the favourite in the imperial palace, the value of which escapes her reckoning. In return, Catherine exacts only a year's absence. At the end of a year the ex-favourite will be better able to realise the situation. As for Catherine, 'she will never forget all that she owes to the family of Gregory Orlof, nor the talents with which he is personally endowed, and how useful they may be to the nation' She desires only 'a mutual repose, which she will do her best to preserve.'

It may be that in this way of accommodating things there is a little fear of what might be the result of hostility on the part of a family to which she herself has given such power in her empire; but is there not also a genuine tenderness? Eleven years later, on hearing of the ex-favourite's death, Catherine wrote—

'The loss of Prince Orlof put me into a fever, with such delirium during the night, that I had to be bled.'

It is in June 1783 that she hears the fatal news, and two months after, on her way to

Frederikshamn to meet the King of Sweden,
she stipulates beforehand that he will not speak
to her of this catastrophe, which still moves her
to the very depths of her being   She is the
first to speak of it, with an effort to conceal the
agitation which so distant a past never fails to
awaken in her mind.   Nevertheless, she has
found several successors to the lover whom she
had replaced even before his death.   Is it a mere
infatuation, as Grimm at first supposes, which, in
1778, throws her into the arms of Korssakof?

'Infatuated? infatuated?' she replies to her
confidant.   'Do you not know that this term is
out of place in speaking of Pyrrhus, King of
Epirus' (the name she gives to the new favourite),
'a peril to painters, a despair to sculptors?   It is
the admiration, sir, it is the enthusiasm, that the
masterpieces of nature inspire!   Things of beauty
fall and are dashed to pieces like idols before the
ark of the Lord, before the character of this
mighty man.   Never does Pyrrhus make a movement which is not either noble or graceful.   He
is radiant as the sun, he radiates light.   All that
is not effeminate, but male, all that one would
have it: in a word, it is Pyrrhus, King of Epirus.
It is all in harmony; nothing is out of place: it
is the effect of a mingling of the priceless gifts
of nature; art is not absent, but artifice is a
thousand leagues away.'

We may admit that the sentiment which inspires this language in her is neither very deep
nor very delicate.   And indeed Korssakof is a
mere hector.   But take another actor in this
drama of passion, Patiomkine, the man of genius,
and read what follows.   It is a letter from the

favourite, written after a lover's quarrel of a few days' duration. Catherine replies in the margin, point by point. A sort of treaty of eternal peace and love is thus signed and sealed by the reconciled lovers :—

In Patiomkine's handwriting—

'Permit me, dear love, to tell you how I think our quarrel will end. Do not be surprised that I am concerned in regard to our love. Besides the numberless favours you have showered upon me, you have also given me a place in your heart. I would be there alone, and above all who have gone before, for none has loved you as I love you. And as I am the work of your hands, I would find rest in you also; I would have you delight in doing me kindness; I would have you toil for my happiness, and find in it a solace from the serious tasks that are laid upon you by your high position. Amen.'

In Catherine's handwriting—

'The sooner the better.

Do not be concerned.

Hand washes hand. Sure and firm.

He is and will be. I see and believe it. I rejoice at it. That is my greatest joy.

That will come of itself.

Let calm return to your mind, and your feelings have free course; they are loving, and will find the best way themselves. End of the quarrel. Amen.'

This is no commonplace exchange of vows, and the two beings who, placed at the summit of human greatness, speak of their love in these terms are no vulgar debauchees. All the dreamy, troubled, and imperious disposition of Patiomkine manifests itself in these lines, as does the temperament, at once practical and exalted, of Catherine.

It is by her judgment that the sovereign generally rules the favourite, it is by his ardour that he often carries her away. A great part of their correspondence has been published. There never was such a correspondence between two persons so linked by a common destiny. The turns of phrase generally employed by Catherine, especially during the early years of their connection, could not be paralleled, perhaps, in their excessive familiarity, in the correspondence of no matter what *jeune galante* of the time. We will not dwell on, 'I embrace you a thousand times, my friend,' 'Forgive me if I am troubling you, my heart,' 'Do you see, my soul?' little as one expects to find these tender expressions from the hand of an Empress. But here is a note which ends, 'Good-bye, my bow-wow.' 'Good-bye, my gold pheasant,' we read elsewhere. Or again, 'Good-bye, papa.' There are frequent squabbles : Patiomkine has a troublesome disposition, and is sulky or furious at the least excuse. She writes to him thus : 'If you are not more amiable to-day than you were yesterday, I—I—I—well, I really won't eat my dinner.' Is there an allusion, in this other note, to the project that this irascible lover professed at one time of going into a monastery ? We know not. 'A plan,' writes Catherine, 'which had been formed four or five months ago, with which even N. B., the town and suburbs, were acquainted ; a plan for plunging a dagger into the breast of his friend, on the part of one who loves us the most, who has our happiness always at heart ; does such a plan do credit to the mind and heart of him who has conceived it and would put it into execution ?'

The favourite, as one may imagine, is himself not behindhand in tender flowers of speech. Only, and it is a curious trait of this astonishing idyl, in all the abandonment of his amorous warmth, he never for a single instant forgets the distance between them. His turns of phrase, often more passionate and intense, always preserve a certain solemnity, never follow those of Catherine in their rather trivial freedom. 'If my prayer is heard, God will prolong your days to the utmost limit, O thou merciful mother!' That is his most customary style. He never, as a rule, uses the *tutoiement* except in this form of invocation, in which he seems to address her, the work of whose hands he feels himself to be, as he would address God. We have other fragments of love-letters of Patiomkine, not addressed to Catherine, in which he reveals himself as an accomplished virtuoso, mingling Oriental fantasy with the reverie of the North, and the delicacy of the most exquisite models that the West has furnished.

'O my life, O sister soul of mine, · how can words tell thee of all my love? Come, O my mistress (*soudarka maïa*), hearken, O my friend, my joy, my treasure without price, gift unparalleled that God has given me! . . . Darling (*matouchka goloubouchka*), give me the joy of seeing thee, the delight of rejoicing in thy heart.

I kiss with all my love thy pretty little hands and thy pretty little feet.'

It is not to Catherine that Patiomkine writes that. *Matouchka* she is, indeed, but at the same time, and always, *gossoudarinia* (sovereign), before whom one bows with his forehead. in the dust, even when speaking of love ; never *goloubouchka* (darling) nor *soudarka* (mistress).

Called to the post of favourite in 1774, Patiomkine makes way, two years later, for Zavadofski. The lover gives place, but the friend remains ; and the engagement entered into at the beginning is not broken as yet. It will scarcely be so, even when, just before the death of the Prince of Taurida, Zoubof, installing himself as master in the palace as well as the heart of the sovereign, leaves no room for one who had formerly ruled *alone.* Till that time there is scarcely a difference to be traced in Catherine's manner towards the brilliant adventurer, whom she allows to rule over her court, command her armies, govern her empire, though she has already broken off her more tender relations with him ; and she accepts from him new lovers, while showering upon him not only riches and honours, but the most unmistakable signs of an unbroken affection.

' Good-bye, my friend ; take care of yourself ; I embrace you with all my heart. Sacha sends greetings.'

This is dated June 29, 1789, and Sacha is Mamonof, the reigning favourite, and the creature of Patiomkine.

' *Sachenka* greets you and loves you as his own soul,' we read in another letter, dated May 5, 1784 ; ' he often speaks of you.'

In September 1777, Patiomkine receives from the sovereign a present of 150,000 roubles. In 1779 he receives an advance of 750,000 roubles as his annual pension of 75,000. In 1783 Catherine pays to his account 100,000 roubles to hasten on the erection of a palace that he is building, which she will buy from him for several millions, and of which she will make him a present immediately after. He is Field-Marshal, he is Prime Minister, he is Prince, he has all the distinctions, all the posts, all the honours, all the powers, that there are to be bestowed. At the time of the annexation of the Crimea, during the second Turkish war, he acts as master, without guidance and without control. He does as he pleases, follows his own devices, and Catherine is like a little girl who bows before the decree of a superior genius. He leaves her without news for months together; he does not even trouble to reply to her letters. Then she complains, but timidly, almost humbly :—

'I have been between life and death all the time that I have had no news of you. . . . For God's sake and for mine, take more care of yourself than you have done in the past. I am afraid of nothing, except that you may be ill. . . . At this moment, my dear friend, you are no longer a private person who lives as he likes and does as he pleases : you belong to the state, to me.'

Tender appellations, that of 'papa' among others, find their place once more in the former lover's letters. The Empress is herself again in the frequent moments of discouragement into which the conqueror of the Crimea is always thrown by a momentary reverse. In 1787 an attack of the Turks on Kinburn makes him think of resigning his command. Catherine will not hear of it.

'Strengthen your mind and soul against all

that may befall, and be assured that you will overcome everything with a little patience, but it is a weakness indeed to wish to quit your post and hide yourself away.'

A few weeks later a storm destroyed part of the fleet brought together by Patiomkine at Sebastopol. This time he would not only abandon the army, but evacuate the Crimea.

'What is it you say?' writes Catherine. 'No doubt you thought so at the first moment, fancying that all the fleet had perished, but what would become of the rest of this fleet after the evacuation? And how can you begin a campaign by the evacuation of a province which is not even threatened? It would be better to attack Otchakof or Bender, thus substituting the offensive for the defensive attitude, which you yourself say is less politic. Besides, it is not only against us that the wind has blown, I imagine! Courage! courage! I write all this to you as to my best friend, my pupil and scholar, who at times shows more resolution than I, but at this moment I have more courage than you, because you are ill and I am well. . . . I think you are as impatient as a child of five, whilst the affairs under your charge at this moment demand an imperturbable patience.'

She adds that he may return for a time to St. Petersburg. Is he afraid that some one will play him an ill turn during his absence? 'Neither time, nor distance, nor any one in the world will ever change my way of thinking in regard to you, nor the feelings I have for you.'

This freedom of action that Catherine allows to the man in whom she has placed her confi-

dence, this way of closing her eyes on his proceedings, in order to pay him the greater compliment, is only the application of a system that
we know already. Occasions are not wanting,
however, on which the will of the Empress and
her personal intervention are exercised in a direct
and effectual manner. There are then frequent
disagreements between the two, and neither
friendship nor love hinder Catherine from insisting on her authority being obeyed. The ill-
temper of the favourite comes out plainly enough :
he is now sharp, now sulky : 'I tell you,' he
writes, 'what is for your interest ; after that, do
as you please.' 'You may get angry if you like,'
replies Catherine, 'but you must admit that I am
right.' The causes of disagreement are sometimes of a rather delicate nature. An inspector
of the troops has been nominated by Patiomkine. Catherine opposes the choice, which
she conceives to have been made for a particular reason. This is how she reasons the matter
out :—

'Allow me to tell you that the miserable face
of his wife is not worth the trouble you will have
with such a man. Nor have you any chance
there, for madame is charming, but there is
nothing to be gained by paying court to her.
That is a well-known fact, and an immense
family watches over her reputation. My friend,
I am accustomed to tell you the truth. You do
the same with me when there is occasion for it.
Oblige me in this instance by choosing some one
more suitable for the post, one who knows the
work, so that the approval of the public and of
the army may crown your choice and my nomina-

tion. I like to give you pleasure, and I do not like to refuse you anything, but I should like that in a post of that sort, every one might say, what a good choice, and not, what a wretched choice, of a man who does not know what he has to do. Make peace, after which you can come here and amuse yourself as much as you like.'

Catherine forgot to add that meanwhile she was amusing herself on her side, and that this time she had not consulted her 'friend' on the nature of the new amusement that she had found for herself. Zoubof appeared on the horizon and proclaimed himself a formidable rival in the conquest of the imperial favour, and even of the part that friendship had left to his predecessor. Tied to the other extremity of the empire, Patiomkine bounded with rage; he declared that he would soon return to St. Petersburg, 'to have a tooth taken out' (*zoub* means tooth in Russian) which troubled him. He did not succeed in his attempt. He came back only to witness the definite triumph of the enemy. He returned to the South, chafing at his fate; he was struck to the heart, and soon death came to spare him the last humiliations of disgrace. Catherine, nevertheless, had taken all the trouble in the world to make him look favourably upon her new choice, and the letters in which she gives voice to this anxiety are not the least curious of the collection from which we have already made many extracts. Compliments, kind attentions, delicate flatteries, even unexpected outbursts of tenderness, follow one another, coming to the friend already sacrificed, on the part of the victorious lover, of 'the child, the

'little blacky,' as she delights in calling the new
favourite, with the caressing ways that age has
not taken from her.   'The child,' she writes,
'thinks you are cleverer and more amusing and
more amiable than all those about you; but keep
this quiet, for he does not know that I know
that.'

But Patiomkine is not to be wheedled.   He
sees his prestige escaping him, he feels that
this time the place is taken altogether, and not
only the corner of the imperial palace, near her
Majesty's private rooms, which he had let go so
lightly, but that other sanctuary as well, which
the vows of bygone days had led him to hope
would retain a place for him for ever.   That too
he was going to lose !

Once already he had had a serious cause **for**
anxiety.   Among his rivals there had been one,
before Zoubof, whom Catherine seemed to have
loved as she never loved before or after.   It
seems to have been the fate of this extraordinary
woman to exhaust, in all their diversity, the
whole range of sentiments and sensations, **and**
the entire order of the phenomena of passion.
The love that she experienced for Lanskoï was
utterly different from that which she had for
Patiomkine, or for any of those who filled her
life, so rich in varied impressions.   But Lanskoï
was not ambitious, and it was not given to Catherine to keep him long.   On June 19, 1784, the
young man who for the last four years had made
the joy of her existence, in whom all her thoughts,
all her affections, and all her desires were con-
centrated, the most petted, the most caressed, the
most fêted of favourites, was attacked by a

mysterious disease. The German physician Weikard was hastily summoned from St. Petersburg to Tzarskoïe-Sielo. He was a savant of the pure Teutonic breed, little used to delicate discretion in his dealings. Sitting on the patient's bed, Catherine anxiously questioned him.

' What is it ? ' she asked.

' A bad fever, Madame, and he will die of it.'

He insisted that the Empress should leave the patient, judging the malady to be contagious. So far as we can conjecture, it was a quinsy. Catherine never hesitated an instant between the counsels of prudence and those more imperious ones of her heart. She was soon taken with a troublesome uneasiness of the throat. She braved it all. Ten days later Lanskoï expired in her arms. He was only twenty-six. Hear the lament of the lover from whom the loved one has been taken by death :—

' When I began this letter, I was in hope and joy, and my thoughts came so swiftly that I knew not what became of them. It is so no more : I am plunged into the depths of sorrow, and my happiness has fled : I thought I should have died of the irreparable loss that I have just had, a week ago, of my best friend. I had hoped that he would be the support of my old age : he was attentive, he learnt much, he had acquired all my tastes. He was a young man whom I was bringing up, who was grateful, kind, and good, who shared my sorrows when I had them, and rejoiced in my joys. In a word, I have the misfortune to have to tell you, with tears, that General Lanskoï is no more, . . . and my room, so pleasant before, has become an empty den, in

which I can just drag myself about like a shadow.
Something went wrong with my throat the day
before his death, and I have a raging fever;
nevertheless, since yesterday, I have got up
from bed, but so feeble and sorrowful that at
the present hour I cannot look on a human face
without my voice being choked with tears. I
cannot sleep or eat; reading wearies me, and
writing is too much for me. I know not what
will become of me; but I know that never in
my life have I been so unhappy as since my
kind, my best friend has quitted me. I have
opened my drawer, I have found this sheet that
I have begun, I have written these lines, but I
can no more.'

This is on July 2, 1784. Only after two
months does Catherine resume her correspondence with Grimm.

'I confess to you that all that time I was
incapable of writing to you, because I knew that
it would make us both suffer. A week after I
had written to you my letter of July, Count
Fedor Orlof and Prince Potemkin came to me.
Up to then I could not endure to see any one;
these took me just in the right way: they began
to howl with me, and then I felt at my ease with
them; but it took a long time to come to it, and
thanks to my sensibility, I had become insensible
to everything but this one sorrow; and this
seemed to increase and take fresh hold at every
step, at every word. Do not think, however, that
despite the horror of the situation, I neglected
the least thing which required my attention. In
the most awful moments I was called upon to
give orders, and I gave them, in an orderly and

sane manner : which particularly struck General
Saltykof. More than two months passed without
any respite; at last some calmer hours have
come, and now calmer days. The weather having
become wet, the rooms at Tsarsko-Selo have
had to be heated. Mine have been heated with
such violence that on the evening of the 5th
September, not knowing where to go, I called
out my coach, and came straight here without
any one's knowing it; I have put up at the Hermitage, and yesterday, for the first time, I went
to mass, and consequently, for the first time also,
I saw everybody and was seen by everybody;
but, in truth, it was such an effort that on getting
back to my room I was so overcome that any one
but I would have fainted. . . . I ought to re-read
your three last letters, but I really cannot. . . . I
have become a most sad creature, and speak
only in monosyllables. . . . Everything distresses
me . . . and I never liked to be an object of
pity.'

An English orator, Lord Camelford, has said
that Catherine honoured the throne by her vices,
while the King of England (George III.) dis-
honoured it by his virtues. The expression is
somewhat strong; but it may be admitted that
vices capable of manifesting themselves in so
touching a form deserve something other than
absolute condemnation.

IV

Favouritism, as practised by Catherine, was
not without its serious inconveniences. On
December 1, 1772, the French minister at St.

Petersburg, Durand, writes to the Duc d'Aiguillon that, according to reports coming from the palace, 'the Empress is so singularly occupied with the affair of M. Orlof, that for nearly two months she has attended to nothing else, she reads nothing, and scarcely ever goes out.' Two months after, the crisis is not yet over. 'This woman does nothing,' says one of the courtiers to Durand; 'so long as the Orlof faction is in power, there is nothing to be done.' Now these crises are frequent. In February 1780 the English ambassador Harris, coming to Prince Patiomkine to question him in reference to an important memorandum which has been in the Empress's hands for some time, is told that he has come at a wrong time: Lanskoï is ill, and the dread of his death so paralyses the Empress that she is unable to fix her attention on anything. All her thoughts of ambition and of glory are forgotten; all care for her own interest or her own dignity leaves her; she is completely absorbed in this one anxiety. And Prince Patiomkine expresses his fear lest Count Panine should profit by the occasion to bring his ideas into play, and give a new direction to the foreign policy. Three years later, it is an illness of the Prince himself that throws the Sovereign into a state of such distress, that the Marquis de Vérac, on the point of leaving St. Petersburg, cannot obtain his farewell audience. Those about the Empress, seeing her eyes red with the tears that she cannot restrain, beg her not to appear in public. The audience is put off.

When favouritism does not bring affairs to a standstill, it sometimes puts their guidance into hands as little suitable as possible to manage the helm, those of Mamonof or Zoubof, for example. And it is not merely the hasty advancement of the favourites themselves, becoming generals, marshals, ministers, from one day to another : the high personages thus created with a wave of the wand have in turn their dependants. They have also their enemies whom they seek to put in the background—as Patiomkine did with the illustrious Roumiantsof, thus depriving the empire of its finest soldier. Sometimes they push forward an ambitious man in order to get rid of a rival. In 1787 Mamonof is alarmed by the appearance at court of a young Prince Kotchoubey : he arranges to have him sent as ambassador to Constantinople ! The favourite gone, the consequences of his elevation still last. After the death of Patiomkine, his secretary, Popof, replaces him as head of the government of Iekatierinoslaf. He settles everything off-hand by the magic formula : ' Such was the will of the late Prince.' He inherits the secret of this will. and remains the instrument of his 'maker,' as he calls the deceased. Now, Count Rastoptchine, a good judge, declares that this man, though, during the lifetime of Patiomkine, he had governed the whole empire in his name for ten years, had no aptitude for affairs. Besides, he had other engagements. Rastoptchine never noticed in him more than one quality : the strength of his physical constitution, which enabled him regularly to pass his days and nights in gambling. Meanwhile, he is appointed general, chevalier of three orders, and incumbent of posts which bring him in 50,000 roubles a year. In February 1796

Rastoptchine writes: 'Never were crimes so frequent as they are now. Impunity and audacity are pushed to their utmost. Three days ago, a certain Kovalinski, who had been secretary of the War Commission, and had been dismissed by the Empress for pillage and cor-ruption, was appointed governor at Riazan, because he has a brother blackguard like himself who is in favour with Gribolski, Plato Zoubof's chancellor. Ribas alone steals 500,000 roubles a year.'

Favouritism is expensive. Castéra has made out a formidable sum-total on account of ten principal heads of affairs, adding a doubtful supernumerary, Vysotski.

Amounts received—

	Roubles.
The five Orlofs, ...	17,000,000
Vysotski, ...	300,000
Vassiltchikof, ...	1,110,600
Patiomkine, ...	50,000,000
Zavadofski, ...	1,380,000
Zovitch, ...	1,420,000
Korssakof, ...	920,000
Lanskoï, ...	7,260,000
Iermolof, ...	550,000
Mamonof, ...	880,000
The brothers Zoubof,	3,500,000
Expenses of the favourites,	8,500,000
Total,	92,820,000

This comes, at the then rate of exchange, to more than 400 millions of francs. This is much the same as the calculation of the English am-bassador Harris.

From 1762 to 1783 the Orlof family received, according to him, 40,000 to 50,000 peasants and 17 million roubles in money, houses, plate, and jewels. Vassiltchikof, in twenty-two months, received 100,000 roubles in cash, 50,000 in jewels, a furnished palace with 100,000 roubles, plate worth 30,000, a pension of 20,000, and 7000 peasants; Patiomkine, in two years, 37,000 peasants, and about 9,000,000 roubles in jewels, palaces, pension, and plate; Zavadofski, in eighteen months, 6000 peasants in Ukraine, 2000 in Poland, 1800 in Russia, 80,000 roubles'-worth of jewels, 150,000 roubles in cash, plate worth 30,000, and a pension of 10,000; Zovitch, in a year, an estate worth 500,000 roubles in Poland, another worth 100,000 in Livonia, 500,000 roubles in cash, 200,000 in jewels, and a commandership in Poland, with an income of 12,000 roubles; Korssakof, in sixteen months, 150,000 roubles, and, on his leaving, 4000 peasants in Poland, 100,000 roubles to pay his debt, 100,000 for his equipment, 20,000 roubles a month to travel abroad.

These figures need no comment. In July 1778 the Chevalier de Corberon wrote from St. Petersburg to the Comte de Vergennes—

'The new favourite Corsak' (such appears to have been the individual's original name) 'has just been made chamberlain. He has received 150,000 roubles, and his fortune, which will not last, will be at least brilliant for him and burdensome for the state, which has to suffer for it. This nuisance, so often repeated, spreads dissatisfaction and discontent in the public mind, and the result might be dangerous if Catherine II. were not more powerful and more farseeing than those about her. There are murmurs, but she rules through all, and the ascendency of her mind is her salvation. . . . Lately, in a Russian house, some one calculated how much had been spent on favouritism during the present reign : the total came to 48 million roubles.'

But it was not merely a question of money. Prince Chtcherbatof has excellently characterised the demoralising influence of an institution which brought into prominence excesses of this kind at the highest point of society. The favourites of Catherine might well, from the absolute point of view, seem only the equivalent of the mistresses of Louis XV., but the absolute is out of place both in morals and in politics, the difference of the sexes will probably always make, in this connection, an enormous difference in the relative bearing of the same facts, and if Marie-Antoinette found painful surprises awaiting her at the court of her father-in-law, these were probably nothing to the impression made on the second wife of Paul, Maria Fedorovna, when her residence at St. Petersburg had brought her in contact with the official scandal of the imperial palace. Besides, the mistresses of Louis XV. were not supposed, in France, to transact the business of royalty.

One of Kosciuszko's campanions in arms, Niemcewicz, speaks in his memoirs of having visited in 1794 the houses constructed for the passage of the Empress on her tour in the Crimea, in 1787. The Empress's bedroom was everywhere made after a uniform plan. Beside the bed was a square of glass ; on touching a spring it moved, and another bed, that of Mamonof, appeared. Catherine was then fifty-nine! Shamelessness carried to this height was surely a school of vice.

There was certainly, in this strange woman, a colossal disregard of her situation in regard to the eternal laws of womanhood. For it must be observed that there was in her in no sense an affectation of cynicism, nor even an obliteration of the moral sense, nor even depravation of mind. Favouritism with all its consequences once excepted, Catherine is severe in regard to moral questions, and very susceptible in regard to outward decency. She values chastity, and at times is even prudish. One day, on the way to Kief, she requests the Comte de Ségur, who is in her carriage, to repeat some verses. He recites a piece, 'a little free and gay,' he tells us, 'but nevertheless decent enough to have been well received at Paris by the Duc de Nivernais, the Prince de Beauveau, and ladies as virtuous as they are amiable.' Catherine at once frowns, stops him midway by a question on quite another subject, and turns off the conversation. In 1788, the Admiral Paul Jones, whom she has summoned to her service from England, is accused of having taken liberties with a girl belonging to the court. He is immediately dismissed, notwithstanding the dearth of men capable of taking the command. For a similar reason the English ambassador Macartney is obliged to leave his post. In 1790, chatting with her secretary over the events that have been taking place in France, Catherine inveighs against the actresses, whom she accuses of having depraved the morals of the nation. 'What has ruined the country,' she declares, 'is that the people fall into vice and drunkenness. The comic opera has corrupted the whole nation.'

She is conscious of not having taken to drink herself, and of having done nothing to corrupt the morals of her country.   But she thinks it quite natural to write to Patiomkine that his successor Mamonof—*Sachenka*, as she calls him —'loves him, and looks upon him as a father.' And she is in nowise embarrassed in asking her son and daughter-in-law for news of the King Poniatowski, whom they have seen in passing through Warsaw.   'I think,' she writes, 'that his Polish Majesty would have some difficulty in remembering my face as it was twenty-five years ago by the portraits you showed him.'

'One could never venture,' writes the Prince de Ligne in his portrait of the sovereign, 'to speak ill of Peter I. nor of Louis XVI. before the Empress, nor the least thing in regard to religion or morals.   Scarcely could one venture on anything in the least risky, however glossed over ; at which, however, she would laugh quietly.   She never permitted trifling, either of this kind or in reference to any one.'

A ukase instructing keepers of public baths to have separate compartments for the two sexes, and not to allow any men in the women's quarter, except those required for attendance, and doctors, bears the signature of Catherine.   An odd exception is made in favour of painters, who would study their art in the feminine compartments.

Certain accusations have nevertheless been brought forward, associating the last years in particular of the Empress with infamous tastes and habits.   Besides the 'set' admitted to the private receptions at the Hermitage, another more limited 'set' had been formed, comprising, in addition to the two brothers Zoubof and Peter Saltykof, some women whose names we prefer to omit. The name of Lesbos has been uttered in regard to these gatherings, and the name of the Cybele of the North affixed to the other glorious titles of Catherine the Great. We are averse to discuss such imputations. We cannot believe that Catherine has ever justified them, though we dare not say that she has not, in a sense, deserved them. Is not this outrage to her memory a just expiation? Maria Theresa was not a woman to give credence to calumnies without proper examination. She could also be indulgent, needing no indulgence on her own account. Nevertheless she wrote in 1778—

'The Grand Duke, it is well known, like his supposed father and the Empress, is utterly debauched.'

From the sovereign and mother, by way of the lover, the scandal thus attained the son also.

The sudden death of Catherine, coming as it did, was perhaps another expiation. For a long time past her excesses had been thought to be telling on her robust health. In a despatch of May 1774, Durand, the French *chargé-d'affaires*, speaking of the anxiety of the favourite on account of the Empress's health, wrote—

'He is well aware of what few people know, that the Empress had a fainting-fit a day or two ago, lasting more than half an hour, just as she was about to take a cold bath; that her most trusty servants have noticed curious twitches and movements that she has been subject to for some time; that by the use of cold baths and of tobacco she has moments of absence of mind and

ideas quite opposed to her natural ones. All
that I infer at present from these symptoms is
that she is affected with hysteria.'

In 1774 these conjectures were premature.
Twenty years later Catherine justified them.

We ask the pardon of our readers for having
raised the veil cast by time and oblivion over
these details.   For all we have done we have had
but one reason, and we desire but one excuse—
the sincerity that, in default of other merit, we
have brought to our task, a task whose difficulties
and dangers we have by no means ignored, but
one which has appealed to us in spite of all, as it
has interested, we hope, others as well, by reason
of the variety, the complexity, and the originality,
perhaps unique, of facts which are purely a
matter of history, and which yet might challenge
the best attempts of the most fertile imagination.

FINIS

Printed by T. and A. CONSTABLE, Printers to Her Majesty,
at the Edinburgh University Press.

Lightning Source UK Ltd.
Milton Keynes UK
UKOW06f1839010216

267565UK00009B/161/P